BROADCASTING AND AUDIO-VISUAL POLICY IN THE EUROPEAN SINGLE MARKET

Richard Collins

John Libbey

LONDON • PARIS • ROME

British Library Cataloguing in Publication Data

Collins, Richard
   Broadcasting and Audio-visual Policy in
   the European Single Market
   I. Title
   384.54094
   ISBN 0-86196-405-5

Published by

John Libbey & Company Ltd, 13 Smiths Yard, Summerley Street, London SW18 4HR,
England.
Telephone: 081-947 2777: Fax 081-947 2664
John Libbey Eurotext Ltd, 6 rue Blanche, 92120 Montrouge, France.
John Libbey - C.I.C. s.r.l., via Lazzaro Spallanzani 11, 00161 Rome, Italy

Printed in Great Britain by Whitstable Litho Ltd, Whitstable, Kent, U.K.

BROADCASTING AND AUDIO-VISUAL POLICY IN THE EUROPEAN SINGLE MARKET

Richard Collins is Head of the Department of Communications and Music Technology, London Guildhall University

Contents

Acknowledgements

This book began as an investigation into the European satellite television channels, Eurikon and Europa, which were established in the 1980s by consortia of public service broadcasters under the aegis of the EBU. However, I realized that to understand how these channels came into being, lived and died required study of changes in European broadcasting regulation in the 1980s. I turned towards a study of the European Community and discovered that no account of the Community's policies existed. Reading Community documentation I soon realized that the story was more complicated and extensive than I had expected. There was no unitary Community policy, rather an intense struggle between rival policy visions and their institutional bearers, some of the most important of which had no specific responsibility for the audio-visual and broadcasting sectors at all.

This book represents my preliminary ordering of a mass of primary Community documentation. My understanding of this material was greatly assisted by the insights I gained from interviews with officials of the Commission of the European Communities, UK Departments of State and Members of the European Parliament. I have also benefited from discussions with Matteo Maggiore, Jean-Claude Burgleman and Caroline Pauwels and with my former colleague, Gareth Locksley, now translated to an office in the lair of the ultra-liberals, all of whom generously shared their knowledge of the Commission of the European Communities with me.

Discussion of my papers *Unity in diversity: The European single market in broadcasting and the audio-visual* delivered at the 1992 PICT Conference, and *Difference and community. Cultural and media policy in Canada and the European Community*, delivered at the Conferences of the Gesellschaft für Kanada-Studien/and the British Association for Canadian Studies Conference on Canada and Europe in 1992 helped me to clarify my thoughts on Community broadcasting and audio-visual policy. Certain themes of this book were foreshadowed in articles published in

vii

Broadcast, Media Policy Review, Cardozo Arts and Entertainment Law Journal, The Journal of Common Market Studies and in my pamphlet on *Broadcasting and audio-visual policy* for the University of North London Press' European Dossier Series.

I owe particular thanks to the ESRC and to the Department of Media and Communications at Goldsmiths' College for their support without which this study could not have been undertaken. These expressions of gratitude signify more than the conventional pieties which customarily precede academic publications for the generous and constructive response of both the ESRC and the Department of Media and Communications at Goldsmiths' College which enabled me to retrieve what promised to be a comprehensive personal disaster and to survive a troubled time. I am very grateful to the Council and its officials (notably Catherine Roberts and Steven Schwenk) and to Goldsmiths' and its officers (notably Ivor Gaber and Roy Vickery). These exceptional debts noted, there are more conventional acknowledgements to be made: that they follow my expressions of gratitude to those who provided the context essential to this study (and to reconnect with nearest and dearest) does not mean that my thanks to those mentioned below are less sincere than to those named above. For I owe particular thanks to Manuel Alvarado (who encouraged me and assisted me in preparing this work for publication) and to Avis Furness (whose oversight of the library of the European Parliament in London is exemplary).

Colin Aggett, Monique Auban, Ulf Bruhann, Janey Buchan, Joan Burch, Jean Cerentola, James Curran, Harry Dennis, Jane Dinsdale, Michael Elliott, Patrick Fallon, Margot Frohlinger, Alf Game, Saturnin Munos-Gomez, Pierre Hivernat, Stig Hjarvard, Laurie Keating, Josephine Langham, Gareth Locksley, Matteo Maggiore, Mariano Maggiore, Les Massey, Caroline Pauwels, Christian Pinaud, Patricia Rawlings, Rachel Reynolds, Ryclef Rienstra, Elisabeth Rohmer, Kevin Saldanah, Ivo Schwartz, Sheila Sheehan, Roger Silverstone, Jack Stuart-Clark, Michael Type, Keith Waghorn, George Waters, Harald Wendelbo, and Karen Williams also gave me essential help and I thank them for it.

The research on which this study is based was carried out when I was a Senior Research Associate in the Department of Media and Communications at Goldsmiths' College, University of London under a research grant (R00023 2159) awarded by the Economic and Social Research Council.

Richard Collins
November, 1993

Introduction

This treaty marks a new stage in the process of creating an 'ever closer union' among the peoples of Europe (Treaty on European Union, Title I, Article A).

Britain in Europe

The reference to 'ever closer union' in the 1991 Treaty on European Union, the Maastricht Treaty, echoes the same provision in the Treaty of Rome; the notion of 'ever closer union' although unobtainable (by definition) has long been enshrined as a goal for the European Community (now to be known as the European Union). Progress towards the goal of 'ever closer union' represents a considerable challenge to all the member states of the European Community but sets peculiarly difficult problems for the United Kingdom. For the UK, more than any other Member State of the Community (Denmark possibly excepted) has resisted the European unionist project and has sought to construct the European Community as a pragmatic association of sovereign states in a free trade area rather than as a unified Europe super state. Hence the customary British synonym for the European Community of 'the Common Market'.

The struggles between rival interests in the European Community and rival visions for Europe are evident in the course of the European Community's broadcasting and audio-visual policy[1]. The mass media and communications are believed to be

---

1 In this study I have often used the terms *broadcasting* and *audio-visual* synonymously. This choice requires some explanation for broadcasting denotes television and radio and the audio-visual denotes film, broadcasting and recorded sound. However, what I and the European Community usage usually mean by broadcasting and/or audio-visual policy is policy for the film and television sector. The Community has not developed an explicit policy for radio, although some controversial provisions of the Commission's Draft Directive on Broadcasting [Commission of the European Communities, 1986a] pertained to radio, and whilst film and television policy strictly cannot be reduced to each other, it is customary for Community usages to recognize the intimate interdependence of film and television. Thus the European Parliament's *Report on the European film and television industry* (European Parliament, 1989) refers, in its title and text, to a single film and television industry and recognizes that the main outlet for films is now television and not the cinema (European Parliament, 1989, p. 5).

particularly important both for the post-industrial European economy and for social cohesion in a European Community in which European citizens' assent is required to a controversial sharing of sovereignty between long established sovereign entities – the European 'nation states' which make up the Community – and the supranational Community itself. The narrow majorities for ratification of the Maastricht Treaty on European Union in France, Denmark and the United Kingdom testify to the difficulty of commanding popular assent to the European project and to the importance of the mass media (and television in particular) in the struggle over the future of Western Europe.

John Major's governments have made dramatic changes to the established European policies of the United Kingdom. In contrast to the sceptical and often hostile stance towards the European Community of his predecessor, Major has committed the United Kingdom to stand at 'the heart of Europe'. The Prime Minister, in euphoric mood, referred to the United Kingdom's supposed Game, Set and Match victory at Maastricht in December 1991, but a sober and more balanced assessment was made by Ian Davidson of the *Financial Times*. The UK's victory, Davidson said, was compounded of:

> ... blunders based on a profound failure to devise a European strategy which can mesh plausibly with the other forces in place. And that failure in turn is the direct consequence of the defensive and adversarial vocabulary adopted consistently for the past 40 years by almost the entire political class in Britain towards the European Community (*Financial Times*, 12.12.1991, p. 3).

In the same newspaper, Robert Mauthner had earlier described the UK's aloofness from the continuing process of European integration as one of the most incomprehensible features of its post war history (*Financial Times*, 4.12.1991, p. 21). Davidson's and Mauthner's judgements, that the UK is the persistent odd man out, are echoed by academic commentators, one of whom gave his study of the United Kingdom's relationship with the European Communities the eloquent title *An awkward partner. Britain in the European Community* (George, 1990). Nowhere more than in respect of audio-visual policy has the UK differed from many of its European partners. Not only has the UK consistently opposed the development of the pro-active audio- visual and broadcasting policies advanced by the Commission of the European Communities and by other Member States (notably by France) but it has not agreed that Community policies for the audio-visual sector are required at all.

In consequence the UK has customarily appeared negative, refusing to initiate broadcasting and audio-visual policies, opposing the initiatives of the Commission and other Member States and, at best, offering grudging assent to Community decisions. Davidson's ascription of a 'defensive and adversarial vocabulary' towards the European Community to the UK's political class is well exemplified in the story of the development of the Community's broadcasting and audio-visual policy. Yet, no more than the UK, can the European Community be regarded as a unitary entity with singular policies and a shared policy vision. Telling the story of the European Community's broadcasting and audio-visual policy involves tracking the evolution of two distinct policy visions each translated into action through different Community institutions, working in alliance with, and opposition to, Community Member States and other European institutions (notably the Council of Europe and the European Broadcasting Union).

The complex history of European Community broadcasting and audio-visual policy can be (over)simplified by describing it as driven by the interaction between three dynamics: the opposition between policies designed to foster cultural unity and policies designed to foster cultural diversity within the Community, the opposition between liberal (market) and administered (interventionist or *dirigiste*) means to achieve desired policy goals, and opposition between institutions (within and without the Community) that have sought to augment their own influence and power (and diminish that of other rival institutions) both to realize desired policy outcomes in the audio-visual domain and as part of a more extensive power dynamic. Liberal doctrines for broadcasting and the audio-visual have been exemplified pre-eminently by the UK and by Directorates General III and IV (Internal Market and Competition) of the Commission for the European Communities and interventionist doctrines by France and by Directorates General X and XIII (Culture and Information Technology) of the Commission for the European Communities. Each institutional/policy paradigm cluster has at different times advocated audio-visual and broadcasting policies promoting unity and promoting diversity.

The UK and the European Communities[1]

Strictly speaking the European Community is three communities and should properly be referred to as the European Communities. The first of the three, the European Coal and Steel Community, was founded under the Schuman Plan and established by the Treaty of Paris in 1951. It was this Treaty, concluded by France, Germany, Italy and the Benelux states, which laid the foundations for the establishment of the two further Communities that came into being with The Treaty of Rome of 1957. The Treaty of Rome established both the European Atomic Energy Community and the European Economic Community. These three communities, Coal and Steel, Atomic Energy and Economic, together constitute the European Community. The Treaties of Rome, the Single European Act of 1985 and the Maastricht Treaty on European Union of 1991 are the basis of what could be called the European Community's 'constitution'.

In 1972 Denmark, Ireland and the UK joined the six founding members of the

---

1 Title II, Article G of the *Treaty on European Union* (the Maastricht Treaty) provides, *inter alia*, for the official designation of the European Economic Community as the European Community. However, approved Brussels usage, post-Maastricht, is now 'European Union' rather than 'European Community'.

Communities, in 1981 Greece, and in 1986 Spain and Portugal became members. Further accessions to the European Community can be anticipated: Austria, Finland and Sweden are likely to achieve an early acceptance into the Community, then perhaps Norway and Switzerland and later (with less certainty) Cyprus, Malta, Turkey and the 'Visegrad' states of the Czech Republic, Hungary, Poland and Slovakia.

The European Community, however, is only one of a number of pan-European institutions which have shaped, and will continue to shape, the broadcasting and audio-visual landscape of Europe. The Council of Europe, the European Broadcasting Union, and even the Audio-visual Eureka, have all had important roles to play and these will be examined in later chapters. Nevertheless, in the alphabet soup of pan-European institutions, it is the European Community that has borne a major responsibility for shaping the broadcasting and the audio-visual landscape in Europe. Its rule-making and pro-active initiatives in the broadcasting and audio-visual sphere have had a striking impact on European states inside and outside the Community. Community competition policy has had, for example, a major effect on the long established practices of the European Broadcasting Union to which the public service broadcasters of all European states belong.

The United Kingdom has been hostile to the Community from its earliest days. Indeed the UK attempted to forestall establishment of the nascent European Community by promoting the European Movement from which the Council of Europe developed (and which the United Kingdom saw as an alternative focus for Europe). The UK's strong support for the Council, and equivocal commitment to the Community, reflects the characteristic British preference for participation in confederations, and for co-operation through intergovernmental agreements rather than for federations which entail the pooling of sovereignty. Jean Monnet, the 'father' of the European Community, testified eloquently to the incompatibility of the UK and EC visions of Europe when he cited the National Executive Committee of the Labour Party's rejection of the Schuman Plan in the 1940s. Labour's rejection of the Community was grounded in sentiments of community and collective identity that primarily linked the UK to an international anglophone world. Only secondarily, if at all, was there any sense of identification with Europe.

> In every respect except distance we in Britain are closer to our kinsmen in Australia and New Zealand on the far side of the world than we are to Europe. We are closer in language and origins, in social habits and institutions, in political outlook and in economic interest (cited in Monnet, 1978, p. 315).

The Labour Party (then the party of government in the UK) rejected the European Coal and Steel Community's (ECSC) *Haute Autorité* (High Authority) and thereby repudiated the *Haute Autorité*'s jurisdiction over the UK's newly nationalized coal and steel sector. It did so because of a fundamentally different perception of the cultural and historical experiences, and the economic interests of the UK and the six members of the ECSC; Belgium, France, Germany, Italy, Luxembourg, and the Netherlands.

As is well known, however, the UK's perception of its economic interests eventually shifted and it sought membership of the European Community. After two rejections of its candidacy (largely due to the opposition of France) the United Kingdom, together with Denmark and Ireland, joined the Community in 1972. However, differences in sentiment and in cultural identity and in language, origins, social habits, institutions and political outlook have continued to differentiate the UK from some of its partners, and from mainstream European values and sentiment.

To be sure the United Kingdom was, and is, not alone in having a less than harmonious relationship with the European Community but George's term, 'awkward partner', is still appropriate. The UK does not see the Community in the same way as many other members and, in respect of broadcasting and audio-visual policy, differences of sentiment and perception are consolidated by differences in economic interest. Yet, the UK is not always 'awkward'. When the European Community's policies accord with the image of the Community that the UK believes it joined (basically that of a group of states collaborating in a free trade area) then the UK is a notably conscientious, indeed enthusiastic, Community partner. Indeed, the two most awkward partners in the Community, Denmark and the UK, are the most diligent Member States in implementing Community directives.

The UK's awkwardness is most apparent in its characteristic resistance to the efforts of other Community members to extend the Community's reach beyond the limits of a free trade zone and towards political, and cultural, integration. The UK wants a Community unified in its markets but diverse in its political institutions. Davidson comments, 'the antithesis between high politics and pragmatic trade liberalization has been the most consistent single theme in the running policy debate between the members of the Community, and it has regularly pitted the United Kingdom against the original Six'[1] (*Financial Times*, 19.1.1993, p. v). These conflicts over the political destiny of the European Community, and the extent and pace of political integration, have, and will continue to have cultural consequences. For in official Community circles and in many, but not all, member states the belief in a nationalist congruence between polity and culture is widespread.

European Union and the nationalism question

Nationalism has been characterized by Minogue (1967, p. 8) as the 'foremost ideology of the modern world'. It is an ideology grounded in the linked propositions that nations should be sovereign in their own states, and that nations are communities of individuals linked by sentiments of shared identity, that is, by a

---

1 That is the six original members of the European Communities: Belgium, France, Germany, Italy, Luxembourg and the Netherlands.

common culture. As Gellner puts it 'Nationalism has been defined in effect as the striving to make culture and polity congruent, to endow a culture with its own political roof, and not more than one roof at that' (Gellner, 1983, p. 43). But historically the term 'Europe' has signified a geographical expression rather than a strongly felt collective identity. Europe embraces multiple national communities, each of which more or less strongly differentiates itself from adjacent national communities. Consequently the collective identity signified by the term 'European' has, in the past, been much weaker than those signified by terms such as 'French', 'Irish', 'Serb' or 'Basque'. Indeed the strongly marked sentiment of national identity possessed by many Europeans is closely related to the evident differences between their own particular national community and that of their neighbours. Moreover, nationalism is very much a European ideology and phenomenon. It emerged in the post medieval period when a strong self-consciously national community, endowed with political sovereignty, came to be seen as a normative form of political organization and collective identity. The intellectual, economic and military hegemony of Europe generalized national and nationalist sentiments across the globe.

The growth of the nation state has usually depended on the anathematization of difference within the state. Each European state increasingly assumed the character of a monoglot, ethnically and religiously singular community. Although there are still multi-national states in Europe (Spain and the United Kingdom) nations which had no states (Wends, Macedonians, Bretons) multi-lingual states (Belgium, Finland) and nations living in more than one state (Germans, Irish, Hungarians) these cases have tended to be seen as deviant exceptions to the nationalist norm.

After the First World War the Versailles and Sèvres Treaties enshrined the principles of the nation state and national self determination in the post-war settlement which attempted to establish a stable European order on the basis of President Wilson's Fourteen Points. As the Empires of the defeated belligerents broke up the trans-national Austro-Hungarian and Ottoman Empires were replaced by a 'Europe des Patries'. The horrifying transmutation of the Wilsonian idealism of national order into mass slaughter on a unprecedented scale (in the 'ethnic cleansing' institutionalized by the Nazis) led, after the Second World War, to a determination to rebuild post-war Europe on supra-national lines. East of the Elbe the Red Army implanted proletarian internationalism as the official ideology, west of the Elbe more pedestrian aspirations prevailed and the banal bureaucratic initiative of the European Coal and Steel Community provided the foundations for the supra-national European Community.

The eastern 'super state' of the Soviet Union and its satellites, imposed by conquest, has now disintegrated. The western super state has not. Unlike the political order of Europe East of the Elbe, post war Europe West of the Elbe built its supranational structures without conquest and unconstrained by duress. Although both political orders, East and West, depended on a submerging or sharing of the political sovereignty of nation states the sharing of sovereignty in Western Europe took place, more or less, voluntarily, that in the East, more or less, involuntarily.

The chief western initiative, the creation of the European Communities, was designed to reduce the sovereignty of European nation states and hence their capacity to wage war against each other. As Robert Schuman stated in 1950, the European Coal and Steel Community makes 'it plain that any war between France and Germany becomes not merely unthinkable, but materially impossible' (cited in Pinder, 1991, p. 1). The European Communities are the offspring of the Second World War; and the roots of many of the differences between the UK and its European partners lie in their very different experiences of the most recent in the succession of large scale orgies of mutual slaughter carried out in Europe in the name of nationalism.

The UK did not suffer defeat and occupation in the Second World War, nor has it experienced defeat, occupation and the invasion of its territory[1] for centuries. The founding fathers of the European Community have testified to the importance of such experiences to the foundation of the Community[2]. Walter Hallstein (the first President of the European Commission who held office from 1958 to 1967) stated 'It took the boundless excesses of nationalistic policy in the Second World War, and the equally total disaster they caused, to make obvious that in politics and in economics also, the countries of Europe must sink or swim together' (Hallstein, 1972, p. 18). The UK's approach to the Community stems, at least in part, therefore, from profound differences between its historical experience and that of the founders of the European Communities.

Monnet made a similar point. He recognized the importance of other differences in outlook and experience between the UK and the founders of the Community (notably the UK's commitment to free trade and its long established parliamentary democracy) but believed the crucial difference was in the experience, and therefore the meaning, of the Second World War. The UK's wartime experience might have been to the UK's advantage but, at least in Monnet's eyes, it ill-fitted the United Kingdom for the post-war order.

> ... they had not known the trauma of war-time occupation; they had not been conquered; their system seemed intact. In reality they suffered – paradoxi-

---

1 The Channel Islands apart.
2 The European Communities were not the only transnational European institutions to be created as a consequence of the Second World War. The sentiments which led to European bonding in and through the Coal and Steel Community, Euratom and above all the European Economic Community, also contributed to the establishment of the EBU. An Irish broadcaster, Muiris MacConghail, commented: The notion of the EBU derives from a generally shared communion of views amongst the foundation services in the European broadcasting area, after the Second World War, that structured co-operation between broadcasting organizations of post-war Europe and was in keeping with the notion of European reconstruction. Like other initiatives of co-operation at this time in the area of economic and social development, broadcasting co-operation and the role of the EBU was well intentioned, visionary even. (Telex to Miro Vilcek in connection with the EBU Perez group study on public service broadcasting 23.9.1982).

cally – from not having had their pride broken and their factories destroyed (Monnet, 1978, p. 452).

Monnet's and Hallstein's judgements were supported by British commentators. Lord Cockfield[1] stated that the Community's objective 'was the preservation of peace in Europe' (in Crouch and Marquand, 1990, p. 1) and described the Treaty of Paris (which established the first of the European Communities - the Coal and Steel Community) as a product of war-time traumas. The Treaty promised its signatories, he argued:

> ... to substitute for age old rivalries the merging of their essential interests: to create, by establishing an economic community, the basis for a broader and deeper community among peoples long divided by bloody conflicts (Crouch and Marquand, 1990, p. 2).

Francois Duchene (formerly the Director of Monnet's Documentation Centre of the Action Committee for a United States of Europe) echoed Cockfield. Moreover, Duchene asserted the importance of France's exclusion of the UK from the Community (France twice vetoed UK applications to join the Community) as a root cause of the UK's 'awkwardness' in the Community. Duchene stated that a French policy based on the *entente cordiale* as insurance against Germany precluded European integration: Britain had to be disconnected (Crouch and Marquand, 1990, p. 10).

The Community developed to suit the needs and interests of its original members and the UK acceded to membership of an organization devised to serve interests which were not always the same as its own. This is most easily shown by examining the status of the UK as, not only a net contributor, but the second largest contributor to the Community's budget. Germany contributed a net 5.55m ECU, and the UK a net 3.38m ECU to the Community budget in 1990 and France, the next net contributor, contributed 1.79m ECU. Other States which enjoyed a higher GDP per head than the UK were net beneficiaries of the Community's budget[2]. Indeed, on the Commission's figures (Commission of the European Communities, 1991c, p. 8), the UK enjoys a GDP per head (adjusted for purchasing power parities) which is only the fifth highest in the Community. As Biehl stated, the UK 'became the second biggest net payer in the EC system despite the fact that its GDP per capita has been below EC average for many years in the past. Clearly the principles of fair burden sharing and of *Finanzausgleich* (financial equalization) seem to have been violated ... the mirror image of the British situation is that some of the richer member countries are net receivers despite the fact that their GDP per capita is higher than the British' (Biehl in Crouch and Marquand, 1990, p. 95).

---

1 The Rt. Hon. the Lord Cockfield was a Vice-President of the Commission of the European Communities between 1984–1988 and responsible for the internal market (DG III).
2 1990 European Community payments and receipts. (Source *Financial Times* 10.2.1992, p. 12 using Commission of the European Communities statistics).

Fitzgerald (in Crick ed, 1991, p. 11) observes that the UK has the lowest proportion of its population working in the agricultural sector (3 per cent) of any EC Member State – yet the CAP (Common Agricultural Policy) accounts for 'a very large proportion' of the EC's spending[1]. Here is an obvious source of awkwardness between the UK and its Community partners. Fitzgerald also notes (in Crick ed, 1991, p. 20–21) that the UK is exceptional among Community Members in having a first-past-the-post electoral system and that the UK's Constitutional arrangements are quite unique in the Community:

> Britain's unwritten constitution is based upon the theory of the sovereignty of the Crown in Parliament, in relation to which the people of the United Kingdom are subjects rather than citizens. No other European country has a constitution of this type. This has influenced profoundly the psychology of both politicians and people in Britain (Fitzgerald in Crick ed, 1991, p. 18).

These differences, Fitzgerald argues, underpin the 'striking contrast between the adversarial British approach and the more consensual approach to politics that is characteristic...of many other EC countries' (in Crick ed, 1991, p. 20). Above all Fitzgerald argues that what is most striking about the UK's post war relations to Europe is 'the persistent failure of the British political system to carry through successfully the process of objective analysis of the character of British interests and of the optimal means of pursuing them' (in Crick ed, 1991, p. 12). Fitzgerald's view is shared by Davidson who referred to the comprehensive post-war failure, in respect of Europe, of the British political class (see above p. 2). Moreover Crouch and Marquand argue that the United Kingdom's established attitudes and behaviour fit it particularly ill for the Community of the future in which 'the economism of the original Monnet approach to European integration' is 'now out of date. The questions that cry out for answers now belong unmistakably to the sphere of high politics which the Monnet approach sought to circumvent' (Crouch and Marquand, 1990, p. xi).

The Community's founding fathers, Monnet among them, espoused a kind of economic determinism, whereby economic integration would necessarily, they believed, engender political interdependence. Monnet described the creation of the Coal and Steel Community as 'the basis for the building of a new Europe through the concrete achievement of a supranational regime within a limited but controlling area of economic effort' (Monnet, 1978, p. 316). Hallstein, in the foreword to his *Europe in the making* (Hallstein, 1972) stated 'The need is for political unity in Europe' and later (p. 20) discussed the development of European unity as 'largely political'. By contrast, the UK's political class (to use Davidson's term) has customarily viewed the Community as an economic project encumbered

---

1 In 1992 the CAP accounted for 35.3bn ECU of the Community's overall budget of 66.8bn ECU. In 1999 the Community's budget is projected to amount to 84.1bn ECU of which 38.4bn ECU will be committed to agriculture (*Financial Times* 14.12.1992, p. 2).

by parasitic political accretions, rather than as an essentially political project to be achieved by economic means.

The UK view of the Community as a free trade zone chimes with the enthusiastic embrace of the single market initiative, but determined opposition to pro-active industrial policy-making, by the UK. However, as the post-Maastricht debate has shown, Monnet's original vision of a Europe united through economic interdependence has now been transcended and transformed into a new project of European political union. The structure of the Community itself, a loose and contradictory agglomeration of federalist and intergovernmental structures and working arrangements, does not fit well with the new vision. The United Kingdom, however (which is not alone in finding Community institutional arrangements unsatisfactory and which has probably fought hardest against the loss of political sovereignty implicit in Monnet's vision) finds it particularly difficult to accommodate to a post-Monnetian idea of political, financial and military integration. In consequence, the United Kingdom is a powerful advocate of 'widening' the Community by extending membership to other European states, in opposition to those who argue for a 'deepening' of the Community by fostering the 'ever closer union' prescribed in the Treaties of Rome and Maastricht (notably in the political and cultural domains) among the existing member states before the Community is opened to new members.

Whether or not Crouch and Marquand are right that 'high politics' are required if the Community is to resolve the problems which it faces, political goals are now high on the Community's agenda. The Commission's five year plan for 1993–7 makes quite clear the supremacy of the political over the economic. It states 'How could the main objective of the European venture – political union – be achieved without the backing of a prosperous and dynamic economy? Unless this condition is fulfilled, it would be futile to promise success in the reinforcement of economic and social cohesion within the Community' (Commission of the European Communities, 1992, p. 14).

Damaging though Monnet regarded the dyed-in-the-wool protectionism of the French political class to have been, the French assumption, that political and economic interests and actions are interdependent, has clearly underpinned the Community's evolution. Story states 'French diplomacy regularly takes the lead in Brussels as champion of protectionist stances in international trade negotiations' (Story in Crouch and Marquand, 1990, p. 5). Simon (1992, p. 2) similarly observes that 'The traditional image of the French State is one of deep involvement, not to say intrusion, into economic affairs and private industry as opposed to other European countries like Italy or the UK'. The French approach developed under the 'ever closer union' provision in the 1957 Rome Treaty (and reiterated in the Maastricht Treaty) the provision which has been used to legitimize the *engrenage* (creeping incrementalism) whereby Community jurisdiction and authority have expanded. As the *Economist* (25.1.1992, p. 55) pointed out, even the Community's move towards free trade has offered opportunities to *dirigistes* who have interpreted free trade as necessitating comprehensive harmonization of regulations and thus new rule-making.

The UK vision of the European Community as a free trade area has not only long misrecognized the aspirations of other members (and poorly accommodated the interests of the Community's permanent officials) but increasingly misrecognizes the reality of the Community[1]. In spite of Major's commitments to putting the UK at the heart of Europe and to ratification of the Treaty on European Union, the UK still remains too close to the view of Europe voiced by Mrs Thatcher for the comfort of most other Community Member States.

The policy matrix

Shared commitment to the goals of political and economic union for Europe has not put an end to manoeuvring within the Community by Community Member States for political and economic advantage. The UK is not the only European Community Member State to pursue self interest. Indeed Duchene comments that self-interest has characterized French membership of the Community from its inception. France, he states, was 'violating the principle of equality ... demanding privileged status for France; and changing the rules she herself had earlier defined ... (and this) has been a recurring feature of French policy within the Community. The Community was created to safeguard the French from a more-than- equal Germany. But recurrently they have tried to exploit their position as its initiators to claim more-than-equal status themselves' (in Crouch and Marquand, 1990, p. 15).

Since Colbert in the seventeenth century, France has used political power and resources to foster national economic development and thrown up strong 'national champions' to serve French interests in international trade. The French have pre-eminently identified the state itself as the expression of the collective will and the interests of a singular and homogeneous national community. In an era of increasing international interdependence and shared sovereignty, which in post-war Europe has been manifested in the European Community, it is not surprising that France sees the Community as the new state, which requires a coherent, singular and homogeneous population and strong political direction of the economy if it is to prosper. The Community is the key international arena in which French interests (rather than collective European interests) themselves must be pursued. Fittingly, Monnet's ashes were interred in the Paris Pantheon in 1988.

Recent developments in the European Community have shown that political developments have moved from the economistic forms pioneered by Monnet to what

1 Only Denmark and Luxembourg had fewer respondents than the UK who answered affirmatively to the question 'In general are you for or against efforts being made to unify Western Europe?'. However even in Denmark (where enthusiasm for integration was lowest) 66 per cent of respondents answered that they were either 'very much' for or 'to some extent' for European integration. (Commission of the European Communities, 1991g, p. A 10).

Crouch and Marquand (1990, p. xi) call the sphere of high politics. Crouch and Marquand, however, highlight concern (1990, p. viii) that 'it is not self-evident that the Community's existing institutional structure is strong enough to bear the weight which these developments will place upon it'. This view is widely held in the Community, hence the long standing pressures to include the cultural domain (including the audio-visual) among the Community's competencies and which resulted in the inclusion of Clause 128 in the Treaty on Political Union negotiated at Maastricht in 1991.

In this area too the experience of the UK leaves it out of step with its Community partners. The UK (together with Ireland, Spain and Portugal) is a subordinate member of a large international language community but, unlike all other member states (except Ireland) the UK is also a member of the world's wealthiest language group. This has particular relevance for the audio- visual industry. The combination of membership of the world's wealthiest language community and the status of London as one of the world's three principal centres for media production, have given the UK and its audio-visual sector different perspectives and interests to those of the rest of the Community. No less than in agriculture do the UK's interests in the audio-visual sector differ sharply from those of its most important Community partners.

For most of the period of its membership of the European Community, the UK has had a positive balance of trade in film and in television programmes (CSO, 1991). This contrasts to the experience of its European partners. In an official publication of the Commission of the European Communities Maggiore (1990, p. 45) estimates that the UK accounted for more than 68 per cent of the Community's audio-visual exports in 1985[1]. Moreover London has become an important base for 'footloose'

---

[1] Maggiore states that UK audio-visual exports amounted to 335m ECU in 1985. However the UK Central Statistical Office estimated (CSO, 1992, p. 2) that UK receipts from overseas transactions (i.e. exports) from film and television programmes in 1985 amounted to £370m. Discrepancies between the official UK statistics and other sources are pervasive (see, *inter alia*, the report of the Assises Européennes de l' Audiovisuel which, like Maggiore, cites statistics for the UK which cannot be reconciled with official UK data, [for example Assises de l' audiovisuel, 1989, p. 95 and CSO, 1992, p. 3]).

Country	Payments (billion ECU)	Receipts (billion ECU)	GDP per head (Av 100)
Belgium	1.76	0.99	103.0
Denmark	0.77	1.20	107.2
Germany	10.36	4.81	113.4
Greece	0.56	3.03	53.0
Spain	3.67	5.38	76.3
France	8.09	6.28	108.6
Ireland	0.37	2.26	67.3
Italy	6.10	5.68	105.2
Luxembourg	0.07	0.01	128.7
Netherlands	2.62	2.93	103.1
Portugal	0.50	1.10	55.4
UK	6.53	3.15	103.7

European satellite television ventures. Moeglin (citing Truffart, 1991) observes that in 1990, of 12 transnational European television channels, 5 transmitted in English, another used English as one of its three languages, a seventh used no language and an eighth used several languages (including English). Of 96 national and regional television channels in the European Community 24 used English, far more than those using any other single language (Moeglin, 1991, p. 17). From the London perspective this appears to be a UK success and a benign consequence of the Single Market. From the standpoint of other Community capitals English language dominance is profoundly threatening.

The UK is sometimes regarded as the Trojan Horse for American audio-visual interests[1]. The symbiosis with the USA which the UK's audio-visual sector has achieved and the (relative) equanimity with which UK policy makers look forward to the restratification of audio-visual markets under the influence of technological and regulatory change is viewed with alarm by many of the UK's partners in the European Community. In France the growing presence of American films[2] and television programmes led to a recurrent play on the acronym, PAF. PAF (which came into common usage in France in the eighties) signifies *Paysage audio-visuel francais* but, more sinisterly, it came also to mean *Pourrisement audio-visuel français*. France with its strong cinematic tradition has led those in the Community who have sought an interventionist audio-visual policy to counteract the American and anglophone threat[3].

Today the achievement of the Community's political goals are widely perceived to depend on changes in European culture and consciousness, and here the European audio-visual industries assume a central importance. Those who wish to advance European political union have to confront the pluralistic and polyglot character of Europe, a character inimical to the 'ever closer union' enjoined in the Rome Treaty and which is profoundly disturbing to those European unionists who view Europe through the spectacles of nationalist theory and philosophy.

European unionists have sought to support growing European political structures with a corresponding European culture and consciousness shared by European citizens. Their efforts are directed to realizing in Europe what Gellner defined as the core of nationalism: 'homogeneous cultural units as the foundation of political life' (Gellner, 1983, p. 125). Thus Monnet's mysterious[4] statement to the effect that'if we were to begin again the building of Europe, we would begin with culture', has taken on a talismanic status. For European unionists audio-visual and broad-

---

1   The perception of the United Kingdom as a Trojan Horse is particularly marked in respect of the audio-visual sector but not confined to it. In respect of the automobile industry, for example, the UK is often seen as a Japanese Trojan Horse.

2   See Sorlin, 1991 for an excellent account of the complex relationships of European and American cinema.

3   The major exception has been where representations of sexual activity and sexual difference – issues of 'taste and decency' – are concerned.

4   'Mysterious' in that, whilst it is often cited – see *inter alia* [Commission of the European Communities, 1984, p. 10] – I have never seen its source identified.

casting policy has come, as the Commission stated (Commission of the European Communities, 1992c, p. 3) to the forefront of European concerns.

The UK, of course, tends to see things through the other end of the telescope to that used by France. The 'European state' is, in the characteristic British view, likely to hang together better as an association of separate entities than as a homogeneous cultural, political and economic unit. This reflects the United Kingdom's experience as a multi-national state embracing distinct national communities and significant differences in the language and law used in different parts of the UK. The United Kingdom believes that Europe will develop better through an intensification of competition and micro-economic change rather than, as Colbertian *dirigistes* tend to emphasise, through macro-economic change. Of course, the UK's own particular interests, especially in the audio-visual field, will also be best served by such a strategy!

The UK's audio-visual and broadcasting policy reflects its general orientation to the Community. It has strongly supported the Commission's initiatives to establish a single broadcasting market, and the UK was one of the first four member states to report its compliance with the provisions of the *Television without frontiers* Directive[1] (Council of the European Communities, 1989) to Brussels. By contrast, the UK customarily drags its feet when pro-active industrial policy measures are proposed and has strongly opposed any extension of the Community's competence to cultural issues, particularly in relation to broadcasting and the audio-visual sector. It sought to frustrate extension of Community competence into the cultural field when negotiating the text of the Maastricht Treaty on Political Union and to block inclusion of Article 128 in the Treaty.

---

1 A Directive is a Community legislative instrument which is implemented through national legislation in Member States. The *Television without frontiers* Directive was adopted by a qualified majority vote (Belgium and Denmark voting against) in 1989, it came into effect on 3.10.1991. Its requires free circulation of TV programmes within the Community, establishes a common basis for regulating advertising (including prohibition of tobacco advertising on television) and promotes European television programme production (especially by independent producers).

1

The broadcasting and audio-visual policy of the European Community: an overview

European media policy ... is a touchstone for judging whether the Member States, and public broadcasting corporations, are prepared to take European unification seriously and adopt a common policy on the media (European Parliament, 1985b, p. 35).

Media Policy is a crucial issue for Europe because broadcasting and the audio-visual industry cannot easily be separated from questions of culture and identity and they, in turn, bring into focus the conflict between those who view Europe as a Europe of nation states linked together in a convenient free trade area, and those who envisage a Europe moving towards a European consciousness, as yet nebulous and undefined. As we saw in the introduction, the nation state is a deeply-rooted political entity in Europe and the move towards any supra- national identity, especially in terms of culture, inevitably provokes, and will continue to provoke, fear and suspicion in many quarters. A highly committed strand of European opinion advocates closer union, in cultural as well as economic terms, and sees this as an ideal which will bring in its wake a final end to Europe's bloody and war-torn past. For others, this is at best naive, at worse self-serving. Debates about the media in Europe, therefore, involving culture as they do, are not only interesting because of what they reveal about different policies but also because of what they uncover about the complexes which the protagonists nurture about each other. In part, it is this which has made the media policy debate so emotive and fractious.

The European Community's broadcasting and audio-visual policy can only be understood by examining in some detail the power and prerogatives of the various

15

institutions of the European Community and the extent and limitations of their capacity to define policy for the broadcasting and audio-visual sector. Media policy in the Community has evolved through a complex interweaving of initiatives and responses of the European Parliament, the Commission of the European Communities and the Member States. The process has not been straightforward.

The political structure of the European Community

The political structure of the European Community includes a parliament (the European Parliament) a supreme court (the Court of Justice) and an executive (the Commission of the European Communities). It thus follows a well established western tradition of division of powers between legislature, judiciary and executive. However, not only does the European Community include unfamiliar institutions (such as the Economic and Social Committee, the Council of Ministers and the Court of Auditors[1] but, most important, the balance of power between the European Community's institutions of government is different to that customarily found in Western democracies. Thus the European Community is not so easy to understand as might first appear.

The executive of the European Community is the Commission of the European Communities, which has considerable power. The Parliament is relatively weak. Parliament's main power is its right to dismiss the Commission. However, it may exercise this power only through an affirmative vote of two thirds of its members and may not selectively dismiss a single Commissioner, or Vice-President or, indeed, the President of the Commission, but only the Commission in toto. Moreover the Community has an additional body which is less familiar to citizens of western democracies, this is a Council of Ministers, composed of a representative of each of the governments of the Community's Member States[2]. The most important loci of power in the European Community are the Commission and the Council. Community policy is customarily initiated by the Commission which consists of the permanent officials of the Community. Proposals from the Commission, when they are of general applicability or of particular importance, must be ratified by the Council of Ministers. However, although the Council of Ministers is described by the Community as its 'decision maker' (Commission of the European Communities, 1992b, p. 37) if proposals are not initiated by the Commission then the Council 'is paralysed' (Noel, 1988, p. 23). Moreover, the Council is only empowered to amend a Commission proposal if the amendment is unanimously agreed by Council Members. A Commission proposal, on the other

---

1 The Court of Auditors monitors the Community's budget and expenditure, the Economic and Social Committee is a consultative body made up of representatives of various areas of economic and social life, and the Court of Justice ensures that Community law is followed.

2 Voting in the Council of Ministers is weighted. Luxembourg has two votes, Denmark and Ireland each have three votes, Belgium, Greece, the Netherlands and Portugal each have five votes, Spain has eight votes and Germany, France, Italy and the United Kingdom each have ten votes. The total number of votes is thus seventy six and a qualified majority is fifty four votes.

hand, may be accepted, but only in toto, by a majority vote in the Council. As Noel (1988, p. 24) states, 'the Commission is always in a position to sway the outcome'.

The powers of the Commission are vividly exemplified in the Community's broadcasting policy. The most important of the Community's acts in respect of broadcasting[1] has been the establishment of a single market. This came about through the *Television without frontiers* Green Paper and Directive (Commission of the European Communities, 1984a and Council of the European Communities, 1989). These were both initiated by Commission officials in one of the Commission's Directorates General, DG III[2]. The single broadcasting market was neither proposed by the Parliament, nor the European Council or the Council of Ministers.

The four Directorates General (DGs)[3] of the Commission of the European Communities whose work bears most directly on broadcasting are; DG III (Internal Market and Industrial Affairs) DG IV (Competition), DG X (Audio-visual, Information, Communication and Culture) and DG XIII (Telecommunications, Information Industries and Innovation).

> DG III was the lead directorate for the Community's most striking initiative in the media field to date, the *Television without frontiers* Green Paper which was designed to establish a single European Community television market[4].

> DG IV is a peculiar case because, in spite of having no specific responsibilities for the broadcasting and audio-visual sector, its competition policies have had a very profound impact on the sector.

> DG XIII is concerned with telecommunications (including satellite and High Definition Television – HDTV) policy and sponsored the Community's Green Paper on communication satellites (Commission of the European Communities, 1990e) and the Community's Directive on satellite television transmission standards (Council of the European Communities, 1986 and 1992).

---

1   There are significant differences and regularities in Community usage of the terms 'broadcasting' and 'audio-visual'. A useful, but not infallible, presumption is that use of the term 'broadcasting' implies a liberal, market orientated, policy whereas the term 'audio-visual' suggests a more pro-active and *dirigiste* emphasis. Indeed Jean Dondelinger, when the Commissioner responsible for DG X, stated explicitly that the economic imperatives which have governed the Community's efforts to establish a single broadcasting market are inappropriate to the audio-visual sector.
The European film and television industry is among the sectors most seriously endangered by competition from other markets more accustomed to a free and easy diffusion of broadcasts over large areas. The role of the Commission is, of course, that of providing consistent means for policy and co-ordination at Community level. It is also that of actively supporting a sector little-adapted to purely economic competition (Dondelinger, 1989, p. 3).

2   In 1993 responsibility for policies relating to the media and the internal market (and the Commission officials concerned with formulating and implementing these policies) were transferred from DGIII to DG XV.

3   Other directorates, notably DG I, and DG XXI are also involved in audio visual policy. DG I, the Directorate for External Relations, is concerned *inter alia* with international trade in services (a contentious issue in the Uruguay Round of GATT negotiations) and DG XXI, the Directorate for Customs Union and Indirect Taxation, also has interests in broadcasting matters.

4   In late 1992 DG X was given responsibility for the implementation of the Directive (Council of the European Communities, 1989) which derived from the *Television without frontiers* Green Paper.

DG X has specific responsibility for the audio-visual industries and is the host directorate for the Community's MEDIA 95 programme.

The co-ordinating group of Commissioners responsible for harmonization of policy for broadcasting and the audio-visual, is chaired by the Commissioner responsible for DG X. DG X is also responsible for preparation and documentation of Commissioner meetings. The group meets regularly and, until the end of 1992, included the President of the Commission (Delors) and the Vice-Presidents and Commissioners responsible for DG I, External Relations (Andriessen), DG III, Internal Market (Bangemann), DG IV, Competition (Brittan), DG X, Audio-visual, Information, Communication and Culture (Dondelinger), DG XIII, Telecommunications, Information Industries and Innovation (Pandolfi) and DG XIX, Budgets (Schmidhuber).

A new Commission, appointed in late 1992 and in office until 1995, allocated responsibilities as follows; DG I, External Relations (van den Broek), DG III, Internal Market (Vanni d' Archirafi), DG IV Competition (van Miert), DG X, Culture and Audio-visual (Deus de Pinheiro), DG XIII Telecommunications and Information Technology (Bangemann), DG XIX, Budgets (Schmidhuber).

The Council of Ministers maintains a sub-committee on audio-visual policy which meets the Commission approximately every second month; but the meetings are convened by the Commission. The European Parliament has a Committee on Youth, Culture, Education, the Media and Sport which has responsibility for broadcasting and audio-visual matters but there is no regular contact or co-ordination between the Parliament and the Commission's Directorates on broadcasting and audio-visual policy (Sources: Interviews by the author November, 1991; Burgleman and Pauwels, 1991). The dominant body shaping policy in the area is therefore the Commission but the Commission is not a singular body with a unified policy.

DG III and, *a fortiori* DG IV, have a markedly more liberal, market orientation than the other directorates concerned with broadcasting and the audio-visual. They are often described as 'ultra liberal' by *dirigistes* and are regarded as particularly powerful. On the other hand, DG X, which is considered to be less powerful[1], and

---

1 It is not easy to identify which Directorate has responsibility for the allocation and administration of particular budget lines in the Community's annual budget. The budget is a notoriously opaque document and not all Directorates publish individual annual reports.

However an indication of the relative importance the Community attributes to 'hardware' (the province of DG XIII) and 'software' (DG X) can be found through a comparison of the 1990 outturns (payments) for the budget lines for Culture (B 3-2) – of 8,794,168.13 ecu and for Projects in the Field of Information Technology and Telecommunications (B 5-40) – of 29,905,225.84 ecu and Towards a Large Market and an Information and Communication Society (B6-52) – of 533,448,262.46 ecu. The 'hardware' programmes, located in DG XIII, are clearly more generously budgeted than are the 'software' programmes of DG X. (OJ L 26 3.2.1992 pp 318, 319, 914).

But comparison of budgets for the MEDIA programme (DG X) with those for IT and *(contd)* Telecommunications and Innovation and the Information Market (DG XIII) show that the disparity between the spends (shown in ecu) of the two Directorates are diminishing (see Table, p. 17).

MEDIA (B3-300)	Commitments	Payments
1990	11,091,999.70	9,038,357.84
1991	32,459,000.00	19,459,000.00
1992	48,262,000.00	32,000,000.00
OJ L 26 3.2.1992 p. 710		

(B5-40) Projects in Information and Technology and Telecommunications	Commitments	Payments
1990	26,633,261.83	25,610,512.20
1991	40,172,000	27,472,000
1992	39,623,000	38,250,000
OJ L 26 3.2.1992 p. 824		

Innovation and the Information Market (B5-50)	Commitments	Payments
1990	23,393,752	13,548,598.36
1991	30,583,000	27,783,000
1992	36,162,000	31,600,000
OJ L 26 3.2.1992 p. 825		

DG XIII, which is very influential, are Directorates which have advocated political intervention in the market. They have done so on a variety of grounds including; the economic and cultural importance of television, the power of new technologies to transform the audio-visual landscape, the necessity to develop powerful defences against external cultural and economic threats to Europe's television industries and television viewers, and the endemic failure of broadcasting and audio-visual markets. Indeed the MEDIA[1] programme (a Community programme which originated in DG X) has published arguments suggesting that the single broadcasting market (the goal and ideal of the free marketeers and enshrined in the *Television without frontiers* Directive) has been a Trojan horse permitting a dangerous American assault on Europe[2].

Clearly the different emphases of DG III and DG IV, on one hand, and DG X and DG XIII, on the other, echo other divisions within the Community, notably those between Community Member States.

---

1 An acronym for Measures to Encourage the Development of the Audio-visual Industry, MEDIA 92, later metamorphosed into MEDIA 95, required establishment by a unanimous vote of Community member states because cultural, including media, initiatives are not numbered among the specific provisions of the Community Treaty. Thus, under Article 235, unanimity is required for any action on such matters.

2 Under the title *Audio-visual opportunities in the single market* Roberto Barzanti (whilst President of the European Parliament Committee on Youth, Culture, Education, Media and Sport) stated, in the Newsletter of the MEDIA 92 programme: 'The American production and distribution model is best suited to the single market economy. It is better prepared to harvest the economic fruits of the single European market than any other national cultural industry in the Community' (Barzanti, 1990, p. 1). A similar argument was put by an official of DG III (interview with the author 11.11.1991) who stated that only the distributors owned by the United States were organized on a Community-wide basis and thus only they were able to benefit fully from the creation of a single market.

The UK has customarily agreed (interview with UK Official 10.2.1992) with the Netherlands, Ireland and Portugal (and sometimes with Germany) on broadcasting and audio-visual policy issues whereas France and Greece are usually at the opposite end of the policy spectrum to the UK. Italy seldom takes an active part in debates and the UK 'never' agrees with Luxembourg. The customary alliances on broadcasting and audio-visual policy questions make a 'fuzzy match' with alliances on other Community policy issues. 'Northern' states, notably Germany, the United Kingdom and the Netherlands, often take a 'liberal' free market, approach to Community affairs. 'Southern' states, notably France, but also Greece, and sometimes Spain and Italy, favour a *dirigiste* and interventionist approach. There is a related correspondence in the language customarily used in different Community Directorates: DG X and XIII usually use French, DG III and DG IV use English.

A (French) Commission official (interviewed by the author 7.11.1991) characterized the UK and France as the 'ideal types' of the opposed liberal and interventionist approaches and believed that 'The Information Industries will be central to this policy debate.'

Media policy and the European Community: how it has evolved

Strictly speaking, the Community has had an audio-visual policy only since 1988 when the Council of Ministers formally testified at its Rhodes meeting (for a fuller discussion, see Chapter Eight) to the importance of 'co-operation to develop Europe's audio-visual capacity' which would 'contribute to a substantial strengthening of a European cultural identity' (in Commission of the European Communities, 1990b, p. 7)[1].

However, the absence, before 1988, of an *official* policy (i.e. sanctified by the Council of Ministers) did not prevent the development of Community policies nor did it stifle debate between rival interests and viewpoints. The birth of the Community's broadcasting and audio-visual policy can, in fact, be dated as far back as 1982 when the European Parliament adopted the Hahn Resolution – the Resolution on Radio and Television Broadcasting in the European Community (European Parliament, 1982a – for analysis of the Hahn Resolution see Chapter Two). Community policy has also developed in conjunction with other European institutions, notably the Council of Europe and the Audio-visual Eureka, through European 'Variable Geometry' (the term used to describe the furthering of policy through a variety of European institutions, notably, but not exclusively, the Coun-

---

1   The Council reaffirmed its commitment to the audio-visual sector at subsequent meetings in 1989 at Madrid and Strasbourg (see Commission of the European Communities, 1990b, pp. 8–9). At Rhodes the Council of Ministers acknowledged the French Government's role in developing the Community's audio-visual policy, and in particular the part France had played in orchestrating the meeting in Paris (which was to take place the following year) variously known as the Audio-visual Eureka or the Assises de l'audiovisuel.

cil of Europe, rather than through the institutions of the European Community alone)[1].

The audio-visual and broadcasting policy of the European Community can be seen, over the years, to have focused on three distinct but interdependent sectors:

On *hardware* (notably the setting of television transmission standards);
On *software* (notably the production and distribution of films and television programmes);
On the *restructuring and harmonization of the television broadcasting market.*

Within all three sectors, however, media policy has evolved in a complex and unpredictable way. Shifts in policy and practice in one sector have often had unanticipated consequences in another. Shifts in the balance of power and activity between Community institutions; changes in the priority given to different sectors in the overall domain of broadcasting and audio-visual policy; alterations in the Community's high policy goals; and modifications to the instruments chosen for the realization of policy goals have all shaped the evolution of Community broadcasting and audio-visual policy. In addition, the Community's policies on broadcasting and the audio-visual sector are not only influenced by political dynamics within the Community itself but, like those of individual states, they are influenced and limited by the Community's international relations[2].

The Community's broadcasting and audio-visual policy was described by a Commission official (interviewed by the author on 11.11.91) as having three 'legs':

The establishment of rules (notably through the issue of Directives);
The promotion of film and television production (and promotion of the circulation of resulting works);
The development of the technological competence and productive capacity of the Community.

This 'triptych' is set out in the *Communication from the Commission to the Council and Parliament on audio-visual policy* (Commission of the European Communities, 1990). The 1990 'Communication' identified the European audio-visual market as

---

1   The Commission has stated that its audio-visual policy proposals had been influenced by discussions at the Assises de l'audiovisuel (Audio-visual Eureka) held in Paris in 1989. Also, the regulatory regime, established under the Community's Directive on television broadcasting (Council of the European Communities, 1989) is interdependent with the Council of Europe's Convention on Transfrontier Television.

2   The GATT Uruguay round negotiations have been particularly important. The European Community wished to remove the audio-visual and broadcasting sectors from the general provisions of a GATT in services by establishing an annex for them. The issue was, at the time of writing, opposed by the United States and Japan and is so far unresolved. However the outcome of GATT (and the status of the audio-visual and broadcasting sectors in GATT) and therefore the shaping of Community policy, will be affected by the trading-off of interest in one sector to secure goals in another. Thus the future course of Community audio-visual policy may well be determined by the outcome of GATT negotiations on agriculture, textiles, public procurement and services. Certainly the audio-visual sector is 'in play' internationally. The *Financial Times* (22.1.1993, p. 4) identified the audio-visual sector as one where the European Community must make concessions if it is to achieve its goals for other sectors and bring the Uruguay Round negotiations to a successful conclusion.

a failed market and declared that political intervention was required to redress the market's deficiencies. The European market was perceived to be 'dominated by American and Japanese firms', vitiated by 'structural constraints' and deficient in comparison to that of the United States. The Commission argued that there were scant incentives for broadcasters in Europe to produce programmes for secondary markets or to market programmes vigorously. Moreover, a plurality of European producers were faced with a few powerful monopsonistic distributors and yet, in spite of the dominance of monopsonist distributors, Europe had too few distributors who were 'capable of bringing out a film or videocassette in all European countries at the same time with adequate promotion budgets'. Accordingly the Commission proposed that 'promoting the emergence of ... distributors must become one of the priorities of Europe's audio-visual sector' (Commission of the European Communities, 1990, p. 18).

The Commission's response to its own damning analysis was also to call for changes in the 'rules of the game'; it proposed measures to support the emergence of more distributors, harmonization of national copyright laws to ensure pluralism in the European audio-visual sector and development of a secondary market for films and television programmes (Commission of the European Communities, 1990, pp. 3–4). The Commission also advocated continued development of the MEDIA programme (see below for a discussion of the MEDIA programme) and a prioritization of support to Small and Medium-Sized Enterprises (SME's) to achieve 'the restructuring of the audio-visual industry and ...promote a balance between the large and small national industries' (Commission of the European Communities, 1990, p. 4). In respect of technology, the Commission trailed a new Directive on satellite television transmission standards and a Community programme for development of High Definition Television (HDTV).

The motifs in the Commission's 'Communication' were all familiar; initiatives had already been undertaken in respect of all the elements in the audio-visual triptych well before the formal establishment in 1988 of the audio-visual as a domain of Community competence. There were also many precedents for the concern voiced by the Commission in its 'Communication' about the penetration of the European audio-visual space by exogenous films and television programmes and the perceived linked decline in pluralism in Europe's media markets.

Despite its aspirations, the Community has found it difficult to develop policies which would preserve and develop small enterprises, artisanal production, 'quality' products and production in small language communities while at the same time permitting the production of television programmes, films, videos that are fully competitive with imports. To date, it has found no satisfactory means of resolving this conundrum and of reconciling rival interests. Community enterprises which have successfully established themselves on a large scale within the Community or in a competitive international audio-visual market (or both) inevitably have a different viewpoint from those which perceive themselves to be threatened by the Europeanization (or the internationalization) of the broadcasting and audio-visual sector. English-language producers can, in varying degrees, more readily sell their films and television programmes to the world outside the Community than can other Community language groups. Language is a key indicator to the side of the argument which a Member State supports.

Ironically the major factor stunting the growth of small enterprises has been, according to many commentators, the Community's own policy of 'the free circulation of services'. Of all the goals which the Community has defined for its audio-visual and broadcasting sectors the *Television without frontiers* idea has come closest to realization through the establishment of a single market for television (see Commission of the European Communities, 1984a and Council of the European Communities, 1989). Yet this successful initiative has, at the same time, been a key factor in eroding long established European audio-visual policies and orders. The single market initiative, therefore, despite its relative success, has not enjoyed unanimous support from all Community members[1]. Support for compensatory action (within both Community and national contexts) to counteract the effects of market integration has risen following adoption of the *Television without frontiers* policy[2].

Two themes therefore distinguish the development of European Community broadcasting and audio-visual policy: creation of a well functioning, integrated, competitive European *market* for broadcasting and the audio-visual and *intervention* in the Community's audio-visual and broadcasting market(s) to redress what have been perceived as undesirable outcomes of the single market. Broadcasting and the audio-visual has therefore been a notable site where one of the 'grand narratives' of the Community has been played out, the battle between interventionists and free marketers, between '*dirigistes*' and 'ultra liberals'.

Paradoxically, the voluminous literature[3] of reports, resolutions, communications

1 See, for example, the Commission's action against the German Film Industry Support Act discrimination against non-German EC nationals. *The week in Europe*, WE/4/92, 30.1.1992, p. 2.
2 Community broadcasting and audio-visual markets remain imperfectly integrated notwithstanding the promulgation of the *Television without frontiers* Directive, the Community's commitment to 'ever closer union', the Maastricht Treaties and the Single Market initiative. Whilst Community measures have undoubtedly permitted and promoted integration of audio-visual markets (e.g. between France and the Walloon Community in Belgium and between the Netherlands and the Flemish Community of Belgium) the most important factor which structures audio-visual markets is the difference in language and culture between different groups of Community citizens. Whilst barriers to entry to the UK market for a German satellite television channel have been very significantly reduced as a consequence of Community policies UK viewers still watch minute amounts of German television.
3 Below is a highly selective list of chief documentary landmarks marking the development of Community policy: The Hahn Report and Hahn Resolution (European Parliament) both of 1982; *Realities and tendencies in European television: perspectives and options* (Commission) 1983; *Television without frontiers* Green Paper (Commission) 1984; The Framework Report and Resolution (*A framework for a European media policy based on the commission's green paper on the establishment of the common market for broadcasting, especially by satellite and cable*) (Parliament) 1985; *Television without frontiers* Draft Directive (Commission) 1986; Directive on satellite television transmission standards (MAC standard) (Council) 1986; Action Programme to promote the audio-visual industry (MEDIA) (Commission) 1986; *Television without frontiers* Directive (Council) 1989; Communication on audio-visual policy (Commission) 1990.

23

and papers which have marked the evolution of Community broadcasting and audio-visual policy have resulted in only three definite initiatives:

On satellite television transmission standards;
The creation of single broadcasting market;
A programme of support for audio-visual production and distribution (Council of the European Communities, 1986, 1989, 1990, 1992).

It should also be stressed that DG IV (the Competition Directorate of the Commission of the European Communities), despite having no specific responsibilities for broadcasting and audio-visual policy, has played a decisive role by using its powers of regulating economic activity to foster competition in broadcasting.

The politics of audio-visual policy

European Community media policy has evolved within the framework established by the major European treaties and declarations, notably the Treaty of Rome and the European Convention on Human Rights (which although promulgated under the aegis of the Council of Europe has been signed by all Member States of the European Community). However the legal foundations on which Community policy has been built have, thus far, been insufficient to support comprehensive initiatives in the cultural – including audio-visual – field. In consequence Community institutions, notably the Commission, supported by the Parliament (and in particular by its Committee on Youth, Culture, Education, the Media and Sport) and some Member States has sought specific cultural powers either by revision of the Treaty of Rome or, latterly, by inclusion of a culture article in the Maastricht Treaty on European Political Union.

However some Member States, notably Denmark and the UK, have opposed revision of the Rome Treaty on the grounds that 'cultural policy should remain an exclusively national competence' (European Parliament, 1989, p. 14). Thus far the objections of the dissenting minority of Member States to cultural policy initiatives have prevailed. Article 235 of the EEC Treaty, the Treaty of Rome, provides that Community action on matters not explicitly mentioned in the Treaty (including culture) requires unanimity in the Council of Ministers[1].

The combination of Danish concern to ensure that Community powers do not extend into an area which it regards as the exclusive province of the national government, and the desire of the UK (and Germany) to ensure that Community spending on culture does not grow, have seriously limited Community initiatives in the broadcasting and audio-visual sector.

In consequence the Community's actions in the broadcasting and audio-visual sector have had to be undertaken either as strictly economic measures which are

---

1 The UK was opposed to the culture article in the Maastricht Treaty. However, rather than incur opprobrium and weaken its bargaining position on other issues deemed to be more important, it sought to minimize the competence of the culture article (Article 128) rather than oppose it completely.

permitted under the EEC Treaty (the most notable instance here has been the *Television without frontiers* policy which established a single Community broadcasting market) or by using the Commission's limited discretionary spending powers (the most notable example here being the Community's MEDIA 92, latterly MEDIA 95, programme).

Unity *vs.* diversity

The first signs of a Community policy for the audio-visual and broadcasting sector can be discerned in the early 1980s. Two main tendencies were then evident. The first, and better known, was liberal, directed towards establishment of a single competitive broadcasting market in the Community (without necessarily presuming what the resulting market would deliver). This tendency centred on the *Television without frontiers* Green Paper (Commission of the European Communities, 1984a) and ultimately resulted, five years later, in the promulgation of the Community's directive on television broadcasting (Council of the European Communities, 1989). Liberal attempts to create a single market were opposed by some important policy actors who sought to redress what they perceived as the failures of European broadcasting and audio-visual markets, notably the single television market created in consequence of *Television without frontiers.*

Interventionist policies, however, were by no means straightforward. Initially, intervention was advocated to redress the perceived failure of Community broadcasting and audio-visual markets and to foster a single European culture (i.e. the European market delivered too much diversity). Latterly, however, interventionists have sought to compensate for what they perceived to be an undesirable reduction in diversity (i.e. too much unity) in the integrated television market. Establishment of the MEDIA Programme, to support audio-visual production and distribution (Council of the European Communities, 1990) and inclusion of European content quotas (to protect European producers) in the broadcasting directive (Council of the European Communities, 1989) constituted the principle interventionist measures in the domain of software (production and distribution of film and television programmes).

The second focus of the interventionists, on hardware, has been more significant and established, for reasons of electronics industrial policy, an integrated Community satellite television market. In 1986 the Community issued a Directive on satellite television transmission standards (Council of the European Communities, 1986) to establish MAC satellite transmission standards as a Community norm. It acted in order to restructure what was perceived to be a failed satellite television market and establish a market based on a single technical standard, to facilitate the incremental development of HDTV in Europe, and to support the European consumer electronics industry. However prioritization of a particular standard, D2-MAC, meant that transnational, Community wide, television services reaching audiences of different language communities became more difficult to implement than would have been the case had a different standard been preferred[1]. Promotion of a single hardware market militated against the creation of a single Community software market.

Analysis of European Community broadcasting and audio-visual policy must explore the themes of rivalry between liberal and *dirigiste* approaches, the relationship (and cross impacts) of hardware and software oriented policies (and the linked, but not wholly isomorphic conflict between emphasis on economic and cultural goals for broadcasting and audio-visual policy) and changes in emphasis from cultural unity to cultural diversity as a Community policy goal.

In the middle 1980s, the rationales advanced by *dirigistes* for intervention in Community broadcasting and audio-visual markets changed strikingly. Formerly the role of broadcasting in fostering European *unity* was emphasized. Latterly preservation of *cultural diversity* came to the forefront. Formerly the importance of the media as a means to *disseminate political information* was highlighted: latterly their economic and cultural importance has been judged more important. Jacques Delors' address to the European Parliament at the opening of its 1985 session (after taking up office as President of the Commission of the European Communities) signals this shift, Delors emphasized cultural (and economic) rather than political aspects of audio-visual policy.

> 'Do you know, ladies and gentlemen, that what we might call the culture industry will tomorrow be one of the biggest industries, a creator of wealth and jobs? Under the terms of the Treaty we do not have the resources to implement a cultural policy; but we are going to try to tackle it along economic lines. It is not simply a question of television programmes. We have to build a powerful European culture industry that will enable us to be in control of both the medium and its content, maintaining our standards of civilization, and encouraging the creative people amongst us' (Delors, 1985, p. 64).

Delors' emphasis on the economic reflects both a recognition of the strictly economic importance of the cultural industries and the necessity for any cultural or political dimension to Community policy to be packaged within an economic rationale[2]. For the Treaty of Rome gave the Community (and most importantly the Commission) jurisdiction in the economic but not in the cultural sphere. By stressing the economic importance of the cultural industries Delors was able to bring the cultural industries within the Commission's realm of authority. However,

---

1   The Directive authorized use of three MAC standards, C-MAC, D-MAC and D2-MAC. But D2-MAC was the only standard approved for both cable and satellite use. D2-MAC was better fitted to use on many existing cable systems than were either C or D MAC standards, however D2-MAC has capacity for only two stereo (or four mono) sound channels. Provision of multilingual services, aimed at audiences in more than two separate language communities, were thus rendered difficult.

2   However it is striking that Delors' speech to the European Parliament in 1992 (Commission of the European Communities, 1992) – the main theme of which was the Maastricht Treaty – makes no mention of culture.

outside the European Community (notably at the Assises de l' audiovisuel)[1], Delors has strongly asserted the *cultural*, as well as the economic, importance of the audio-visual and broadcasting sectors.

Recently the main thrust of the Community's audio-visual policy has been directed to ensuring that audio-visual and broadcasting policy does not reduce pluralism but, on the contrary, helps to strengthen it 'by encouraging, in particular the diversity of the programmes offered to the public' (Commission of the European Communities, 1990, p. 21). But there is no consensus on how best the goal of pluralism is to be achieved. 'Ultra liberals' in DG III and IV have sought to ensure that public broadcasters are unable to exploit their dominant position and that Member States do not privilege their own country's productions (or their own nationals). *Dirigistes*, however, have perceived the single market itself as the main threat to pluralism and consider public broadcasters to be bastions of pluralism against emergent commercial media concentrations. The concern for pluralism led to the publication of a Green Paper (originating in DG III) on pluralism and media concentration in the internal market (Commission of the European Communities, 1992g).

Thus both *dirigiste* and liberal policies for the Community audio-visual and broadcasting sectors are now asserted and developed under a common banner of pluralism (diversity). This recent emphasis is in clear contrast to that of the 1980s when in *Realities and tendencies* (Commission of the European Communities, 1983) *Television without frontiers* (Commission of the European Communities, 1984a) and in the *Hahn report* (European Parliament, 1982a) a restructured broadcasting order based on the new technology of DBS and the new single market structure was advocated as a powerful agency for the creation of unity in the European Community.

The Community's audio-visual policy is not the product of a single and unified Community vision of the audio-visual sector. Rather it is the result of the tortuous interaction of differing priorities and perspectives of several distinct power centres, notably the Member States of the Community, the European Parliament and rival power centres within the Commission of the European Communities itself. As Community officials in DG IV confirmed (interview with author 11.11.1991) the views and interests of DGs are different. In consequence the story of the European Community's broadcasting and audio-visual policy is complicated and difficult to tell.

---

1   The Assises de l'audiovisuel were held in Paris in 1989 and were jointly sponsored by the Government of France and The Commission of the European Communities.

2

Origins of an audio-visual
policy for Europe

The so-called audio-visual field includes from a political point of view, a wide range of issues – from the free circulation of services to the support of the European consumer electronic industry, and from the preservation of the cultural identity of countries to regulations on copyright and competition (Dondelinger, 1989, p. 3)[1].

Community audio-visual and broadcasting policy has focused on three distinct, but interdependent sectors; on hardware, notably the setting of television transmission standards; on software, notably film (and to a lesser extent television programme) production; and on a mediating third sector, distribution (principally television broadcasting)[2]. Community policy has often appeared contradictory because the Community has attempted to integrate and improve the competitiveness of the Community's markets and then moved to countervail the results of this integration through interventionist policies. Broadcasting and audio-visual policy has, therefore, been an arena for one of the great ideological struggles in the Community between liberals on the one hand and interventionists on the other. Thus far, however, the struggle has been

---

1   Jean Dondelinger, when Commissioner responsible for DG X, explicitly stated that the economic imperatives which governed the Community's efforts to establish a single market are not appropriate to the audio-visual sector. 'The European film and television industry is among the sectors most seriously endangered by competition from other markets more accustomed to a free and easy diffusion of broadcasts over large areas. The role of the Commission is, of course, that of providing consistent means for policy and co-ordination at Community level. It is also that of actively supporting a sector little-adapted to purely economic competition.' (Dondelinger, 1989, p. 3).

2   Although the tendency in the Community has increasingly been to consider film and television under a single rubric of the 'audio-visual', films (and video-cassettes) are treated as 'goods', and are therefore subject to Articles 30–37 of the EEC Treaty (which deal with the free circulation of goods) whereas broadcasting was established to be a service in the Sacchi case of 1974 and is therefore subject to Articles 52–56 of the EEC Treaty (which deal with free movement of services and freedom of establishment).

unequal, for interventionists have been hampered by the Community's lack of jurisdiction in cultural matters.

The Culture Article of the Maastricht Treaty represents the culmination of a long struggle to place cultural matters within the Community's competence. Both the European Parliament and the Commission of the European Communities advocated the addition of a specifically cultural clause to the EEC Treaty. The 'Culture Article' in the Maastricht Treaty on European Union is the result.

Some Member States, notably Denmark and the UK, however, have been, and are, deeply opposed to the inclusion of culture within the competencies of the Community. Denmark's and the UK's opposition to the extension of Community competence to the cultural domain is based on the presumption that '... cultural policy should remain an exclusively national competence' (European Parliament, 1989, p. 14). It is not only Denmark and the UK that have qualms about the extension of Commission jurisdiction into the cultural domain, Germany and Belgium too have resisted closer cultural union (although their opposition has been less determined than that of either the UK or Denmark).

The limits to Community competence, and the consequential effective veto powers exercised by single member states in cultural (and hence audio-visual) policy matters under the Treaty of Rome, has meant that several significant audio-visual initiatives have been launched outside the formal institutional context of the Community, using European 'variable geometry'. The audio-visual Eureka of 1989 and the Eurimages production fund (established in 1988 under the aegis of the Council of Europe but described by Wangermee (1989, p. 2) as 'interesting but provided with derisory resources') are the most striking examples of 'variable geometry'[1].

The liberal vs. *dirigiste* debate

As we have seen in Chapter One two main tendencies in the European Community's television and audio-visual policy developed in the early 1980s. The first, and better known, was the liberal policy thrust directed to the establishment of a single broadcasting market in the Community (without necessarily presuming what the outcomes of the resulting market would be). From this developed the *Television without frontiers* Green Paper (Commission of the European Communities, 1984a) and, ultimately, the Community's directive on broadcasting (Council of the European Communities, 1989). Commentators on Community broadcasting and audio-visual policy (see, *inter alia*, Negrine and Papathanassopoulos, 1990) have rightly identified this single market initiative as the most important of the Community's actions in the audio-visual field so far. The establishment of a single market for television (the major factor affecting the distribution and circulation of audio-vis-

---

1 See also the Paris Symposium on European Cultural Identity of 1988 (SIICE, 1988).

ual products within the Community) is associated with the work of DG III and DG IV.

However, the second interventionist policy thrust arose out of attempts to redress the perceived failures of European broadcasting and audio-visual markets. This policy cluster is associated with DG X and DG XIII and with the European Parliament. Within the overall interventionist approach there were two foci; one on software and the other on hardware (see Chapter 1 for discussion). Intervention in the software sector has increasingly sought to compensate for the undesirable reduction in diversity in the integrated market. This tendency can be dated from the Schall report (European Parliament, 1980) and the Parliament's Resolution of 18.9.1980 on radio and television broadcasting in the European community (see below for a fuller discussion). In recent years, interventionists have referred more and more to 'audio-visual' rather than to a television (or broadcasting) policy and have focused attention on the European audio-visual (including film) production industry and its needs[1]. The Community's most important initiatives in respect of production of audio-visual software is the MEDIA programme. This interventionist policy cluster is associated with DG X.

The second focus on hardware has seen a significant interventionist attempt to establish an integrated Community satellite television market. The attempt to establish MAC satellite transmission standards as a community norm (Council of the European Communities, 1986) was undertaken in order to redress what was perceived as the chaotic operation of the satellite television market. The intention was to establish a satisfactory market for some of the European consumer electronics industries and to permit the incremental development of HDTV in Europe (for a fuller discussion see Chapter 1). This policy cluster is associated with DG XIII.

Although issued with a 'health warning' that 'The contents of this publication do not necessarily reflect the official views of the institutions of the Community...' DG X's European File Document *European Community audio-visual policy* (Commission of the European Communities, 1992c) represents the principal audio-visual policy concerns of the *dirigistes* within the Community. Its starting point is the changing audio-visual landscape in the Community where the cinema sector is in decline but where the supply of television viewing opportunities is increasing as new channels are established, and programme imports grow.

The Commission claims that audio-visual policy is '... in the front-line of its concerns' (Commission of the European Communities, 1992c, p. 10) because 'much hangs on ... audio-visual policy: it will have industrial, technological and cultural repercussions. The latter are vital for the preservation of the diversity of European culture and identity' (Commission of the European Communities,

---

1   Note for example the change between 1984 and 1986 in the titles of the European file publications from *Towards a European television policy* (European File 19/84) to *Television and the audio-visual sector: towards a European policy* (European File 14/86).

1992c, p. 3). It is paradoxical, but not extraordinary, that the Commission's policy statement in 1992 (the year of the single market) and the conclusion of a treaty on European political Union, should emphasize diversity. The Commission's contemporary emphasis on diversity contrasts with the emphasis it placed on unity a decade before. This shift in emphasis can be understood if we examine how the European Parliament reacted to broadcasting and audio-visual issues in the past decade.

The role of the European Parliament

Unlike the legislatures of Community member states, the peripatetic European Parliament[1] has little power. The European Community has a very powerful executive but a weak legislature. Indeed the weakness of the European Parliament has led to the European Community being described as having a 'democratic deficit' (Commission of the European Communities and European Parliament, 1990, p. 6). The most significant of the Parliament's powers are those it exercises over the Commission's discretionary expenditure[2].

The European Parliament is also empowered to call Commission officials to account for their work and policies before its committees and through Parliamentary questions. However, as a Conservative UK Member of the European Parliament (MEP) ruefully remarked 'The Commission tries to do as much as it can without involvement of the Parliament' (interviewed 6.11.1991).

Not only is the Parliament weak in comparison to the Communities' major power centres, the Commission of the European Communities and the Council of Ministers, but its Committee charged with responsibility for the media (including television) is generally regarded as having low status and little influence. UK MEPs, from both Conservative and Labour parties (interviewed in November 1991) commented that the Committee on Youth, Culture, Education, the Media and Sport enjoyed the lowest status of any of the European Parliament's Committees. One Labour MEP observed that it was described by Denmark as 'the illegal Committee'[3]. The other said 'its work means sod all. It's the bottom of the pile in terms of

---

1 Plenary sessions of the Parliament are held in Strasbourg. However its Secretariat is in Luxembourg and its committees meet in Brussels. The European Community's Court of Justice and Court of Auditors are located in Luxembourg whereas the Commission of the European Communities is permanently located in Brussels. The Community's Economic and Social Committee (an advisory body made up of representatives of interest groups such as trades unions, employers' associations and consumer groups) is also located in Brussels. The European Parliament has been directly elected by citizens of the European Communities in quinquennial elections since 1979.

2 The Single European Act (signed in 1986) came into force in 1987. It established a 'co-operation procedure' between Commission and Parliament which strengthened the Parliament's powers vis-à-vis the Commission. The Commission has now to secure the Parliament's assent to its expenditure on 'non-obligatory items' and the Council of Minister's assent in respect of 'obligatory' expenditure. For a useful summary of the contemporary constitutional issues in the Community see *Financial Times* 13.8.1991, p. 2.

3 A reference to Denmark's recurrent argument that, Culture being part neither of the Rome Treaty nor of the Single European Act, Community assertion of jurisdiction in Culture was *ultra vires*.

importance, at the end of the day the Council of Ministers will decide, end of bloody story.'

A Conservative MEP characterized the work of the Committee on Youth, Culture, Education, the Media and Sport as 80 per cent examination of proposed legislation (i.e. responding to Commission initiatives) and 20 per cent 'own initiative' work. Characteristically the Committee responds to the Commission's agenda for the Community rather than setting the agenda itself. Mary Banotti, the Vice Chairman (sic) of the Committee on Youth, Culture, Education, the Media and Sport confirmed that the Parliament's role was essentially reactive by stating that the Committee 'does play a significant part in amending Community legislation' (Banotti, 1992, p. 6). Few MEPs have a specialized knowledge or interest in the media. The Parliament's views on media (and other matters) therefore tend to be set by a few expert members. As Banotti testified 'each Committee contains a very mixed group of people in terms of experience and specialized knowledge. One or two people tend to deal with a piece of legislation and the others concur with their conclusions' (Banotti, 1992, p. 6). None of the UK MEPs interviewed in 1991 regarded the media as one of their primary interests or areas of expertise. Indeed only the Chairman of the Committee[1] and two of its substitute members[2] were thought to have the media as a particular area of interest and expertise.

Nonetheless, as de Vries put it (European Parliament, 1987, p. ii) 'limited powers do not necessarily imply limited influence'. Indeed, in spite of the Community's 'democratic deficit' and the weakness of the 'illegal committee', strong claims have been made for the importance of the European Parliament's influence in developing Community broadcasting policy. Gijs de Vries (a senior Dutch Liberal Democrat MEP who was President of the European Parliament Intergroup Television) claimed that Community audio-visual policy was initiated by the Parliament rather than by the Commission or the Council. The Parliament, he claimed, 'prompted the Commission into publishing, first the Interim Report, and in 1984, the Green Paper on the Internal Market in broadcasting ... Parliament has thus *de facto* initiated legislation' (European Parliament, 1987, p. ii). Roberto Barzanti, formerly Chairman of the Parliament's Committee on Youth, Culture, Education, the Media and Sport, echoed de Vries' claims for the importance of the Parliament. Barzanti described the Parliament's Hahn Resolution (see below) as the *première pierre* in Community audio-visual and broadcasting policy (interview with author 8.11.1991) and elsewhere, Barzanti has advanced strong claims for the importance of the Parliament's contribution to policy making. He stated:

> Le parlement européen est depuis toujours chef de file parmi les institutions européennes pour affirmer le rôle de la communauté dans les débats et les initiatives qui se produisent en Europe autour du secteur audiovisuel. Il s'agit,

---

1 Then the Italian Member of the Party of the Democratic Left, formerly the PCI, Roberto Barzanti.
2 Dieter Schinzel a German member of the SPD and Karsten Hoppenstedt a German member of the CDU.

bien évidement, d' un secteur de l' industrie: mais il s'agit aussi, et dans aussi une mesure du moins aussi importante que l'autre, d'une activité culturelle (Barzanti, 1990a, p. 35)[1].

However, de Vries has argued that not only has the Parliament initiated Community audio-visual and broadcasting policy but that the Parliament remains the locomotive of Community media policy. Certainly the Parliament continues to urge comprehensive Community initiatives in respect of the audio-visual sector; the Committee on Youth, Culture, Education, the Media and Sport has established a close alliance with DG X and has consistently advocated *dirigiste* measures for broadcasting and the audio-visual; for example 'The European Parliament consistently called for a comprehensive Community media policy, which not only removes legal and technical barriers to a common market for broadcasting but also supports European audio-visual products' (European Parliament, 1987, p. 22)[2]. But its influence, as is that of DG X, is weak in comparison to that of 'ultra liberals'.

The Parliamentary publication titled *Audio-visual policies of the Community. The role of the European Parliament* (European Parliament, 1987) usefully lists the major documents and resolutions which have marked the development of Community audio- visual policy (and the Parliament's role in particular). It does so under three main heads: Television without Frontiers, Satellite Television, and The Audio-visual Media Industry. It defines the objectives of European Community audio-visual policy as ensuring that:

> The access of every Community citizen to the greatest number of programmes broadcast by the various channels of the Community in conformity with the treaty;
> The establishment of a common market in broadcast services. This is of vital importance to Europe both culturally and economically;
> A community framework for broadcasting regulation having regard to international technological developments in broadcasting and telecommunications;
> The promotion of television programmes with European content to supplement the existing national one (European Parliament, 1987, p. 3).

and to:

> Redress the structural economic weaknesses of the programme production sector in the Community;
> Maintain European identity and diversity, working for a better balance among the small and large cultural areas in Europe;

---

1 'For a long time, the European Parliament has led European institutions, in discussions and in practical initiatives, in developing an active role for the Community in the audiovisual sector. The audio-visual is certainly an industrial sector but it's no less important as a cultural activity.'
2 John Woodward the Chief Executive of the Producers' Alliance for Cinema and Television (PACT) stated (interview 13.9.1991) that de Vries was 'deceiving himself' and that the Commission rather than the Parliament remained the decisive locus of European Community power in respect of the audio-visual sector.

Increase mobility of persons, equipment and products of the European audio-visual industry;

Obtain better co-operation within Europe on the financing, production and distribution of audio-visual programmes and a closer partnership between cinema and television (European Parliament, 1987, p. 20).

In contrast, a UK MEP stressed that the Parliament's broadcasting policy priorities were first of all industrial and protectionist. Another stated that 'by and large it's about manufacturing TVs. Broadcasting is low down on the list of priorities. The story is one of fear of competition, from Japan in hardware and competition, from America in films and programmes' (interview 7.11.1991).

The European Parliament's contribution to the development of a Community audio-visual policy began with the Schall report, which was adopted by the Parliament in January 1981 (OJ C 28. 9.2.81, p. 74). The Schall Report criticized the Community's information policy and stated that, '23 years after the signature of the EEC Treaty, the level of information about the Community among the citizens of the Member States remains low and that neither the Commission nor the European Parliament have so far been able to carry out their duty to provide information on a scale commensurate with the importance of the European Community and its objectives' (OJ C 28. 9.2.81, p. 74).

Accordingly the Schall report emphasized the importance in information work of radio, television and film material to reach a mass audience (OJ C 28. 9.2.81, p. 76) and advocated pro-active measures by the Community, notably the establishment of a European television company or the creation of a European television channel, to promote the Community and its activities and institutions to Community citizens.

The Hahn Report, and the consequential Hahn resolution, followed publication of the Schall report and were adopted by the Parliament in 1982 (European Parliament, 1982 and 1982a). The Schall and Hahn initiatives testified to the Parliament's growing recognition of the importance of television and the audio-visual sector. These landmark documents of the early 1980s embodied an assumption that television is a profoundly influential medium. Television, the Parliament presumed, had the properties of a powerful social glue with the potential to cement the Community more closely together by bringing information about the Community's political institutions and practices to its citizens. Television could foster support for the Community and advance the 'ever closer union' enshrined in the Treaty of Rome. By representing the culture and civilization of Europe to Community citizens, television would engender a truly European consciousness and a collective European identity capable of transcending the established limited, national identities of Community citizens.

Television was thus a vital element in securing the Community's future and consequently merited direction, protection and support rather than abandonment to the chance outcomes of the market. Indeed the Parliament's Political Affairs

Committee stated explicitly (in its contribution to the Hahn Report) that it feared broadcasting becoming 'an article of merchandise in the framework of the Common Market' (European Parliament, 1982, p. 23). The Parliament's Political Affairs Committee was particularly alarmed by the prospect of satellite broadcasts flooding the Community 'in unlimited quantities as though they were a commercial product' (European Parliament, 1982, p. 24). The Parliament, and the Committee on Youth, Culture, Education, the Media and Sport in particular, were therefore hostile both to establishment of a single Community broadcasting market and to the Commission's increasing use of competition regulations to restructure Community broadcasting markets.

Roberto Barzanti, when Chairman of the European Parliament's Committee on Youth, Culture, Education, the Media and Sport (at a felicitously named conference 'Coherence in Diversity. The Challenge for European Television' held in Luxembourg in 1989) refuted application of regulations and competitive regimes similar to those applied to other industrial sectors in the cultural industries. 'On ne parle, quand même, pas de viande ou de grain: la disparation de la production dans une région, une nation ou un continent sur la base de la concurrence equivaudrait à la fin de l' autonomie culturelle et de la liberté d'expression.' (Barzanti, 1990a, p. 36)[1].

Barzanti echoed arguments made the previous decade by the Parliament's Political Affairs Committee which had stated that the free operation of a broadcasting market was inimical to the central values of the Community. But rather than emphasising, as did Barzanti, that cultural identity and freedom of expression were important values threatened by a market regime for broadcasting, the Political Affairs Committee argued that:

> ... the maintenance of public order is as important to the Member States, in protecting their own fundamental rights and preserving their cultural and political identity, as the principle of a free flow of information. Unrestricted cross-border commercialization is dangerous ... regulation should embody the structural guarantees necessary for independence without which a European broadcasting war will inevitably break out which may destroy the cultural values of our Community (European Parliament, 1982, pp. 24–25).

The European Parliament's Committees, whether affirming the super ordinate value of order or that of freedom, have characteristically opposed development of a liberal, market-based, broadcasting and audio-visual regime within the Community. The Parliament has rather argued for a broadcasting regime of 'positive freedom' – freedom to – rather than the regime of 'negative freedom' – freedom from – (see Berlin, 1969) based on the values enshrined in the European Conven-

---

1 'After all, we're not referring to grain or to meat; eliminating production in a region, a nation or a continent through competition is tantamount to the end of cultural independence and freedom of expression.'

tion on Human Rights which provided the doctrinal underpinnings for the vision proposed two years later by liberal interests in *Television without frontiers*.

The Hahn Report (see below for a full analysis) described by Barzanti as the *Première pierre* in the edifice of Community audio-visual policy, advocated a Community broadcasting regime based on regulation and pro-active initiatives by political authorities. Hahn's vision was pre-eminently one of a broadcasting order of 'positive freedom' created to serve the cause of European unity and to redress the deficiencies of media markets. The authors of the report believed that the desired outcomes could not be realized through the free operation of markets. The Hahn Report and Resolution may thus be seen as an attempt to forestall the *Television without frontiers* initiative (which emanated from DG III of the Commission of the European Communities in 1984). The European Parliament was therefore a key institutional location from which an interventionist audio-visual policy for the European Community was put forward. This policy perspective foregrounded political, and latterly cultural, objectives for the broadcasting and audio- visual sector rather than the economic objectives foregrounded by liberals.

The Hahn Report and Resolution

In September 1980 the Parliament referred to its Committee on Youth, Culture, Education, Information and Sport a resolution tabled by Wilhelm Hahn[1] and others on *Radio and television broadcasting in the European Community*[2]. The Committee appointed Hahn as rapporteur to formulate its *Report on Radio and Television Broadcasting in the European Community* (European Parliament, 1982) which was submitted to the Parliament on 23 February 1982. The Hahn Report, as the report is invariably named, contained two draft resolutions (one from Hahn and another from Schinzel[3] which were subsequently composited to form the so called Hahn resolution adopted by the Parliament later in 1982 (European Parliament, 1982a).

Hahn identified the mass media, and television in particular, as instruments through which the European Community could become a genuine 'political community'. The Hahn Report stated that 'Information is a decisive, perhaps the most decisive factor in European integration' (European Parliament, 1982, p. 8) and that 'The instruments which serve to shape public opinion today are the media. Of these, television, as an audio-visual means of communication, is the most important' (European Parliament, 1982, p. 8). The Committee judged that the political

---

1 Hahn was a German Christian Democrat refugee from East Prussia.
2 The resolution was also referred to the Committees on Budgets, Political Affairs and Legal Affairs. The Committee on Budgets did not submit a view on the resolution. The reports of the committees are in The Hahn Report (European Parliament, 1982).
3 Schinzel's resolution was on 'The threat to diversity of opinion posed by commercialization of the new media'. In October 1992 the European Parliament adopted a further report drafted by Schinzel which advocated establishment of a European Media Council and other measures to counteract concentration of ownership in the European media.

integration which it desired was unlikely to be achieved whilst 'the mass media is controlled at national level' (European Parliament, 1982, p. 8).

The Committee's emphasis on political union reflected long-standing and powerful sentiments which are especially prevalent in the officials and political class of the Community. O'Brien (1992, p. 3) has referred to the disparity between the formal, confederalist, constitutional status of the Community and the federalist and integrationist emphases of its officials, emphases which he exemplified citing the Commission's document *European unification: the origins and growth of the European Community* (Commission of the European Communities, 1990f, p. 25) which defined a fundamentally political goal and character for the Community: '... economic integration is not meant to be an end in itself but merely an intermediate stage on the road to political integration'. Community audio-visual and broadcasting policy has been shaped by the same process. As the Schall and Hahn reports reveal, integrationist sentiments were important factors in the early definition of broadcasting and audio-visual policy in the Community.

The Hahn Report gave particular attention to the new technology of satellite television. As well as *threatening* a broadcasting war, as the Parliament's Political Affairs Committee (European Parliament, 1982, pp. 24–25) had foreseen, in which European culture might be annihilated, satellite television also *promised* (if suitably guided) hope to European integrationists. The Hahn Report suggested that 'television satellites will lead to a reorganization of the media in Europe; the new technical facilities will break down the boundaries of the national television networks and enforce the creation of wide-ranging transmission areas' (European Parliament, 1982, p. 8). Hahn, echoing the Schall report of two years before, stated that 'what is needed to match the scope offered by future technical facilities is in fact a European television company or at least a European television channel' (European Parliament, 1982, pp. 9–10).

A profound belief in the power of a new communication technology, satellite television, was common to both the pessimistic vision of the Political Affairs Committee and the hopes expressed in the final Hahn Report which considered several vehicles for the realization of the unionist hopes including a pan-European television company. However Hahn concluded that establishment of a new pan-European television company was not realistic (European Parliament, 1982, p. 11) and that therefore the creation of a 'joint European channel' should be encouraged under the auspices of the European Broadcasting Union (EBU). The Hahn Report envisaged that the European channel would not be transmitted from a dedicated satellite but 'via the fifth channel that will in future be available to the Member States on their satellites' (European Parliament, 1982, p. 11). The committee referred approvingly to the EBU proposal (first canvassed at the meeting of the EBU New Developments Committee in Venice in 1980 by Vittorio Boni, when Head of RAI's International Department) to establish a European satellite television channel. It was from this proposal that the EBU's first satellite ventures, Eurikon and Europa, actually developed and which subsequently led to the establishment of the EBU sponsored channel Eurosport in 1989 and Euronews in 1993)[1]. The Parliament therefore strongly supported the EBU's nascent pan-European initiative Eurikon[2].

Hahn's vision of pan-European television was based on a proposal by the West German public broadcasting company ZDF. ZDF had proposed a mixed schedule for a European programme service, of a kind very familiar to viewers of European public service broadcasting but which embodied the Committee's notion of European culture embodied in 'unity in its diversity of forms' (European Parliament, 1982, p. 9).

The ZDF proposal was described as follows.

> The experts of the ZDF have given a convincing presentation of how a European television channel might look in detail and their proposals are quoted below:

>> The following types of programmes could be presented from a European angle:
>> – News bulletins: these should present world news in the traditional sense and, in addition, one news bulletin could present the day's events from a European viewpoint;
>> – A European magazine programme: such a programme could present the European problems which are of particular concern to the man (sic) in the street, either on film or live. The emphasis in such a magazine programme would therefore be the human dimension in Europe;
>> – Feature films, current affairs reporting or historical documentaries: priority should be given to exchanges of programmes between countries. The contributions should increase understanding of internal developments in the countries of Europe and of European interdependence;
>> – Live reports from the European Parliament and Council of Ministers: there could be live link-ups with several foreign broadcasting companies;
>> – Language teaching;
>> – Cultural programmes: cultural programmes from the whole of Europe could be shown – something which rarely occurs in the television time

---

1   The experimental Eurikon channel was transmitted in 1982 by a consortium of EBU members from Austria, Germany, Italy, the Netherlands and the United Kingdom. Europa was established by a consortium of public service broadcasters (from Germany, Ireland, Italy, the Netherlands, Portugal) in 1985 and was closed down the following year. It was judged to be particularly relevant to the Commission's audio-visual and information policies, especially in two fields: (i) the use of the difficult technique of *multilingual broadcasting*; (ii) the elaboration of multinational editorship for the production of a *genuine European information*, at a time when extra-European broadcasting specialized in news – like the CNN (Cable News Network) of Mr Ted Turner – want to set foot on the European market (Commission of the European Communities, 1986b, p. 4). The Commission supported Europa in the hope that it would contribute to the achievement of two of the Community's enduring policy goals: political integration, which was assumed to depend on increased cultural integration, and the associated goal of the Europeanization of the content of European television.
2   For discussion of the EBU's satellite television ventures see *inter alia* Collins, 1993, Papathanassopoulos, 1990, Wright, 1983.

currently available. This would mean that more existing European pro-
grammes could be shown in German versions and would also serve to
encourage a further development, namely co-productions bringing the
television systems and the viewers into contact with the whole of Europe.
In this type of co-production, for example, the French could report on
Kracow, the British on Estremadura and the Dutch from Transylvania;
  – Programmes on travel and foreign countries;
  – Educational and scientific programmes;
  – Programmes for the children of immigrant workers: there are many
immigrant workers from European countries living in the Federal Republic of Germany and the question is being raised increasingly why no
children's programmes are broadcast for these groups. The European
channel could make this possible;
  – Entertainment: this would primarily mean the extension of the different types of shows presenting songs and European games and quiz
programmes;
  – Music and theatre: live transmissions of major cultural events throughout Europe (from theatres, opera houses, etc.);
  – Sport: an additional European channel would extend facilities for
more live coverage of sporting events;
  – Live transmission from European centres: on a European channel it
would be possible to devote a whole day's transmission time to a programme of outside broadcasting from one place, incorporating news,
entertainment and sport (European Parliament, 1982, p. 15/16).

Subsequently ZDF advocated not the mixed channel format which Hahn cited but
more focused, thematic, pan-European satellite television channels, notably a
sports channel.

This vision of European union was found much more congenial by the Parliament
than the single market advocated under the rubric of *Television without frontiers*.
Hahn supported a European television channel with both political and cultural
rationales albeit the authors of the report recognized that the legislative foundations of the Community provided few footholds for cultural initiatives[1].

---

1 The Political Affairs Committee, to which the Hahn and Schinzel resolutions had been remitted, was
   unequivocal in its judgement that media matters were outwith the remit of the Parliament and
   Commission. It stated 'There is no provision for media policy in the Treaties of Rome' (European
   Parliament, 1982, p. 22) and affirmed that historically such matters had been the concern of the
   Council of Europe (rather than the Parliament or Commission). The Legal Affairs Committee, though
   more constructive in its attempts to find a basis for action by Parliament or Commission than was the
   Political Affairs Committee, supported the judgement of the Political Affairs Committee. It argued
   that, though Article 100 of the EEC Treaty did not provide a foundation for media policy, Article 235
   might do so. More recently, e.g. in the Council Directive on the co-ordination of certain provisions
   laid down by law, regulation or administrative action in Member States concerning the pursuit of
   television broadcasting activities (often known as the *Television without frontiers* Directive) the EC has
   had recourse to the EEC Treaty and to its provision 'establishing an ever closer union among the
   peoples of Europe' to legitimize the growing Community activity in the audio-visual field.

The main text of the report states that:

> The Treaties of Rome relate to the Common Market and are limited to the economic and agricultural fields and their repercussions on the world at work ... However, both the complexity of the resulting technical mechanisms and the concentration on specific aspects have impeded the emergence of a European awareness. The concept of 'Europe' had definite negative connotations in the sense of an uncontrolled and frequently absurd bureaucratic machine (European Parliament, 1982, p. 9).

Accordingly Hahn found other grounds on which to base the proactive media initiatives it wished to foster and referred to the statement of the President of the European Commission the previous year:

> Europe's future is, of course, not only a question of economics ... this political community will not be created without a common political will ... without action by the Member States, without the involvement of the citizens of Europe, without cultural projects or an information policy, these high-flown ambitions will probably be only short-lived (European Parliament, 1982, p. 9).

The Hahn Report proposed that the Commission report on the media by mid 1983, this recommendation was supported by the Parliament in its resolution (the Hahn resolution, the text of which is reproduced as an appendix). From the Parliament's Report and Resolution flowed the Commission's interim report *Realities and tendencies in European television: perspectives and options* (Commission of the European Communities, 1983).

3

Pan-European television

The audio-visual sector is the new-born child of traditional activities such as film production, broadcasting and the electronics industry. These sectors are both public and private and fall under the categories of both industry and culture ... The dimensions of the sector are not impressive as yet. In 1985, its turnover was estimated at ECU 15,400 million in Europe, representing 0.4 per cent of the GNP of the European Community. Television accounts for 58 per cent of this total, and 120,000 people are employed in the whole of the industry (Maggiore, 1990, p. 11).

Realities and tendencies in European television

The European Commission's Interim Report, *Realities and tendencies in European television: perspectives and options* (Commission of the European Communities, 1983) was inspired by the Parliament's Hahn Resolution (European Parliament, 1982a) and was drafted in DG X. In its report the Commission stated that new telecommunications technologies (in particular DBS) would internationalize European television by 1990 and that technological changes would both 'afford the citizens of Europe greater opportunities to learn about, appreciate and participate in the cultural unity of our continent' and offer competitive advantages to Europe an industry and culture (Commission of the European Communities, 1983, p. 5). Accordingly the Commission proposed a policy with four main foci:

To devise ...

> A general framework for the 'European system' with (sic) will be constituted by the satellite cable and traditional network, and to examine the economic and financial aspects of the new situation, including the question of advertising;
>
> In industrial policy, the aim must be to adopt uniform technical standards and to support European industry;
>
> Integration at European level of the programme market, in terms both of

production and demand – including the integration of cinema and video production;
Action ... to maintain the pluralism of cultural identities that go to make up the cultural unity of Europe (Commission of the European Communities, 1983, p. 5).

The Commission argued that television was 'the field where the new technologies – satellites, cables and video – will have by far the heaviest impact on existing structures' (Commission of the European Communities, 1983, p. 7) and, following on from the Hahn resolution, specifically nominated the EBU's pan-European television satellite experiment Eurikon ('the common European programme') as constituting one of 'the first steps in the areas mentioned' and committed itself to 'provide political and material support and a reference framework for this initiative by the EBU and its members' noting that 57 per cent of Community citizens supported a European television channel (Commission of the European Communities, 1983, p. 6).

The Commission's report focused on 'consideration of the practical possibilities of getting a European television programme onto the screen' (p. 8) thus responding to the proposals of the Schall and Hahn reports (European Parliament, 1980 and 1982) and the provisions of the Hahn (and later the Arfé and Hutton resolutions [European Parliament, 1982a, 1984a and 1984c]).

However the Commission introduced a new theme and emphasized that, increasingly, the anticipated massive expansion of European television distribution capacity[1] (due to satellite television) would not be matched by a commensurate growth in production capacity. The growing imbalance between production and distribution would suck exogenous programme material into the European market. The imbalance posed what the Commission described as 'a threat of invasion by a foreign culture' (Commission of the European Communities, 1983, p. 11). Concern about the import of exogenous films and television programmes has been a consistent motif in Community policy since publication of *Realities and tendencies*: indeed the first paragraph of the Commission document *European Community audio-visual policy* states that 'a great many imported series, soap operas, documentaries and cartoons are shown on European television' (Commission of the European Communities, 1992c, p. 3). The extent of foreign (principally American) penetration of European audio-visual markets was quantified at the Assises de l' audiovisuel in 1989 as follows:

---

1 Although events did not unfold quite as the Commission expected – the '30 cable television channels, 3 television channels for direct broadcasting by satellite (DBS) and 3 traditional television channels, with 10 hours of transmissions a day on each channel' which the Commission foresaw (Commission of the European Communities, 1983, p. 9) did not become generally available. Nonetheless there was a substantial growth of television distribution capacity in the Community albeit through media different to those foreseen by the Commission. In some localities – notably Spain and the United Kingdom – video cassette recorders were a major force, in others, such as West Germany, additional terrestrial television channels were the principal loci of growth.

In 1988 European countries bought $700 million of American programmes – France bought 228 million, Germany 151 million, Italy 85 million, Great Britain 86 million and the other European countries 93 million – (Assises de l'audiovisuel, 1989, p. 95)[1].

Again and again *Realities and tendencies* returned to the question of European culture and to the role of television (and satellite television in particular) in shaping culture and cultural identity and articulated the twin determinisms, technological and cultural, that run through the Community's broadcasting and audio-visual policy. *Realities and tendencies* states:

> DBS will become a powerful unifying factor. Viewers in one country will be able to share television programmes with viewers in other countries and will thus acquire a new feeling of belonging and involvement. This sharing of pictures and information will be the most effective means of increasing mutual understanding among the peoples of Europe and will give them a greater sense of belonging to a common cultural and social entity. The development of a truly European spirit will therefore become possible in national audiences, who will still, of course, retain their full cultural identity (Commission of the European Communities, 1983, p. 22).

Realities and tendencies articulates the kernal assumptions on which the interventionists' programme for the European broadcasting and audio-visual sectors have rested. First, that technological change, notably satellite television, will reshape European broadcasting and second that the changes in the content and character of European broadcasting consequent on technological change will reshape the cultural, and hence political, identities of European viewers and listeners. On this double determination the case for intervention in European broadcasting rests.

European identity: what is it?

The 1983 *Realities and tendencies* document reveals the Commission's conception of cultural identity to be non-exclusive and plural; European identity can, apparently, be added to national identity without diminishing either. Yet, if this is so, why is the presence of an exogenous, non-European, culture to be feared? If national cultures can non-exclusively co-exist with a European culture why can they not do so with the foreign culture, to which the report referred (Commission of the European Communities, 1983, p. 11)?

Perhaps such questions should not be pressed too far. To demand consistency and rigour in documents which are the result of a continuing process of political

---

1 The individual country totals cited at the Assises do not add up to the overall total cited, and the figure cited for the UK's purchases of American television programmes in 1988 does not correspond to that identified by the UK's Central Statistical Office (which estimated that the UK had purchased £73m of television programmes from North America in 1988 (CSO, 1992, p. 3). This suggests that the Assises estimates should be regarded cautiously.

bargaining and compromise is unrealistic. None the less the precarious coherence of the assumptions on which policy, and policy rhetoric, about television is based is worth noting. As Heath comments 'Nowhere do technological determinism and cultural pessimism meet with so much assent as in attitudes to TV' (Heath, 1990, p. 268).

Cultural Identity is a much abused term. Mattelart *et al.* (Mattelart, 1984, p. 17–18) identify four ways in which the concept of cultural identity leads to misperceptions and misrecognitions. First it leads to inappropriate policy measures; notably the creation of national audio-visual content quotas which, Mattelart and his co-authors assert, create an illusion of effective political action but do 'essentially nothing'. Moreover a quota 'establishes a geographical limit between the here and the elsewhere' (Mattelart, 1984, p. 17). This formulation is not easy to understand but seems to suggest that quotas establish arbitrary boundaries between the protected jurisdiction and the rest of the world and inhibit cultural synthesis and adaptation. Second, quotas serve particular sectional producer interests, the price for which is 'an asphyxiating localism' (Mattelart, 1984, p. 18). Third, the notion of cultural identity engenders a mechanical synthesis between the local and the global whereby a 'national label is stuck on a transnational copy' (*ibid*). And fourth invocation of cultural identity by policymakers can mask a form of cultural imperialism whereby one actor 'presents itself as a champion of a linguistic community and simply treats the latter as a market unified by a common language rather than taking account of its underlying diversity' (*ibid*).

During the early 1980s when the integrative themes of a single market and a unified European culture were dominant in European Community policy making European cultural identity was constructed in terms of unity rather than diversity. The classic nationalist syllogism, that political institutions survive only when they are congruent with cultural communities (states are robust and legitimate only in so far as they are isomorphic with nations and nations are communities differentiated from other communities by cultural difference) informed Community broadcasting policy. If the Community was to survive it needed a common culture and a shared European identity.

Bouke Beumer (a Dutch Christian Democrat MEP who served as Chairman of the European Parliament's Committee on Youth, Culture, Education, Information and Sport) argued for a 'melting pot' concept of Europe – that is for unity rather than diversity – in terms similar to those used in *Television without frontiers*. Beumer supported a European television channel (and a Community film and television production fund) on the grounds that, without such media, the Community risked a weakening of community solidarity and unity as a consequence of too much media diversity[1].

---

1   Although the concepts of a common European culture and shared European identity were often invoked they were rarely defined. I have found only one definition of European identity in a Community document. The European Parliament in its Resolution on the European Community's Information Policy of 1986 defined what are called 'the basic values of European culture' which are

One of the dangers which threatens us is that if we wait too long, there will be a proliferation of European programmes, so that the voice of the European institutions ... will come too late to gain the necessary range and volume, will not come over clearly enough and will not reach the necessary standard (OJ Debates of the European Parliament 12.3.85. N. 2- 324, p. 59).

Beumer's remarks are representative of Community discourse during the first half of the decade 1982–92 when a double determinism governed the Community policy debate. Technological determinism would ensure that new communication technologies (notably satellite television) would transcend and supplant national media. Cultural determinism would ensure that the cultural characteristics of the programmes would be reproduced in the consciousness of those who consumed their output[1].

Hence the support by the Community (and other transnational European institutions such as the Council of Europe and the European Broadcasting Union) for the Eurikon and Europa satellite television channels and later for the European Broadcasting Union's Euronews satellite television channel[2].

Advocates of television as a vehicle for creation of a unified European culture were quickly disabused of their beliefs. Attempts to establish pan-European television services (whether commercial or public service) in the 1980s failed. The conception of a unified European culture (which was thought necessary to complement and sustain a European polity) thereby became hard to sustain as differences in the tastes of European viewers were revealed.

In the first half of the decade (1982–92) pan-European television was believed to be a benevolent friend to the Community. Television would turn national television viewers into Europeans and the mass media would make possible the development of the 'ever closer union' prescribed in the Treaty of Rome. In the second half of the decade the malevolent side of pan-European television came to the fore.

(contd) 'peace, social solidarity, freedom and the rule of law'. (European Parliament, 1987, p. 112). Of course these values are not the exclusive property of Europe and many would argue that they are universals.

1 These ideas, though not so vigorously advocated as heretofore, are not dead.

2 The EBU provides a striking instance of the contradictory policies of the Commission of the European Communities. The EBU's Eurovision system of news and programme exchanges and collective acquisition of programme rights has established the closest approximation that yet exists to a shared European mass medium of communication. In consequence the EBU has received financial and policy support from the Community for many of its initiatives (such as the Europa television channel, Euronews, and the partnership between the EBU and the Commission in BABEL). However the Secretary General of the EBU stated (interview 27.2.1992) 'The Commission will destroy the EBU if it gets its way'. He referred to the persistent challenges to the EBU's practices by the Commission's Competition Directorate, DG IV, on the grounds that the EBU's collective acquisition of rights and exchanges of programmes between members were anti- competitive. (See in particular OJ L 63/32-44 9.3.1991 which records the Commission's judgement that the EBU's partnership with News International in the Eurosport channel infringed Article 85(1) of the EEC Treaty). However, the wind blowing from Brussels to Geneva changed again in 1993. After appointment of a new Commissioner for Competition, the Commission of the European Communities authorized continuance of the EBU's Eurovision programme exchanges (Commission Decision 93/403/EEC, June 11, 1993).

Integrated European audio-visual markets themselves were seen as an enemy of cultural diversity and a threat to the authenticity of the Community's endowment of national languages and cultures. Pan-European television showed both sides of its Janus face as the decade unfolded.

Unity in diversity?

The notion of unity in diversity as the principal defining characteristic of European culture (a term specifically used in the Hahn Report [European Parliament, 1982, p. 9]) is worthy of closer examination because it was so influential and because it reveals the difficulties facing 'closer union' in the cultural field.

The Hahn Report's notion that 'all the Member States and regions must contribute to the channel' (European Parliament, 1982, p. 15) implied a programme schedule for a projected pan-European television channel which would be representative of the Community's diversity. However the potential audience for the service was composed of viewers who, everywhere in the Community, showed strong preferences for their own country's television. The kind of channel envisaged by Hahn was 'supply side' pushed (with politicians and bureaucrats doing the pushing) rather than 'demand pulled' by viewers.

The European Community's polity (and television audience) is undoubtedly culturally diverse. The degree to which it is culturally unified is less obvious. If it is culturally unified then its unity exists only at a level of generality insufficient to differentiate Europeans (or strictly citizens of the European Communities) from other major world communities. European culture in this sense is part of what Gellner (1992, p. 10) called 'Atlantic civilization ... committed to consumerism, pluralism and aversion to ideological enthusiasm'[1], rather as Mrs Thatcher emphasized in her notorious Bruges speech (Thatcher, 1988)[2].

Indeed the shared European experience of difference may simply manifest itself in a shared sentiment of difference rather than in a common sentiment of Europeanness. Many within the Community have opposed the notion of unity in difference, believing it to be inherently contradictory (and even nonsensical) and an insufficient basis on which to construct the cultural unity deemed necessary for the political unification of the Community[3]. The dominant cultural-political theory

---

1 Gellner's list of the attributes of 'Atlantic civilization' can be restated more kindly as commitments to 'peace, social solidarity, freedom and the rule of law'. It was these attributes which were identified as the constitutive elements of European culture by the European Parliament (in the Baget Bozzo Resolution [European Parliament, 1987a]).

2 The links between Europe's two anglophone states and the Anglo-Celtic diaspora in the United States, Australia, Canada and New Zealand are but the most obvious of many examples. An intriguing testimony to the overseas reach of European culture was given by André Fontaine, the editor of *Le Monde*, at the Symposium on European Cultural Identity sponsored by the Government of France in 1988. Fontaine said 'Je me trouvais plus en Europe, à la limite, à Buenos Aires qu'à Paris, parce qu'à Buenos Aires, il n'y a pas des enseignes en anglais' (SIICE, 1988 p. 96) ('I feel more genuinely in Europe in Buenos Aires than in Paris because in Buenos Aires there are no signs in English.')

3 See, *inter alia*, the arguments of Bouke Beumer for a European 'melting pot'. Beumer stated that

which has informed Community debates about culture is nationalism. True, classic one-country nationalism has consistently been opposed by the Community but the arguments made within the Community for European identity, European culture and European union are built on the same structural principles. As has been pointed out in the Introduction, Gellner (1983, p. 43) usefully describes the core of nationalist belief as 'the striving to make polity and culture congruent'. Consequent on this normative notion of the isomorphism of politics and culture (and of political and cultural identities) is the presumption that the creation of a political structure must involve creation of a corresponding cultural entity (if indeed no such cultural structure antedates the new political arrangements).

Thus, those who believed both in the importance of European political union and the necessary interdependence of polity and culture had, either (or both) to identify an antecedent European culture to match the desired European political structures, or create a unified European culture to match European political unity (and here television and the mass media were felt to have a major role to play). The difficulties lay (and lie) in the evident cultural and linguistic diversity of Europe and Europeans and the fact that they shared with non-Europeans many of the values which constitute the common European heritage.

This last was a particular difficulty. If a sentiment of collective identity exists in a sentiment of shared difference from others, then European political and cultural elites faced a problem in trying to find some ways to differentiate Europe from the United States (see for example Delors, 1985). Mrs. Thatcher's insistence on the shared patrimony of Europe and the United States when speaking in one of the temples sacred to European union was scandalous because it uncovered this. European culture and identity, no less than national culture and identity, was left seeming to consist of nothing other than, what Minogue (1967, p. 25) named, 'a collective grievance against foreigners'.

Nonetheless the notion of unity in difference is one to which European policy makers continually had, and still have, recourse. If European culture is to be, as it often is, invoked as a rationale and goal for public policy, then it requires definition. The notion of 'unity in difference' has been convenient for policy makers. It has enabled them to glide over difficult questions. For broadcasters, however, it is not a principle capable of being successfully operationalized in the contemporary European broadcasting market. A broadcaster who schedules programmes, which express the variety of experiences and the range of differences which distinguish Europeans, is unlikely to attract large audiences and is equally unlikely to create a new unity of cultural experience in the viewers (and listeners) for such programmes. Herein lies the problem for broadcasting and audio-visual policy for Europe. Viewers (to a considerable extent in the large European countries and to

(contd) Community policy will only be realized when there is a solid and united body of public opinion which supports it and that development of such a united public opinion is incompatible with media pluralism. (OJ Debates of the European Parliament 12.3.85, N. 2-324, p. 59).

a significant extent in the small countries) are able to watch and hear programme schedules constructed to complement their established and specific cultural tastes and habits.

Viewer responses to the first European transnational satellite channel, Eurikon, clearly recognized the different, European, character of the new programme service but equally clearly preferred their own national services. Indeed viewers' responses to Eurikon programmes suggested that the international and culturally diverse character of the service was alienating. Eurikon viewers tended to perceive Eurikon as 'just another foreign channel' rather than 'our channel' (EBU/OTS, 1983, p. 26). Cultural diversity was clearly experienced but no obvious sentiment of unity was apparent[1].

If we follow Kedourie's reasoning about the nature of the relationship posited by nationalism between language, culture and political identity we can see why the vision of a unified European culture took on a nightmarish quality. According to Kedourie, '... language is the means through which a man becomes conscious of his personality. Language is not only a vehicle for rational propositions, it is the outer expression of an inner experience, the outcome of a particular history, the legacy of a distinctive tradition' (Kedourie, 1966, p. 62).

Language is thus co-extensive with culture and identity. If, as nationalists believe, political structures require to be congruent with cultural communities for them to be stable and legitimate (the core of the argument Hahn and others were advancing in the context of Community audio-visual policy during the early 1980s) then the European Community required not only a common culture but a common language if it was to survive and develop satisfactorily! This idea was dynamite because there was no question that, if there were to be a common language of the Community, it would have to be English. In the face of the starkness of this option there was an immediate retreat away from the notion of a common Community culture. Diversity rather than unity became the slogan on which Community cultural interventionists fought thereafter[2].

A notable attempt to test the fundamental 'nationalist', pro- unity propositions that

---

1 For similar reasons the BBC's World Television Service 24 hour news channel has been seen, not as a triumphant assertion of pan-European media unity and a European champion against the baleful presence of the exogenous CNN news service within the European Community, but (like CNN itself) as an enemy of diversity and pluralism.

2 Caution should be exercised in drawing conclusions from so limited an exercise in audience research as that undertaken in connection with Eurikon. Moreover, whilst *some* conclusions can be drawn in respect of response to programmes to which viewers were actually exposed, it is more hazardous to speculate about how viewers might have reacted had they been exposed to different programmes. It is therefore at least possible that viewers would have exhibited responses consonant with a shared cultural identity of 'unity in difference' had they been exposed to a different diet of programmes. However, the evidence suggests that the responses identified do have a representative character. Harald de Bock (formerly Head of NOS Research, and responsible for the overall co- ordination of Eurikon audience research) commented that 'Austrian, British and Dutch results are remarkably similar ... an overall view is possible' (de Bock undated, p. 1). See Collins 1990 for discussion of the differences in the tastes of European viewers of satellite television.

underpinned European audio-visual policy, in the first half of the past decade is Anna Melich's *Identité Nationale et Média Contemporaines* (Melich, 1990). Melich[1] cast a very sceptical eye over the propositions that there is a close relationship between media consumption and cultural identity and between cultural identity and political identity. She examined the case of Switzerland, but also discussed (Melich, 1990, p. 124–125) four other European responses to 'la faiblesse des télévisions nationales à faire front seules à l'offensive des produits médiatiques extra- européens' (Melich, 1990, p. 124)[2]. She closed her lucid and comprehensive discussion stating: 'A notre avis, ni la pluralité, ni les specificités régionales de la Suisse sont menacées par les nouveaux média' (Melich, 1990, p. 130)[3]. Her conclusion was that the truth of the cultural nationalist propositions on which much European audio-visual policy had been founded had not been demonstrated and that, if conclusions could be drawn in a situation where 'la discussion reste ouverte' and where 'La réponse n'est pas encore definitive, comme tout ce qui concerne notre univers' (Melich, 1990, p. 9)[4], the linkage between media (and television in particular) consumption and the sentiments of collective cultural and political identity shared by consumers was weak.

Two conclusions may be drawn from all this. First that the obvious theoretical incoherence of the Community's audio-visual policy rationale testified to the depth of the sentiments and beliefs of those who advocated it. If such propositions were not firmly believed it is unlikely that they would be advanced so often, and so insistently, because they can not readily be supported on rational grounds. Secondly, the absence of a generalized and sound rational basis for such policies meant that the processes of exclusion and inclusion, which designated some as supporters and others as opponents of audio-visual policies, were likely to be very powerful. Either one was a believer or one was not. This made the debate all the more passionate and vociferous.

The Commission's response to the specific brief of the Hahn resolution; to consider 'the practical possibilities of getting a European television programme on the screen' led it to describe and endorse the EBU's Eurikon venture, which it believed offered 'a concrete basis for possible Community action' (Commission of the European Communities, 1983, p. 26). The Commission believed that the EBU venture would go far to realize what it described as 'the primary objective of the

---

1 Melich's arguments are particularly interesting since she is described as 'Administrateur principal à la Commission des Communautés Européennes'.
2 The weakness of national television when confronted with the offensive by media productions from outside Europe. The four cases she considers are Europa, the MEDIA programme of the Commission of the European Communities, the BABEL programme of the EBU and the MEDIA programme and pan-European television co-productions.
3 We conclude that the new media threaten neither the diversity nor the regional specificities of Switzerland.
4 '... the argument is still unresolved ... there is still no definitive answer, as in everything that pertains to our subject.'

Treaty of Rome which is "to lay the foundations of an ever closer union among the peoples of Europe'" (Commission of the European Communities, 1983, p. 32).

Thus the Commission's report *Realities and tendencies in European television: perspectives and options* (Commission of the European Communities, 1983) advanced Community broadcasting and audio-visual policy in important respects. It asserted that satellite television would become a profound influence on Europe's cultural formation and argued that public policy choices would determine whether DBS would be 'a powerful unifying factor' or the agent of an invading foreign culture. The Commission's concerns about the impact of DBS were emblematic of its concerns about television in general.

Realities and tendencies testified to the Commission's belief that the changing European broadcasting market would increase exogenous programming on European screens and that both European cultural identity and European cultural industries would be damaged if countervailing measures were not taken. In consequence the Commission advocated support for EBU's satellite television channels as a 'concrete basis for possible Community action'. *Realities and tendencies* also foreshadowed two *dirigiste* themes (which later crystallized into specific Community policy initiatives) intervention in support of the broadcasting and audio-visual sectors to preserve European culture (and thus cement European unity) and establishment of common transmission standards for Community satellite television.The first theme was eventually realized in the Community's programme of support for the audio-visual production, distribution and exhibition sectors, the MEDIA programme (see, *inter alia*, Council of the European Communities, 1990 and Commission of the European Communities, 1991c) and the second in the successive Directives on satellite television transmission standards (Council of the European Communities, 1986; Council of the European Communities, 1992).

Realities and tendencies acknowledged the importance of harmonization of broadcasting regulation in the Community and the possible stimulus a single market might provide to the television programme production industry but other sections of the Commission placed a higher emphasis on these matters than did DG X, the sponsoring Directorate for *Realities and tendencies*. *Television without frontiers* (Commission of the European Communities, 1984a) the Green Paper on the Establishment of the Common Market for Broadcasting especially by Satellite and Cable, was published a year after *Realities and tendencies*, and the ideas in it were already current in some sectors of the Community. Yet *Realities and tendencies*, though specifically concerned with satellite television and its powerful potential integrative effect on the Community's television markets, mentioned the Green Paper only once[1].

---

1 At Commission of the European Communities, 1983, p. 8. The mention of the forthcoming Green Paper in *Realities and tendencies* is in a different typeface to that used for the remainder of the interim report, suggesting that knowledge of DG III's single broadcasting initiative came late to those in DG X who drafted *Realities and tendencies*. DG X's absence of attention to DG III's initiative is symptomatic of policy rivalries and institutional discontinuities within the Commission.

The Arfé Resolution

The European Parliament responded to *Realities and tendencies* with the Arfé Report and Resolution (European Parliament, 1984 and 1984a). This endorsed Hahn's support for a pan-European television channel (and Hahn's subsequent proposal for a European fund for television programmes EP Doc 1-1219/83). The Arfé Resolution advocated Community intervention to redress what it described as 'the inexorable trend towards the internationalization of television [which] creates a need for sufficient political integration at Community level to allow timely action to be taken to prevent distortions and imbalances which could not easily be remedied subsequently' (European Parliament, 1984, p. 6).

Arfé therefore recommended that:

- The Community's powers in respect of television be expanded;
- National legislation be harmonized (including that on an anti-dumping policy for cinematographic products);
- A unified television transmission system be established as an essential prerequisite for the production of multilingual European programmes;
- the Community assist the EBU in establishing its satellite television channel (i.e. the Europa channel);
- A Community production fund be established on the lines of a Canadian example[1].

Arfé further advanced a comprehensive shopping list of measures for the development and Europeanization of the broadcasting and audio-visual sectors of the Community including:

- Common frequency and orbital positions for satellite television;
- A central data bank on film and television;
- A European film distribution organization.

The Arfé Report and Resolution marks the official genesis of the ideas of a European Media Observatory and of the MEDIA programme. Arfé also foreshadowed establishment of a European equivalent to CNN; the report referred to a 'European programme exclusively concerned with information – along the lines of a programme that has existed for some time in the United States' (European Parliament, 1984, p. 9). Here, Arfé foreshadowed the Euronews channel. However, although the Arfé Resolution expressed the Parliament's support for the EBU and its satellite television initiatives, it included a provision (Paragraph 7) which 'calls upon the Commission and the Council to formulate rules to ensure that public broadcasting monopolies do not seek to prevent private broadcasters and pro-

---

1 It is not clear which Canadian initiative Arfé thought merited emulation. The text refers to 'the Canadian system of assistance for national television as an experiment worthy of consideration' (European Parliament, 1984, p. 8). However literal interpretation of this formulation could refer only to CBC/Radio Canada, whereas it seems likely that Arfé referred to Telefilm Canada which had been established the same year.

gramme makers from fully contributing to the future developments, and in particular to a European satellite TV channel'.

Concurrent with the Arfé Resolution Alastair Hutton, a UK MEP, tabled a Resolution (European Parliament, 1984c) on the threat to diversity of opinion posed by commercialization of the media. Hutton's resolution took up a number of concerns raised earlier in the Schall, Schinzel and Hahn Reports and resolutions of the Parliament's Committee on Youth, Culture, Education, Information and Sport. But Hutton also stated that 'new broadcasting technology will help efforts to increase European understanding' and, like Arfé, the Hutton Resolution advocated a European television news service. Specifically Hutton proposed a European News Film Organization and asked the Commission to 'consider the arguments for and against being involved with European television companies and other sources in the initial financing of a European News Film Organization' (text from European Parliament, 1984b, p. 8).

Pan-European television was welcomed by the Community as a potential instrument of European integration and as a counter to the threat posed by the increased availability of American television across Europe. Accordingly, the Community supported the successive pan- European channels sponsored by the EBU: Eurikon, Europa and Euronews. Unfortunately for the hopes of European unionists, these channels enjoyed, at best, an uncertain success and the differences in tastes and interests of European television viewers revealed by these channels belied the contention that Europeans shared a common culture (or that if they did, that this common culture could be expressed in television programming).

4

Television in the European single market

I do not know of any other Commission paper which has found so much interest among so many people of all kinds. We have sold thousands of copies and there is still a lot of demand for this paper. So apparently the European Parliament has had an excellent idea to enter this field and apparently there was some substantive, good economic, cultural and industrial reasons finally to deal with these kinds of cultural services (Ivo Schwartz in Great Britain. Parliament. House of Lords. Evidence, 1985, p. 134).

Television without frontiers

The most important of all Community broadcasting initiatives has been the creation of the legislative framework for a single market through the Directive on Television Broadcasting (Council of the European Communities, 1989). The Directive, often known as the *Television without frontiers* Directive, stemmed from the Green Paper on the Establishment of the Common Market for Broadcasting, especially by Satellite and Cable (a Community Green Paper invariably known by its alternative title *Television without frontiers* (Commission of the European Communities, 1984a). *Television without frontiers* both established a basis for common, Community-wide, standards for broadcasting and unassailably established the competence of the Commission in the broadcasting sector.

Before the *Television without frontiers* Directive the framework of Community broadcasting law and regulation had been set by three cases heard by the European Court of Justice; the Sacchi case, the Debauve case and the Coditel/Cine Vog case[1]. These judgements were discussed extensively in the Green Paper (Commission of

---

1 Sacchi, European Court Reports Case 155/73 [1974] 409; Debauve, European Court Reports Case 52/79 [1980] 833; Coditel/Cine Vog, European Court Reports Case 62/79 [1980] 881.

the European Communities, 1984a) which also gave extended consideration to other laws and judgements, such as the European Convention on Human Rights and the EEC Treaty, relevant to the regulation of broadcasting in the European Community.

The Sacchi case established that broadcasting was a service, not a product, and that discrimination on the grounds of national origin of a broadcasting service was unlawful. This judgement meant a cable operator in Biella, Northern Italy, could not be prevented from re-distributing television signals even though the signals emanated from outside the cable network's state of domicile and Italian law granted a monopoly to RAI, the Italian public service broadcaster. The Debauve case focused on whether cable television and terrestrial television should be accorded similar treatment and confirmed that discrimination between signals on the basis of their national origin (and the national origin of advertisements) was unlawful. However, the Coditel/Cine Vog case established that holders of intellectual property rights (e.g. in a cinema film) in one Member State were able to prohibit distribution of such property (by means of the cable relay of transmissions from another member state of the intellectual property in question) in spite of the general sanction for re-distribution of signals confirmed in the Sacchi and Debauve judgements.

Coditel/Cine Vog therefore established that, in spite of a general presumption that circulation of goods and services within the single Community market should be unconstrained, it was lawful for holders of intellectual property rights in one jurisdiction to restrict cross-border circulation of goods and services in which they held rights. Thus the Coditel judgement constituted an important obstacle to the establishment of a single European market in broadcasting[1]. In this case, as in others concerning the harmonization of regulations to establish a single market, the basis on which intellectual property rights are to be harmonized has aroused considerable controversy (for a full discussion see below, p. 71). Indeed, the harmonization of intellectual property regulation remains a vexing problem and the outstanding Community task of re- regulating copyright is sometimes described as writing the missing chapter to *Television without frontiers*.

The *Television without frontiers* Green Paper began with references to the Commission's report of the previous year *Realities and tendencies in European television* and the Parliament's Resolution (the Hahn resolution) of 1982 on television. These documents provided support for the central project of *Television without frontiers*: the creation of a single Community broadcasting market. The Green Paper asserted the importance of broadcasting ... for European integration ... to illustrate the significance of the Treaty establishing the European Economic Community

---

1 In the Debauve and Coditel/Cine Vog judgements the Court ruled against the submissions of the Commission of the European Communities (Michael, 1988, p. 7). Consequently the Commission of the European Communities proposed (in the Draft Directive on Broadcasting [Commission of the European Communities, 1986a] a system of compulsory licensing so that intellectual property rights could not be used to inhibit the circulation of broadcasts from one Community state in others.

(EEC Treaty) for ... broadcasting ... and to submit for public discussion the Commission's thinking on the approximation of ... Member States' broadcasting and copyright law (Commission of the European Communities, 1984a, p. 1).

Both *Realities and tendencies* and the Hahn Resolution had emphasized the importance of television to European integration. *Realities and tendencies* had stressed the importance of 'creating a European television channel' (Commission of the European Communities, 1983, p. 1). The Hahn Resolution emphasized the importance of harmonization of broadcasting regulations (of establishing 'outline rules ... on European radio and television broadcasting ... with a view to protecting young people and establishing a code of practice for advertising' [European Parliament, 1982, p. 110]). However in order to establish a single broadcasting market, the Commission had to establish the legitimacy of its claim to do so. *Television without frontiers* outlined the Commission's now celebrated claim (Commission of the European Communities, 1984a, p. 6) that because broadcasting was an activity carried out for remuneration it therefore fell unambiguously within the scope of the Commission's powers. This argument from economics required the Commission to disavow broadcasting's cultural dimensions, because to concede a central cultural dimension to broadcasting would be to disqualify the Commission from jurisdiction in the broadcasting sector since the Commission was recognized to lack jurisdiction in cultural matters[1].

The Commission's case was well summarized by the United Kingdom's House of Lords Select Committee on the European Communities. The Select Committee's report on *Television without frontiers* stated that the Commission's claim to jurisdiction over broadcasting rested on the propositions that:

(a) Broadcasting is primarily an economic activity which the Commission is therefore competent to regulate under the EEC treaty;

(b) The Community must ensure that the relevant directly applicable provisions of the EEC treaty (particularly articles 59, 60 and 62) should be respected, so as to suppress all discriminatory restrictions on broadcasting from other member state;

(c) Present rules on advertising and copyright are an obstacle to the free flow of television broadcasting between member states (Great Britain, Parliament, House of Lords, 1985, p. 7).

And that, accordingly, a limited number of measures should be adopted as a first step in the establishment of a legal framework for a single Community-wide broadcasting area in conformity with the treaty's objectives (Great Britain, Parliament, House of Lords, 1985, p. 7).

---

1 The Green Paper did admit a cultural dimension to broadcasting but asserted that this was not a powerful objection to its claim to jurisdiction for the activity of the Community has, since the outset, encompassed essential aspects of cultural life in Member States (Commission of the European Communities, 1984a, p. 7).

The Commission had argued that its power to harmonize and integrate the Community broadcasting market rested on its:

(a) Political or moral right to act since broadcasting is relevant to European integration;

(b) Its responsibility under the treaties to intervene in media policy;

(c) That the EEC is the proper forum for action and not national or other regional or global groups (Great Britain, Parliament, House of Lords, 1985).

The Commission's tactics alienated some supporters of an increased role for the Community in the audio-visual sector. Constructing broadcasting as the object of economic, rather than cultural, policy considerations meant that proponents of *Realities and tendencies*, and the European Parliamentarians who had supported the Hahn Report and Resolution, viewed *Television without frontiers* with antipathy. For *Television without frontiers* foreshadowed a European audio-visual order which was very different from that which they sought. It also provoked extensive opposition from public service broadcasters and the governments of most Member States.

The EBU's vigorous opposition was representative of public broadcasters' response to the Green Paper. The BBC, the ARD, ZDF and the EBU all stated that a common broadcasting market was premature, would put established WARC spectrum allocation and administrative arrangements at risk, and objected to the fundamentally economic emphasis of the Green Paper. The European Parliament's report (European Parliament, 1985b) on broadcasting policy referred to the UK ITCA's rejection of the Green Paper on grounds of the Commission's lack of jurisdiction in broadcasting and also referred to the opposition of public broadcasters to the Green Paper.

The UK Government Ministry, the Home Office, responsible for broadcasting at the time of publication of the Green Paper, summarily dismissed the Commission's approach to broadcasting policy by asserting that broadcasting and 'cross frontier traffic in pig meat or banking' (Great Britain, Parliament, House of Lords, 1985 Evidence, p. 2) were so different as to be incommensurable. Indeed the UK House of Lords' Select Committee on the European Communities noted that practically all submissions on *Television without frontiers* had contested the Commission's (and the European Parliament's) right to exercise jurisdiction over broadcasting. The House of Lords' enquiry into the Commission's Draft Directive on European Broadcasting also recorded the almost unanimous opposition of UK witnesses to the extension of Commission jurisdiction into broadcasting and also to the specific character of the Commission's proposals in the draft Directive. However the Committee noted that 'all witnesses supported the principle of transfrontier television' (Great Britain, Parliament, House of Lords, 1987, p. 6) and the Commission's authority was never formally challenged by the UK[1].

---

1 The IBA, in conjunction with the BBC, considered commissioning an expert legal opinion on the robustness of the Commission's position (IBA Information Paper 112(84) p. 2) however its subsequent negotiating position was to express 'sympathy' for the Commission's aims but to question the means

The Green Paper challenged both national prerogatives in broadcasting regulation and the interests of established public service broadcasters. That its programme was, at least in part, realised testifies to the strength of support it commanded elsewhere. Lord Cockfield, the architect of the Single Market programme and the senior UK Commissioner who was responsible for DG III (the Directorate General sponsoring *Television without frontiers*) at the time the Green Paper was published 'attached particular importance to the Directive [that is, the Community legislation which derived from the Green Paper RC], regarding it as the 'flagship' of the internal market programme' (Owen and Dynes, 1990, p. 179). And, of course, the Green Paper was supported by commercial broadcasters and advertisers (notably the European Advertising Tripartite). As the Director General of the World Federation of Advertisers pointed out, 'If an advertiser wants to use television on a European basis he will soon find out that in 50 per cent of Europe time is either extremely tight or not available at all' (de Win, 1985, p. 2). Establishment of a single broadcasting market promised a dramatic increase in opportunities for advertisers and commercial broadcasters.

Television without frontiers included an extensive discussion of the technical, cultural and social, economic and legal aspects of broadcasting, including the broadcasting laws of Community Member States and the framework for Community law and regulation set by the EEC Treaty, Court judgements and international conventions and treaties. This discussion made it clear that substantial revision and harmonization of national laws was required if a single Community broadcasting market was to be established.

Ivo Schwartz, an official in DG III who was credited with the principal 'authorship' of the Green Paper, asserted the importance of the single broadcasting market as a logical expression of the EEC Treaty and emphasized its economic, rather than cultural/political, importance:

> A market capable of amortizing one's own production must be created. National markets must be expanded by laying down the foundations for a real Common Market guaranteed by common rules ... National television programme production limited strictly to national markets cannot possibly be competitive in Europe or elsewhere, especially in the face of an American product whose costs have already been covered in a market of continental size (Schwartz, 1985, p. 23).

Action was required, the Green Paper proposed, because the European broadcasting market would be rapidly restructured as a consequence of technological change and European integration, which new technologies promised, could then

(contd) chosen by the Commission, and defined in the Green Paper, for their realization (see IBA Information Paper 125(85). A year after publication of the Green Paper officers of the IBA advocated adopting (and being seen to adopt) a 'positive approach to the proposals' and took satisfaction that its 'discussions with the Commission and the ITCA's first class lobbying of MEP's, and opinion formers in Europe had resulted in a greater understanding of broadcasting affairs by the European Community's Directorate' (IBA Information Paper 125(85) p. 2).

be more easily realized. The Green Paper declared that 'the rapid development of audio-visual techniques[1] in the Community is regarded in all Member States as exceptionally important for the future coexistence of individuals and nations' (Commission of the European Communities, 1984a, p. 11). It specifically proposed that the Community should establish a single satellite television transmission standard by taking 'the measures it considers necessary to promote adoption of a European standard by the Member States' (p. 15). *Television without frontiers* thus foreshadowed the troubled history of Community attempts to regulate into existence a common standard for satellite television transmissions and to use standard setting as an instrument of industrial policy[2].

The proponents of *Television without frontiers* sought to achieve two goals, each deemed essential to a single market: to ensure that the circulation of broadcast signals and services emanating from Member States was not impeded in other Member States; and to harmonize Community broadcasting regulation so that competition between signals and services took place on a fair and equal basis. The Commission proposed three fields for harmonization of broadcasting legislation in *Television without frontiers* (see Commission of the European Communities, 1984a pp 209–313):

(a) The co-ordination of specific aspects of member states' laws regulating radio and television advertising;

(b) Co-ordination of certain aspects of member states' laws regulating broadcasting in the interests of fair play ('right of reply') and of protecting children and young persons;

(c) Limited co-ordination of member states' copyright laws to ensure that copyright holders' rights to prohibit the simultaneous transmission of programmes coming from other member states are everywhere replaced by rights to receive fair remunerations.

Subsequently, the Commission did not advocate comprehensive harmonization of all the different national laws and regulations which concerned 'fair play' (notably the right to reply) and protection of vulnerable consumers (e.g. children). Schwartz[3] here) indeed sought to reassure those alarmed by the prospect of the disappearance of cherished national standards by stating that 'an approximation of most of these rules is not desirable' (Schwartz, 1985, p. 28).

However creation of a single market proved fraught with difficulty. Not only did broadcasters and governments oppose the comprehensive restructuring of Euro-

---

1 Development was more rapid than the Commission imagined; its notion that a 90cm diameter would be required for DBS receiving antennae was overtaken by events. Most of the DBS antennae installed in Community states are 60cm in diameter.

2 That is the common video transmission standard required for a single market. The D2-MAC standard was eventually adopted.

3 Then Director for the approximation of laws, freedom of establishment, and freedom to provide services of the Commission of the European Communities, subsequently Chief Advisor to the Director General of DG III.

pean broadcasting foreshadowed by *Television without frontiers* but there were intimidating impediments to harmonization of standards. Advertising and programme content standards were eventually harmonized, but harmonization of copyright has proven intractable (see Schwartz, 1985, p. 28).

The importance of harmonization of copyright laws for an integrated market can be illustrated by citing the effect of the Coditel case. Under the Coditel judgement a copyright holder is able to prohibit the distribution of a television signal across national frontiers. The exploitation of intellectual property in one national market provides no lawful basis for the distribution of the work in which that property is embodied in other national markets. Moreover intellectual property rights are established on very different bases in different Community Member States. Thus distribution of television signals across frontiers, in keeping with the principle of the single market, may alienate the rights of a copyright holder.

In its later efforts to harmonize copyright, the Community has chosen to press for harmonization of Community regulations on the basis of the so-called 'transmission' (or emission) theory rather than the rival 'communication' or 'Bogsch' theory. Implementation of the 'transmission theory' would require broadcasters only to acquire programme rights for the country from which a transmission originated, whereas a regime based on the 'communication theory' would require a broadcaster to acquire rights for all the countries in which transmissions were to be received.

Clearly the transmission theory provides the basis for a more competitive Community broadcasting environment, with fewer barriers to entry, than does the rival communication theory. Moreover the 'transmission theory' is likely to better serve free flows of information and communication. For these reasons the 'transmission theory' has been backed by the European Community and the Council of Europe. It is also favoured by the EBU because the rival 'communication theory' presents significant difficulties to broadcasters, not least rendering them liable to litigation if a signal, for which rights have been acquired in one territory, spills over into another territory in respect of which rights have not been acquired. Equally clearly, the communication theory is likely to serve the interests of rights holders better than would the transmission theory. The World Intellectual Property Organization (WIPO) backs it for this reason. Indeed the alternative name for the communication theory, the 'Bogsch' theory, derives from the name of the Director General of WIPO, Arped Bogsch[1].

The most important of the Commission's goals, the core of a European Community *Television without frontiers*, was to ensure that any Community broadcasting enterprise would be able to secure access to any or all Community national television markets for its signal. The Commission argued that this was a consequence of the Treaty of Rome (see, *inter alia*, Bruhann, 1985, p. 2; Schwartz, 1985b,

---

1 For discussion of these arcane matters see, *inter alia*, Ficsor, 1990; Karnell, 1990; Porter, 1991a; Rumphorst, 1990.

p. 26). A single broadcasting market would also serve important cultural and political goals especially the 'ever closer union among the peoples of Europe' defined in the EEC Treaty. Bruhann[1] stated that a single broadcasting market would ensure that Community viewers and listeners:

> ... will have a wider choice of programmes which certainly serves the EEC-Treaty's objective, expressed in its first preamble, to lay the foundations of an ever closer union among the peoples of Europe (Bruhann, 1985, p. 4).

And Schwartz argued that the single broadcasting market would foster the right of freedom of expression guaranteed in the European Convention of Human Rights (Schwartz, 1985, p. 24).

Culturally and socially, the Green Paper stated, new broadcasting technologies, notably satellite television, offered an extension of consumer choice (by bringing broadcasting services from several member states to viewers and listeners) and (enigmatically phrased but unmistakable in meaning) more extensive dissemination of European culture via broadcasting. The Commission asserted that:

> ... the citizens of the Community will welcome the extension of the potential coverage and content of television all the more if the Community is in a position to view the opportunities offered by these new broadcasting techniques as a cultural challenge and to place them within the context of a broad plan for the future of Europe not based on economic precepts alone (Commission of the European Communities, 1984a, p. 23).

Indeed the Green Paper stated 'Cross-frontier radio and television broadcasting would make a significant contribution to European integration' (Commission of the European Communities, 1984a, p. 28). It cited the Hahn Resolution's celebrated syllogism in support of its advocacy of a single market:

> European unification will only be achieved if Europeans want it. Europeans will only want it if there is such a thing as a European identity. A European identity will only develop if Europeans are adequately informed. At present, information vis-à-vis the mass media is controlled at national level (Commission of the European Communities, 1984a, p. 28).

Television without frontiers therefore made the case for a single European broadcasting market in terms very similar to that used by proponents of pan-European television services such as Eurikon and Europa. Not only would European integration be advanced by these new initiatives but so too would cultural exchange between European peoples. The Green Paper further referred to the contemporary proposal for Nordsat (a Nordic countries broadcasting satellite conceived to enhance citizens' of the Nordic countries knowledge and understanding of each other) and to UNESCO's and the Council of Europe's endorsements of the value

---

1 Ulf Bruhann was a senior official in DG III credited with joint authorship – with Ivo Schwartz – of the Green Paper.

of cultural exchange. Television in a single European broadcasting market would, the Commission argued:

> ... become a means of conveying information about political, social and cultural events from one country to another and thus a source of cultural enrichment (Commission of the European Communities, 1984a, p. 30).

Moreover, as well as offering signal cultural benefits and an augmented European consciousness in viewers and listeners, a single European broadcasting market would assist the competitiveness of European television producers and enable them to substitute their products for unwelcome imported works:

> The creation of a common market for television production is thus one essential step if the dominance of the big American media corporations is to be counterbalanced. This is another area where the establishment of a Community-wide market will allow European firms to improve their competitiveness (Commission of the European Communities, 1984a, p. 33).

Having argued for the single market from culture (as well as from economics) the Commission returned to economic considerations and argued that a *Television without frontiers* was required because of the growing economic importance of transfrontier broadcasting. As early as 1984 (at a conference on the Green Paper organized by the UK's Independent Broadcasting Authority) Ulf Bruhann stated (Bruhann, 1985, p. 5) that foreign broadcasters received 'nearly half a million BFR, that is £6.5 million of copyright fees for the cable distribution of their programmes in Belgium'[1] and that (Bruhann, 1985, p. 9) 'advertising money provides nearly half of the total financing needs of all Community broadcasting enterprises'. Moreover, because of differences in advertising regulation in European Community Member States (e.g. differences in regulation of alcohol and tobacco advertising) there were 'real barriers to transborder television' (Bruhann, 1985, p. 6) and thus to development of the single market.

To reduce such barriers the Commission identified a number of specific areas where harmonization was required. It specified:

> – Advertising regulations, in particular the total bans on broadcast advertising in some member states[2] and varying prohibitions on advertising specific items in different member states;
> – National laws concerning the distribution or redistribution of foreign broadcasting signals;
> – National laws on protection of viewers, notably minors;
> – National laws on right of reply;
> – Copyright.

> (From Commission of the European Communities, 1984a).

---

1   Bruhann probably meant to state that 6.5 million Belgian Francs generated £500,000 in revenues for UK broadcasters.
2   Belgium and Denmark.

The fundamental changes to the structure of the European broadcasting industry which would follow establishment of the single market, however, were not all unequivocally benevolent. The Commission recognized that the European integration, which it foresaw would attend creation of a single broadcasting market, would also go hand in hand with an increased division of labour within the Community.

> Moves towards integration, which go hand-in-hand with an increasingly marked division of labour, heighten the need for a cross-frontier exchange of information within the Community ... keener competition within the common market will trigger adjustment processes in broadcasting and in the competing media and will lead to a greater degree of supply specialization (Commission of the European Communities, 1984a, p. 38)[1].

Later 'supply specialization' was perceived to have reduced cultural diversity within the Community and, in order to redress the effects of one of its policies (establishment of a single television market) the Community established a countervailing programme of support for cultural production threatened by supply specialization; the MEDIA programme (see Chapter 6).

The EBU commented that the Green Paper was extremely radical. If the authors' contentions were adopted (that 'a broadcast programme is a purely economic service and the totally free movement of broadcast programmes and broadcasting activities in the Europe of the Ten (Twelve) is to be sought without delay or compromise' (CA 1719 SPG 2787 22.11.1984, p. 3) then, the EBU stated, the Commission's doctrine:

> ... could revolutionize the principles and structures of broadcasting such as have existed since the 1920s in the ten states now EEC members. For other countries it would constitute a body of precedents of very great importance (CA 1719 SPG 2787 22.11.1984, p. 3).

So it proved. From the definition of broadcasting as an economic activity and implementation of the Community's competition regulations flowed the Commission's challenges to the EBU's practices; to Eurosport (and the EBU's collective acquisition of sports rights) to Eurovision and thus to the EBU itself. However other actors endorsed *Television without frontiers* and deprecated the EBU's stance. The European Parliament's Framework Report (European Parliament, 1985b, p. 24) cited the European Bureau of Consumers' Unions as stating that 'Europe's consumer organizations ... are deeply concerned at the frosty reception accorded to the Green Paper by the European Broadcasting Union'.

Although the Commission acknowledged that its proposals would, if implemented, mean fundamental changes to Community broadcasting it sought to alleviate the

---

1 *Television without frontiers* makes it clear that powerful interests were at stake, if 'supply specialization' was to take place. Not least because 'over 100,000 people from a wide range of specialist fields and covering a broad spectrum of skills ... are employed on a permanent basis by broadcasting organizations in the Community ... In addition, many more people are employed in a temporary capacity or on a fee-receiving basis.' (Commission of the European Communities, 1984a, p. 39).

concerns of potential critics. Although establishment of a single market would make more television (i.e. from more than one Community Member States) accessible to Community citizens, access to more television would not necessarily mean more television viewing. The Commission cited experience in Belgium and the Netherlands to suggest that:

> ... the provision of cross-frontier broadcasting is unlikely to produce an increase in viewing and listening (Commission of the European Communities, 1984a, p. 34).

And the United Kingdom's experience was claimed to show that:

> ... a further increase in the choice ... shows that there are no grounds for fears of a drop in the high quality of programmes (Commission of the European Communities, 1984a, p. 36).

Proponents of *Television without frontiers* therefore argued that whilst the cultural effect of a single market would be positive it would also be modest. Whilst granting that 'It is extremely important that each country retain its image and preserve its own identity'. Schwartz challenged the notion that member states would be exposed to 'an out and out cultural invasion. The Commission does not think so, for no member state holds a dominant share of the audio-visual market' (Schwartz, 1985, p. 24–25).

The importance of *Television without frontiers* lay not only its assertion of the economic imperatives of a single broadcasting market but in the Commission's assertion that cultural matters were indeed part of its jurisdiction, albeit via an economic back door (See Jacques Delors, 1985 for similar arguments). Cultural concerns, therefore, came to have an important place in Community broadcasting policy (in spite of the absence in the Treaty of Rome of a basis for a Community cultural policy). Conflicts between the Community's cultural goals (whether seeking cultural unity or cultural diversity) and the economic logic of a single broadcasting market (in which an intensified division of labour and competition would tend to eliminate cultural production by less efficient producers) have, thus far, remained unresolved.

British responses to *Television without frontiers*

British broadcasters did not welcome the Green Paper. The ITCA openly opposed it and its views were representative of UK broadcasting interests. The ITCA's Chairman, David Plowright, then Managing Director of Granada Television, told the House of Lords' Select Committee enquiry on *Television without frontiers* that the ITCA saw no grounds for change to broadcasting regulation and therefore opposed the Commission's initiative.

> Question: The whole tenor of your interesting written submission was, in fact, to me at any rate, that the status quo was working very well and you saw no great reason why it should be altered.

Mr Plowright: 'Quite right' (Great Britain, Parliament, House of Lords, Evidence, 1985, p. 207) .

However, the IBA realized that 'the UK Government may not be opposed to the Green Paper's proposals ... Support for the broadcasting organizations in opposing the Green Paper's proposals cannot therefore be assumed' (IBA Information paper 112(84) p. 3). Nonetheless an internal IBA paper (dated June 1984 and authored by John Harriott, the IBA's Chief Assistant, Policy [Television]) stated that 'For the time being the Foreign Office is willing to take its cue from ourselves and the BBC but ... in the longer term political considerations might come to outweigh those which have to do purely with the character and structure of broadcasting' (Harriott, 1984, p. 1).

British broadcasters had many objections to the Commission's proposals. The IBA feared that 'the attempt to harmonize broadcasting legislation might leave the United Kingdom with a less effective regulatory system and with weaker legislation than it enjoys at present; and there is an evident danger in a common market in which some members have a more *dirigiste* approach to broadcasting than our own, the broadcasting organizations in the UK could become less politically independent than they have been in the past' (IBA Paper 137(84) pp. 2–3).

The BBC shared the IBA's concerns. The BBC Director General stated (in the BBC's internal journal *Ariel* of 12.3.1986) 'In Britain the tradition is that Government keeps its distance from day to day running of broadcasting ... Under the draft Directive ... the EEC would require the British Government, under pain of legal sanction, to order the BBC to allocate its money to programmes of a certain kind. The practical effect would be that for the first time the Government would have to instruct the Corporation to broadcast more of this kind of programme and less of that. We find that an unacceptable proposal.'

UK broadcasters were also concerned about introduction of a 'right of reply' to British broadcasting. Nonetheless the Commission proceeded with its proposals and although lobbying and horse trading had their effect (and the Commission's original proposals were substantially modified) the Green Paper was followed by a draft Directive (published in 1986) and then a substantive Directive (promulgated in 1989).

Eventually UK broadcasters bent to the prevailing wind. The IBA judged that 'on balance, the revised proposals could well help, rather than hinder' (IBA Information Paper 125(85) p. 3). The Commission bent too. Many of the Green Paper provisions which British broadcasters found troubling were modified, softened and deleted by the time the Directive was put into effect.

The Draft Directive

Following publication of the *Television without frontiers* Green Paper, the Commission published a draft Directive on broadcasting in 1986: The Community's Broadcasting Policy. Proposal for a Council Directive concerning broadcasting activities (Commission of the European Communities, 1986a). The draft Directive consisted of the Community's specific proposals for regulation of broadcasting to achieve a single market. The Commission also published an explanation of its policies in an Information Release which accompanied the publication of the draft Directive (Commission of the European Communities, 1986b).

The draft Directive began: 'The main purpose of this proposal for a Directive is to permit broadcasts, particularly television broadcasts, which comply with the Directive's requirements to be received and retransmitted freely in all Member States' (Commission of the European Communities, 1986a, p. 5). The Commission proposed to establish this single Community broadcasting market by approximating the relevant laws of the Member States so as to:

> Promote the exposure within the Community of each Member State's broadcasts;
> Promote freedom of expression within the Community;
> Promote freedom to provide broadcasting services across the internal frontiers of the Community;
> Ensure free circulation within the Community of all broadcasts;
> Promote markets of sufficient size for television productions in the Member States to recover the necessary investment;
> Increase the production of television programmes within each member state; stimulate new sources of television production, in particular the creation of small and medium sized enterprises;
> Promote the distribution (transmission and retransmission) of television programmes of all kinds produced within the Community;
> Ensure the remuneration of authors and other contributors to programmes; stimulate the development of broadcasting as a strategic sector of the Community's telecommunications industry;
> Stimulate the development of a modern communications infrastructure in the Community's economy.

(Commission of the European Communities, 1986a, p. 5/6).

The single market would, the Commission proposed, 'promote several fundamental objectives of the EEC treaty, including a closer union among the peoples of Europe' and:

> ... in addition to the economic goal of providing a large internal market for the Community's broadcasting and associated industries and for advertising, important objectives in the fields of cultural policy, information policy, and policy designed to promote European integration. In essence, by enabling citizens in one Member State to receive directly or via cable, if they wish, unaltered broadcasts originating in others, a cultural interpenetration can be achieved which will make a significant contribution to the European Community's future development as a genuine Community. Each citizen will have ready access to the ideas, information, opinion, art and entertainment that

are available on television in the other countries (Commission of the European Communities, 1986a, p. 7).

The Commission's draft Directive emphasized the importance of cultural, rather than exclusively economic, goals for broadcasting policy in response to the disquiet of those alarmed by the implications of 'supply specialization', the definition of broadcasting as an economic activity and the erosion of time honoured national and public service prerogatives in broadcasting. It identified two principal agencies through which its cultural goals could be realized, a pan-European television channel (and specifically identified the EBU channel, Europa, as a means to realize this policy goal) and a film and television programme co-production fund.

> The economic objectives of the policy thus form part of a wider set of goals of which cultural objectives are an important component. In this way, the Commission's policy on cross-frontier television links up with other initiatives being pursued in the context of Community action in the cultural sector. Two of these are of particular relevance: first the creation of a European television channel ... and possibly a financial participation of the Community in European programmes such as 'Europa-TV'; and second, the 'amended proposal for a Council regulation on a *Community aid scheme* for non-documentary cinema and television Co-productions' (Commission of the European Communities, 1986a, p. 7)[1].

Neither the pan-European television channel nor the co-production fund, two of the four pan-European audio-visual initiatives identified by Melich (1990, pp. 124–125)[2], were successfully realized. Europa closed down the year that the Commission published the draft Directive, and the proposed Community aid scheme for fiction films and television programmes did not receive approval from the Council[3]. The Commission's proposals for the compulsory licensing of intellectual property rights (so that broadcasts could circulate freely between Community states unimpeded by the provisions of the Coditel judgement) was similarly unsuccessful.

The importance of cultural considerations in Community broadcasting policy was further emphasized in the Information release (Commission of the European Communities, 1986b) which accompanied publication of the draft Directive. This stressed the multiple aims of the Directive. Not only was the draft Directive designed to establish a single market, but sought to 'reconcile the requirements of *free movement* of goods and services with the need to maintain a number of *law and order standards* as well as a degree of *cultural quality* in the contents of programmes'

---

1 The Community Aid Scheme for non-documentary co-productions eventually became the MEDIA 92 programme.
2 The other two initiatives which Melich noted were successfully established. They were the MEDIA programme and the FEMA/BABEL programme for re-languaging of audio-visual productions which was itself established in conjunction with the MEDIA programme.
3 European 'variable geometry' came into play and the Council of Europe's 'Eurimages' programme for support of European co-productions was established in 1988.

(Commission of the European Communities, 1986b, p. 1). Taken together, the Commission argued, the measures advanced in the draft Directive would not only achieve '... the realization of an internal market for broadcasting, broadcast advertising and associated industries' together with 'the promotion of the Community's growing political, social and cultural identity' but would also succeed in '... at the same time, respecting and promoting the diversity and the specificity of the audio-visual cultures of its Members' (Commission of the European Communities, 1986b, p. 8).

Comparison of the texts of the Green Paper and the draft Directive shows the extent to which culturalist interests had succeeded in including their perspective and concerns into Community broadcasting policy. In 1985, between publication of the Green Paper and the draft Directive, Jacques Delors had become President of the Commission of the European Communities and, in his first speech to the European Parliament after taking office (Delors, 1985) the new President emphasized the importance of cultural policy and the cultural industries (and specifically mentioned television programmes) for the Community. Delors' personal commitment strengthened the hand of those who, in the memorable words of the UK Home Office, thought different considerations applied in respect of broadcasting to those which applied in respect of 'cross frontier traffic in pig meat or banking' (Great Britain, Parliament, House of Lords, 1985 Evidence, p. 2). However, between publication of the draft Directive (in 1986) and promulgation of the actual broadcasting Directive (in 1989) the balance of forces between the 'economists' and the 'culturalists' changed again.

The Directive on television broadcasting

The Directive (Council of the European Communities, 1989) as promulgated did not contain all the provisions embodied in the draft Directive. Changes in emphasis were evident in the preamble to the Directive, The draft Directive had emphasized television as a broker which could represent the different elements within the Community to each other (in the draft Directive Member States were charged with the promotion of 'the presence of other European cultures in the television programmes of each Member State' [Commission of the European Communities, 1986a, p. 24]). The actual Directive redefined television within the Community as a series of distinct, and autonomous, cultural practices ('... whereas the independence of cultural developments in the Member States and the preservation of cultural diversity in the Community therefore remain unaffected' [Council of the European Communities, 1989, p. 24]). The draft Directive had prioritized unity, the Directive emphasized diversity.

Promulgating the Directive was fraught with difficulties. During the second reading of the proposal for the Directive in the European Parliament 16 amendments were made to the Commission's proposal – many of these were rejected by the Commission because it knew them to be unacceptable to the Community's Member States which, in spite of opposition from West Germany, Belgium and Denmark had formerly hammered out a common position in the Council of Ministers. However at the next meeting of the Council of Ministers France, Greece and the Netherlands added objections to those already registered by West Germany, Belgium and Denmark. Objections to the draft Directive were made on different grounds, the ends of the spectrum being marked by Denmark and France. Denmark asserted its customary minimalist view that the Community has no standing in the regulation of television whereas France wanted more active intervention by the Commission to secure more stringent regulations on European content quotas.

Further changes were made in the course of political bargaining between publication of the draft Directive and promulgation of the Directive. In respect of provisions for the 'Promotion of distribution and production of television programmes' the Commission had proposed a European programme content quota of 30 per cent, rising to 60 per cent, whereas the Directive as promulgated requires 'a majority' of Community programming time[1]. Belgium and the Netherlands unsuccessfully sought to retain the powers they had used to limit redistribution of broadcast signals from other Community Member States via cable networks within the boundaries of their territories[2].

The Commission's complaint to the European Court against restriction by the Governments of Belgium and the Netherlands of redistribution of foreign signals emanating from Community Member States by cable networks in Belgium and the Netherlands *before* approval of the Directive provides an insight into the power plays which attended bargaining over the content of the Directive. The Commission's action indicated that even were the Directive not to be approved (and the votes of Belgium and the Netherlands might have been decisive factors in the 'qualified majority' voting procedure which would govern the acceptance or rejection of the Directive) the governments of Community member states would have no grounds on which to regulate signals emanating from other Community states.

Thus the Commission sent a message that, although the draft Directive might not satisfy the Netherlands and Belgium, they were likely to find the regulatory regime provided by the Directive preferable to the alternative wherein national jurisdiction over broadcasting could not be maintained. Without the Directive, no

---

1   In neither the draft Directive nor the Directive did or does the quota requirement apply to news, sports, games, advertising and teletext programming. The Commission's information release stressed that all established Community broadcasters met its proposed quota standards and that the quota regulations were 'aimed at newcomers in the market' (Commission of the European Communities, 1986b, p. 2).

2   The Dutch authorities required the Dutch language to be used on channels distributed via cable and both the Flemish and Walloon authorities in Belgium were concerned to protect their language communities from exposure to television programme streams in non-indigenous languages and to protect their indigenous television channels (whether public or commercial) from competition for advertising revenue and viewers' attention. The *Television without frontiers* Directive made such regulations impossible to sustain. See, *inter alia*, the two Dutch media law cases heard in 1991 by the European Court of Justice (Commission *vs* Netherlands, Stichting C.A.; Gouda *vs* Dutch Media Commission).

grounds for Community regulation of broadcasting would exist (see Boekwijt, 1989, pp. 4–5).

The final contents of the Directive on television broadcasting (the Directive on the coordination of certain provisions laid down by law, regulation or administrative action in Member States concerning the pursuit of television broadcasting activities [Council of the European Communities, 1989]) reflects compromises between the rival goals and interests of liberals and *dirigistes*, culturalists and economists. It enshrines the objectives of:

- Creating a common market in television broadcasts and programme supply;
- Promoting independent production and distribution enterprises, and in particular by small and medium sized enterprises;
- Stimulating the audio-visual sector in countries with a low production capacity and/or in a restricted language area;
- Establishing minimum standards for television advertising and sponsorship, prohibiting the advertising of certain products, including tobacco, and regulating the advertising of alcohol on television;
- Establishing a European content quota (and enabling Member States to establish specific language regulations and quotas) and protection for the cinema exhibition sector;
- Establishing a right to reply;
- Protecting minors from undesirable programming, especially violent or pornographic programming.

The provisions of the Directive which reflect liberal policy goals are those which establish the regulatory conditions for a single Community television market. Notably those which inhibit Member States from restricting 'retransmission on their territory of television broadcasts from other Member States' (Article 2) and that which establish a 10 per cent quota for independent production (Article 5). Article 5 provides that 'where practicable' a 10 per cent transmission or budget quota (excluding news, sports, advertising teletext and games) is reserved for independent productions. The European Parliament's Barzanti Report (European Parliament, 1990, p. 28) commented that 10 per cent fell far short of what the European Parliament had hoped to achieve in support of independent production.

Although the Directive contains more provisions which support 'interventionist' objectives than liberal objectives, none of the interventionist provisions are of such fundamental importance as Article 2 which has the effect of abolishing the Member States' sovereignty over their national television systems. Moreover the interventionist provisions in the Directive (such as the European content quota) are generally weak. True, Article 7 gives specific protection to the film exhibition sector (a major concern of France) but the articles on European content (Articles 4 and 6) are weak. Indeed the Directive has been described as 'a victory for commercial forces and those who favoured anti-protectionist policies. It could also emerge as a clear victory for US interests' (Negrine and Papathanassopoulos, 1990, p. 76). Although Jack Valenti (President of the Motion Picture Association of America) and other US interests, have vigorously opposed the Directive[1] examination of the Directive suggests there is more to support Negrine's than Valenti's assessment.

The sections of the Directive concerned with the national origin of television programmes are in Chapter III of the Directive in Articles 4 and 6.

Article 4 of the Directive requires that:

> Member States shall ensure where practicable and by appropriate means, that broadcasters reserve for European works, within the meaning of Article 6, a majority proportion of their transmission time, excluding the time appointed to news, sports events, games, advertising and teletext services. This proportion, having regard to the broadcaster's informational, educational, cultural and entertainment responsibilities to its viewing public, should be achieved progressively, on the basis of suitable criteria.

Article 6. 1. states:

> Within the meaning of this chapter, 'European works' means the following:
>
> (a) Works originating from Member States of the Community and, as regards television broadcasters falling within the jurisdiction of the Federal Republic of Germany, works from German territories where the Basic Law does not apply and fulfilling the conditions of paragraph 2;
>
> (b) Works originating from European third States party to the European Convention on Transfrontier Television of the Council of Europe and fulfilling the conditions of paragraph 2;
>
> (c) Works originating from other European third countries and fulfilling the conditions of paragraph 3.

These provisions require some exposition and explanation. Article 6. 1. (a) refers to the former German Democratic Republic (East Germany) Article 6 (b) exemplifies the important interdependence between the regulations and practices of the European Community and the Council of Europe. Effectively this clause, and the following clause 6.1. (c)[2] are the clauses which define the term European for the purposes of the Directive. For the purposes of the Directive 'European' therefore means, at least, any legal or natural person domiciled in any of the member states

---

1 Valenti stated (cited in Canadian Communication Reports 16, 24 December 31.1989, pp. 2–3):
 ... the European Community's broadcast directive ... aims to impose a majority quota on all non-EC material that comes into the European Community television market-place – which, of course, means an impediment and a barrier to a free market-place insofar as American programs are concerned. The President of the United States, the Secretary of Commerce and the United States Trade Representative have been supportive. They have made it clear to the chancelleries of Europe that the imposition of this quota is an intolerable thing to the US.

2 Article 6.3. reads 'The works referred to in paragraph 1 (c) are works made exclusively or in co-production with producers established in one or more Member State by producers established in one or more European third countries with which the Community will conclude agreements in accordance with the procedures of the Treaty, if those works are mainly made with authors and workers residing in one or more European States'.

(twenty-three at the time of writing) of the Council of Europe. Clearly this is a permissive definition. For the article does not require that a European be a natural person. Productions of any European company may qualify as European content for the purposes of the Directive and may not necessarily have been produced by European natural persons. Moreover, for the purposes of the Directive Europe is defined very permissively. As one official (interviewed 18.12.1991) put it 'there is a broad consensus that it is Europe in the cultural sense that is in question, not in the geo-political sense'. Europe extends, therefore, it seems from Iceland to Vladivostock and from the North Cape to the southern Mediterranean littoral[1]. But not only are the format definitions of European content loosely drafted but even these permissive regulations may not be rigorously enforced.

A representative 'culturalist', Matteo Maggiore (the author of a study of the Community's audio-visual sector and of audio-visual policy [Maggiore, 1990] commissioned by DG X) lamented Martin Bangemann's (Vice-President of the European Commission and the Commissioner responsible for DG III) statement that the quota provisions in the Directive were only 'politically binding' and not 'juridically binding'. He also regretted that Bangemann undertook not to proceed unless there were 'very extreme cases' of non-compliance with Article 4 of the Directive (Maggiore, 1990, p. 35).

There were disagreements between EC member states about audio-visual quota requirements. Maggiore states that France and Italy were for, Germany, Denmark and Belgium against. Elsewhere (Maggiore, 1990, p. 108) he states that the United Kingdom, Denmark and Germany were 'most pugnacious' opponents[2]. Gavin (1991, p. 44) states that quota provisions were opposed by the Netherlands and the UK on efficiency grounds, whereas Belgium, Germany and Denmark disputed the Community's competence. All, to varying degrees, were opposed. Moreover there is considerable doubt as to whether all EC member states are able to monitor broadcasting sufficiently well to ensure effective implementation of the provisions of the Directive. Booz Allen and Hamilton (in a report commissioned by DG III) stated that 'several member states either do not support the concept of quotas, resent an EC level intervention in what they believe to be their responsibility or

1 So, too, for the Community's principal programme of support for the audio-visual sector, the MEDIA programme. MEDIA's new (beginning in July 1992) support programme for independent television producers, GRECO, is open to producers in EC states and states which are signatories to the Audiovisual Eureka (Commission of the European Communities, 1991, p. 186). The 26 signatories to the audiovisual Eureka include Turkey and the USSR. It is interesting to note that, although the definitions of Europe and European adopted for European Community regulation are very flexible GRECO (and other MEDIA programmes, such as CARTOON, MEDIA's programme of support for animated films) has adopted the highly specific Canadian points system for determining the eligibility of a production for GRECO support. The point system awards, for example, two points to a production (a production must score 11 points if it is to be recognized as European) for a European director. However GRECO does not define either whether the citizenship or domicile (or both) of personnel is determining or what is meant by 'European'.

2 In the vote on the *Television without frontiers* Directive Belgium and Denmark voted against; the Directive was therefore approved by a qualified majority.

simply do not have the means to monitor and control broadcasters as would be required by the Directive' (Booz Allen and Hamilton, 1991).

Indeed, it should not be forgotten that the passing of regulations, even of loose regulations, is one thing but ensuring adherence to them is another. The *Television without frontiers* Directive came into effect in October 1991. At the time of writing (mid 1992) four (of twelve) European Community Member States have reported that they have complied with the Directive's provisions of which the United Kingdom is one. An interview with a UK official (10.2.1992) established that '... almost all [UK] satellite channels fail to meet the quota' but that the UK proposed only a limited enforcement of the Directive's quota requirements in respect of satellite broadcasters. The official stated that it was unrealistic to expect satellite film channels to screen 50 per cent European content and continued, '... we can't expect them to show Jacques Tati all the time to meet the quota'. However the UK authorities did anticipate requiring Sky One to screen a higher proportion of European content than it was transmitting at the time the interview took place. The official stated 'We are not prepared to go along with their screening of American game shows rather than European because they're cheaper'. However the official confirmed that the main emphasis in UK policy was to ensure that UK terrestrial broadcasters satisfied the requirements of the Directive.

In 1991 DG III was involved in extensive discussions with the Government of France in order to reconcile French national television programme content quotas (which required 50 per cent French programme content) with those prescribed in the Council Directive on television broadcasting (Council of the European Communities, 1989) which requires 50 per cent of programming of Community origin (Article 4.1. OJ No L 298, 17.10.1989, p. 18). However these discussions, and France's revision of its regulations to conform to the requirements of the Directive, took place before the Directive came into effect. The case of national quotas is an example of enforcement responsibilities lying with DG III rather than DG IV. When the organization in question is an enterprise DG IV has jurisdiction, where it is a Member State, then DG III is responsible. However a section of DG IV is responsible for scrutiny of state aid to enterprises and (a different) section of DG IV is also responsible for scrutiny of public broadcasting.

Despite the intention to create a single European television market the most important effect of *Television without frontiers,* and the Directive which stemmed from it, has been to increase competition within the national (or more precisely language) television markets of Community member states rather than to create a single Community wide broadcasting market. The Directive has done little to establish the single market envisaged by the Commission for, even without formal juridical barriers to entry, Community audio-visual markets have remained stratified on largely national and linguistic lines. Changes in regulation and establishment of subsidy programmes have done little to rupture the cultural and linguistic membranes which separate European television viewers.

The missing chapter of *Television without frontiers***: the Community's proposals on copyright**[1]

The European Community's development of a policy on copyright began in 1984 with the Green Paper on the establishment of the common market for broadcasting, especially by cable and satellite, *Television without frontiers* (Commission of the European Communities, 1984a). Creation of a single market for broadcasting necessarily entailed harmonization of copyright law in the Member States of the European Community, for a broadcasting market is a market in which rights to intellectual property are traded. As the Commission stated 'Free movement of broadcasting services in the Community is restricted not only by the broadcasting laws ... but also by copyright' (Commission of the European Communities, 1984a, p. 182). However, in spite of its acknowledged importance, *Television without frontiers*' treatment of copyright was cursory: it considered copyright only in two brief sections.

The first reviewed the impact of the Coditel/Cine Vog and Debauve cases on Community broadcasting markets (and concluded that they permitted 'restrictions to be maintained basically. Hence, the free movement of numerous broadcasting services has been postponed' (Commission of the European Communities, 1984a, p. 184). That is, established copyright laws were inimical to the establishment of a single broadcasting market. The second section considered how 'the obstacles to the free dissemination of radio and television broadcasts arising from the territorial assignment and enforcement of copyright can be dismantled' (Commission of the European Communities, 1984a, p. 305) and canvassed a Directive which would 'permit free movement of services between the Member States of the Community' (Commission of the European Communities, 1984a, p. 328). The Green Paper proposed to achieve 'free movement of services between the Member States' through compulsory (or, as it is sometimes delicately described in European Community circles, non-voluntary licensing) licensing so that the owners of intellectual property could no longer (as the Coditel case had shown they were able to do) prohibit the circulation of audio-visual works from one Community state to another.

However harmonization of copyright law in the Community has proved an intractable problem. There are notable differences in outlook between Member States which are clearly illustrated by the contrast between the English usage of *Copyright* as the right to copy, and the French usage of *Droit d' auteur* which stresses author's rights. All copyright law must mediate between individual and collective interests and between the different interests of consumers of information (who benefit from as wide-ranging circulation of, and access to, information as is compatible with the

---

1 The Green Paper on Copyright and the Challenge of Technology COM(88) 172 final, June 1988, the Follow up to the Green Paper (COM (90) 584 final 17.1.1991) and the Proposal for a Council Directive on rental right, lending right, and on certain rights related to copyright COM (90) 586 final – SYN 319 24.1.1991.

continuance of incentives sufficient to ensure continued production of information) and those of producers of information (who benefit from as stringent restrictions on the free and unremunerated circulation of information as is compatible with continued demand for the protected information). Different countries have struck different balances between these conflicting interests. There are major differences in the length of time over which copyright protection extends in different Community Member States and in the fundamental philosophy on which copyright law is established. The Community's most recent proposals for harmonization (Commission of the European Communities, 1992d) proposes that copyright protection should extend for 70 years and the protection of neighbouring rights for 50 years but the concept of neighbouring rights is unfamiliar to English law.

The Commission's proposal to establish compulsory licensing – a proposal based on a philosophy of right to copy – did not command support. Indeed there have subsequently been powerful movements within the Community's political processes to entrench, rather than abridge, the rights of owners of intellectual property; that is to consolidate authors' rights rather than copy rights. The Commission's proposal (Commission of the European Communities, 1991f, later amended Commission of the European Communities, 1992e) would establish rights, neighbouring rights, for all creative contributors (including directors, scriptwriters and performers) to audio-visual works. The harmonization of copyright laws had promised to achieve the establishment of a single audio-visual market in which works would circulate unrestricted and the intellectual property rights established in Coditel would be taken away. However, in this new situation, where many rights holders may be endowed with *droit d'auteur*, copyright clearance will become practically impossible. Not only are all rights holders to have a right to adequate payment (despite a prior assignment of rights) but the Directive is to have retrospective application. As the Decaux Report (Decaux, 1989, p. 26) observed a copyright regime based on the inalienable *droit d'auteur* might be more equitable but one based on the power of an author to alienate her or his rights is better for making a business of information.

Different Member States have taken radically different attitudes on questions such as: Who is the creator (and therefore the owner) of intellectual property? Do 'neighbouring rights' (an idea which is enshrined in law in some Member States and not in others) blur the question of ownership or does it make the boundaries of ownership more fair and just? 'Neighbouring rights' raises the question of whether collaborators, such as performers in a film or television programme, have rights which derive from their collaboration in the production of the intellectual property. Many other complex questions surround copyright including: how extensive are the rights which are traded when the creator of intellectual property sells her/his rights, and does an author retain inalienable moral rights?

In 1988 the Commission published its Green Paper on Copyright and the Challenge of Technology (Commission of the European Communities, 1988) which began an extensive process of consultation on Community Copyright policy. Later the Commission published a follow up to the Green Paper (Commission of the European Communities, 1991d) a Proposal for a Council Decision concerning the accession of the Member States to the Berne Convention (Commission of the European Communities, 1991e) and proposals for Directives on Rental Right, Lending Right, and on Certain Rights Related to Copyright (Commission of the European Communities, 1991f) and on The Coordination of Certain Rules Concerning Copyright and Neighbouring Rights Applicable to Satellite Broadcasting and Cable Retransmission (Commission of the European Communities, 1991).

The Commission proposals (Commission of the European Communities, 1991e and 1991f) were subsequently amended as: Amended Proposal for a Council Decision concerning the accession of Member States to the Berne Convention for the Protection of Literary and Artistic Works, as revised by the Paris Act of 24.7.1971 and the International Convention for the Protection of Performers, Producers of Phonograms and Broadcasting Organizations of 26.10.1961 (Commission of the European Communities, 1992f) and the Amended Proposal for a Council Directive on rental rights, lending right and on certain rights related to copyright in the field of intellectual property (Commission of the European Communities, 1992e).

A Commission official (interviewed on 11.11.1991) stated that the Community proposals on Copyright regulation were 'to write the missing chapter in *Television without frontiers*'. The official explained that the goals which the Commission sought to achieve through this proposal were to safeguard pluralism, protect encrypted services, prevent the creation of copyright havens in the Community and promote the circulation of tradable information within the Community. Action was necessary because the Broadcasting Directive (Council of the European Communities, 1989) had passed over the question of copyright.

The Copyright Green Paper (Commission of the European Communities, 1988) based Community policy on the recognition that:

> ... intellectual and artistic creativity is a precious asset, the source of Europe's cultural identity and of that of each individual State. It is a vital source of economic wealth and of European influence throughout the world. This creativity needs to be protected: It needs to be given a higher status and it needs to be stimulated (Commission of the European Communities, 1991e, p. 2).

It identified piracy (of recorded sound and images) as a major problem of infringement of authors' (and others') rights. Here authors' and others' (such as broadcasters and record producers) interests (i.e. neighbouring rights) were recognized by the Commission to be congruent.

Community copyright policy has the task of reconciling conflicting interests, notably between authors' rights and neighbouring rights, and harmonization of the different balances struck between these interests in different Community member states. Notwithstanding its recognition, in the Proposal for a Council decision concerning the accession of Member States to the Berne Convention (Commission of the European Communities, 1991e) of a conflict between 'the level of protection sought by some countries and the desire of others to afford the freest possible access to information and culture' (Commission of the European Communities, 1991e, p. 3) it is striking how, in the complicated, and intractable, process of establishing a common Community position on such matters, the Commission has given much less attention to the rights and interests of consumers of information (those most directly interested in a right to copy) than it has to the rights and interests of information producers.

In the Follow up to the Green Paper the Commission asserted that 'protection of copyright and neighbouring right must be strengthened' (Commission of the European Communities, 1991d, p. 3) so as to improve the protection of authors. The Commission sought to balance the interests of authors and holders of neighbouring rights, rather than the interests of producers and consumers of information. It sought a rights regime which ensured a 'high level of protection of copyright and neighbouring rights for the benefit of authors and artists, whilst ensuring that copyright and neighbouring rights do not unreasonably prejudice competition' (Commission of the European Communities, 1991e, p. 3). It assumed that consumer interests and rights would be adequately served if the rights of information producers were satisfactorily protected and competition in information markets secured.

The Commission accordingly recommended that Member States should adhere to the Berne and Rome Copyright Conventions to assist the Community in its fight against piracy and its endeavour to harmonize author and neighbouring rights across the Community (Commission of the European Communities, 1991e, p. 11). However neither Belgium nor Ireland had (by Autumn 1992) ratified the latest provisions of the Berne Convention and nor had Belgium, Greece, the Netherlands, Spain or Portugal ratified the Rome Convention.

The Commission has proposed further developments in copyright regulation within the Community (Commission of the European Communities, 1991d, pp. 37–38). Its Follow up to the Green Paper (Commission of the European Communities, 1991d) foreshadowed a variety of forthcoming initiatives on piracy, distribution rights, data bases and computer programs as well as on broadcasting. In respect of broadcasting the Commission proposed that satellite transmission of a work should be made lawful on the basis of the acquisition of rights in and for the country of establishment of the broadcaster. However, under the regulations it foresaw, cable re-transmission of a satellite signal would be lawful only if rights for the country in which the signal was being distributed had been acquired. Clearly such a copyright regime (though in conformity with that advocated by European institutions such as the EBU and the Council of Europe) would significantly advantage satellite broadcasters *vis-à-vis* cable networks. It would also advantage satellite operators domiciled in 'copyright havens' whether these were located within or outside the European Community.

The Commission's Proposal for a Council Directive on rental right, lending right and on certain rights related to copyright (Commission of the European Communities, 1991f) again emphasized the importance of copyright issues and the primacy of authors' rights:

> ... copyright is a basic instrument of cultural policy ... the primary purpose of copyright is to guarantee the originators of creative literary work a living from their intellectual activity by giving them an exclusive right to the use made of their work and a right to a fair share in the income which others ... derive from it, thereby encouraging literary production and protecting authors (Commission of the European Communities, 1991f, p. 4).

The Commission acknowledged, and sought to redress, what it perceived to be the historic weakness of authors vis a vis publishers and owners of neighbouring rights (Commission of the European Communities, 1991f, p. 46). However, the Commission's concern to strengthen authors' rights led it to neglect consumer rights. Indeed, so strong has been the Commission's emphasis on authors' rights that it identifies non-commercial public lending libraries as a past and possible future threat to authors' rights (Commission of the European Communities, 1991f, p. 5) and to the 'increasingly threatened diversity of culture' (Commission of the European Communities, 1991f, p. 6) which the Commission regards as ultimately dependent on a satisfactory regime for authors' rights.

The Commission therefore proposed general harmonization of Community laws on copyright and related matters and the strengthening of existing rights so as to better protect the holders of authors and neighbouring rights against infringements of their rights.

In respect of broadcasting the Commission's proposals on satellite and cable television (Commission of the European Communities, 1991) began by stating that:

> The draft proposal intends to provide a missing element in the creation of the European audio-visual area since the Directive *Television without frontiers* has been adopted ... without a chapter relating to questions of copyright (Commission of the European Communities, 1991, p. 3).

The Commission noted that the absence of copyright provisions in the Directive violated the wishes of both Parliament and Commission. Moreover, the Commission stated, the absence of satisfactory Community copyright legislation had 'seriously hampered satellite broadcasting [from developing] satisfactorily' (Commission of the European Communities, 1991, p. 4). It therefore proposed two measures: establishing the country of establishment of the broadcaster as the point at which copyright provisions would apply and harmonizing Community rules to establish a common minimum standard of protection so that no Community Member State could become a copyright haven.

However, the UK is likely to become a copyright haven, at least between July 1st 1994 and July 1st 1997. In June 1992 the Council of Ministers reached agreement on the terms of a Directive on rental right, lending rights and certain rights related to copyright (see Commission of the European Communities, 1992e)[1]. One of the most important provisions of the Directive is to establish the director of a film as its author for copyright purposes.

However the UK established its right to waive directors' rights for the first three years of the life of the Directive. Even if the UK's advantages as a copyright haven are of finite duration, the outlawing of copyright havens within the Community is likely to have only limited effect in respect of broadcasting because the propagation characteristics of radio and television signals (especially those transmitted from satellites) are such that any European state (such as Andorra or Monte Carlo, Belarus or Georgia, Malta or Slovakia) might provide a base from which signals could be transmitted under a copyright regime far less onerous than that established by the European Community.

Moreover the establishment of a Community copyright regime which emphasized authors' rights and neighbouring rights would, the UK audio-visual sector believed, be profoundly disadvantageous to the Community's audio-visual industries. The major UK interests (the BBC, ITV, Channel 4, PACT, British Screen Finance, lobbied strongly [*Financial Times* 12.5.1992, p. 8]) against the Commission's proposals on copyright. Notably those which would give actors a right to authorize, or prohibit, the exploitation of audio-visual works in secondary markets by exercising their 'neighbouring rights'. The Commission's proposals on 'equitable remuneration', that is giving neighbouring rights to actors and other contributors to audiovisual works, promise (the lobbyists believed) to 'hamper investment in programmes and put us at a competitive disadvantage with America and Australia' (Clive Leach Chairman ITV European Committee cited in *Financial Times*, ibid). Clearly competitive disadvantage in international audio-visual markets, vis a vis the United States and Australia, was of greater concern to the UK than to other Community Member States.

In respect of cable retransmission of television signals the Commission proposed 'to safeguard and supplement the acquisition of rights to simultaneous, unaltered and unabridged retransmission of programmes via cable ... to promote cross-border cable retransmission and underpin the European audio-visual area' (Commission of the European Communities, 1991, p. 8)[2]. In order to secure compensation for the holders of intellectual property rights the Commission proposed that administration of rights be vested in a central collecting society (Commission of the European Communities, 1991, p. 43). Collection by a collect-

---

1 The Directive (Council of the European Communities, 1992a) was promulgated in November 1992.
2 The Commission noted that its jurisdiction applied only to retransmissions from one member State to another and not to either retransmissions within a member state nor to retransmissions which originated outside the European Community (Commission of the European Communities, 1991 pp. 23 and 35).

ing society would mitigate the difficulties (if difficulties they are perceived to be) presented by an author exercising her or his inalienable rights over intellectual property in which she or he has an authorial stake. However if authors' rights are deemed to be inalienable then they can no more be alienated by delegating their exercise to a collecting society (which would be less likely to vexatiously obstruct the exploitation of intellectual property rights than an individual author might be) than by selling them to a third party.

The measures proposed by the Commission were justified as serving both establishment of a common European audio-visual area (Commission of the European Communities, 1991, p. 26) and promotion of the diversity of European culture (Commission of the European Communities, 1991, p. 26). The Commission regarded harmonization of regulations and increased protection for intellectual property rights as essential to the achievement of both goals. If promulgated, the measures proposed by the Commission would overturn the effect of the Coditel *vs* Cine Vog judgement (which acknowledged the power of rights holders to prohibit the retransmission of a television signal from one Member State to another).

Because of the difficulties of reconciling mutually exclusive rights (the right to copy and the rights of authors) and the different traditions and interests of different Community Member States, harmonization of copyright law, and therefore establishment of the juridical and regulatory conditions for a single broadcasting market in the Community appears to be an intractable, and perhaps insoluble, problem. The Council of Ministers (in December 1991) failed to agree that all Member States should ratify the Berne and Rome Conventions (on copyright and neighbouring rights) by December 1992. However in May 1992 the Council resolved that all Member States should do so by 1995 and formally established a Common position on rental right, lending right and certain rights related to copyright prior to promulgating a Directive (Council of the European Communities, 1992a). Whether any or all of the other proposals[1] for Directives on Copyright and related issues which have issued from the Commission are eventually promulgated remains to be seen. Certainly it is difficult to see establishment of a genuine single market in intellectual property being established in political circumstances which emphasize the principles of subsidiarity and widening Community membership. Copyright may well remain the 'missing chapter' of *Television without frontiers*.

But, even if the Community establishes a common market in intellectual property

---

1 The Proposal for a Council Directive harmonizing the term of protection of copyright and certain related rights. COM (92) 33 final. The Amended Proposal for a Council Directive on rental rights, lending right and on certain rights related to copyright in the field of intellectual property. COM (92) 159 final. The Proposal for a Council Directive on the coordination of certain rules concerning copyright and neighbouring rights applicable to satellite broadcasting and cable retrans-mission. COM (19) 276 final. The Amended Proposal for a Council Decision concerning the accession of Member States to the Berne Convention for the Protection of Literary and Artistic Works, as revised by the Paris Act of 24 July 1971 and the International Convention for the Protection of Performers, producers of Phonograms and Broadcasting organizations of 26 October 1961. COM (92) 10 final.

through harmonization of copyright law, harmonized regulation is not likely to prove sufficient to establish a single Community television market. For it is not only regulatory obstacles that lie in the way of a path to a single market. The perennial question that dogs Community audio-visual and broadcasting policy recurs again. How far can a market which is so sharply differentiated by linguistic and cultural factors be constituted as a single market for the cultural industries and for cultural production?

5

Broadcasting or audio-visual policy? The emerging dichotomy

'If we were beginning the European Community all over again,' said Jean Monnet, its founding father, 'we should begin with culture.' By linking together European culture and the new technologies, which hold the key to future prosperity and employment, a European television policy is now a major imperative (Commission of the European Communities, 1984, p. 10)[1].

---

1 The Monnet quotation is interesting; it is frequently cited yet I have found no attribution which has enabled me to identify its origin. It does not appear in Monnet's *Memoirs* (Monnet, 1978). However the *Memoirs* do record Monnet's conviction that European civilization is not the exclusive property of Europe. In 1966 he wrote:
'We must organize the collective action of our civilization. How can this be done? Only by uniting in collective action Europe and America, which together have the greatest resources in the world, which share the same civilization, and which conduct their public affairs in the same democratic manner (Monnet, 1978, p. 486).'
Walter Hallstein, the first President of the European Commission, did however interpret European culture in ways similar to the contemporary 'unity in diversity' perspective. He stated (Hallstein, 1972, p. 16) stressing the diversity theme: 'our aim is not that Europe should become a melting pot. Europe is variety, and we want to safeguard the riches of its national differences in character, temperament, talent, taste, beliefs and customs.'
However though Hallstein went on to identify the sources of European unity his formulations are no more helpful than were Monnet's in differentiating European culture and civilization from the culture and civilization of North America, the chief contemporary preoccupation of the audio-visual policy makers in the European Community who are concerned to find a rationale for audio-visual import quotas and financial support for the audio-visual sector: 'Who, after all, would wish to deny the cultural unity of the Continent? Western civilization, which today covers the whole vast Atlantic area, has its roots in Europe. It has been shaped by Greek philosophy and Christianity.' (Hallstein, 1972, p. 17).

Towards a European television policy

Following the publication of *Realities and tendencies* (Commission of the European Communities, 1983) and the European Parliament resolutions which had topped and tailed it (European Parliament, 1982a and 1984a) the Commission published an information paper (European File 19/84 *Towards a European television policy* (Commission of the European Communities, 1984). This paper echoed *Realities and tendencies* in describing the European broadcasting environment as changing under the influence of the new technologies of satellite and cable signal distribution. However, like *Realities and tendencies*, it made no reference to the Commission's major initiative of the same year; the *Television without frontiers* Green Paper (Commission of the European Communities, 1984a). This absence is significant and testifies to 'two solitudes' within the field of Community audio-visual policy. Antagonistic currents, one *dirigiste* and one liberal, have each significantly shaped the audio-visual and television policies of the Commission and the Community but have characteristically done so in assumed ignorance of, or active opposition to, the other.

Television without frontiers emphasized the establishment of a single, transnational, broadcasting market in the Community; *Realities and tendencies* advocated transnational satellite broadcasting; *Towards a European Television Policy*, however, emphasized the problems which stem from the internationalization of broadcasting. According to *Towards a European television policy* the 'technological challenge' represented by the new communication technologies of cable and satellite offered a favourable stimulus to the European aerospace, advertising and broadcasting industries, but they also posed 'two challenges to the Community' (Commission of the European Communities, 1984, p. 6). The importance of *Towards a European television policy* is that it marked a new moment in Community policy, whereas *Television without frontiers* and *Realities and tendencies* had both (in different ways) encouraged the internationalization of Community broadcasting. *Towards a European television policy* did not. Its emphasis on the problems, rather than the opportunities, presented by technological change presaged establishment of the Community's subsidy programme for the film and television production sector – the MEDIA programme – which had a distinct emphasis on a national, rather than European frame of reference. 'Diversity rather than unity' started to become the watchword of *dirigiste* audio-visual policy.

The two challenges identified in *Towards a European television policy* (and foreshadowed in *Realities and tendencies*) were the harmonization of television transmission standards, and the encouragement of television programme production; the pre-eminent themes of audio-visual *dirigistes* in the Community. If the Community failed to meet these two challenges then, the Commission anticipated, 'this gigantic new market will be taken over by the American and even Japanese competitors, thereby compounding their economic and cultural penetration of Europe ... The progress of international broadcasting and the preservation of European cultural identity will play an increasingly important part in the construction of the European community' (Commission of the European Communities, 1984, p. 6)[1].

In response to the perceived Japanese and American threats the Commission advocated two responses to these challenges: the technical harmonization of broadcasting standards (through mandatory use of the MAC standard for satellite television transmissions); and the provision of programme production subsidies for the audio-visual sector. These foci refer to twin deterministic presumptions which have underpinned *dirigiste* Community audio-visual policy. First that new technologies necessarily impose (determine) new social relationships and, second, consumption of symbolic culture determines the formation of consumers' cultural and, consequentially, political identities. Thus, if these presumptions are granted, Community broadcasting and audio-visual policy must capture these forces and deploy them to achieve Community ends. *Towards a European television policy* (Commission of the European Communities, 1984) closed with the Monnet citation which heads this chapter.

The separation of Community audio-visual and broadcasting policy

Broadcasting and audio-visual policy in the European Community reflects the complex manoeuvring of different interests, inside and outside the Commission, to realise different policy priorities. Seemingly inconsequential semantic differences signify radically different frames of reference, policy priorities and economic and political interests. The terms 'broadcasting policy' and 'audio-visual policy' which in other contexts may be, if not synonymous, at least mutually inclusive tend, in the context of the Community, to signify radically different perspectives.

In the mid-eighties Community documents began to differentiate between broadcasting and audio-visual policy. Whereas in 1983 *Realities and tendencies* (Commission of the European Communities, 1983) had advocated pro- active measures to support the audio-visual production sector under a rubric of television policy, after the publication of the *Television without frontiers* Green Paper (Commission of the European Communities, 1984a) *dirigiste* policy initiatives tended to be labelled 'audio-visual' rather than 'broadcasting' or 'television'. The term broadcasting had acquired an 'ultra-liberal' flavour. Thus a *dirigiste* statement of 1984 (Commission of the European Communities, 1984) was labelled *Towards a European television policy* but in 1992 an equivalent, updated, statement was published under the title *European Community audio-visual policy* (Commission of the European Communities, 1992c).

---

1 The IBA's internal (and confidential) information paper 18(85) – in which a copy of the EC publication *Towards a European television policy* was circulated – notes the innovatory inclusion of cultural goals in Commission policy. It stated 'The publication is of interest in providing an account of the Commission's reasons for involving itself in broadcasting matters. The article cites cultural as well as economic considerations in arriving at the conclusion that "a European television policy is now a major imperative".'

In 1985 the Parliament adopted a Resolution on A Framework for a European Media Policy based on the Commission's Green Paper on the establishment of the Common Market for Broadcasting, especially by Satellite and Cable (European Parliament, 1985). This Resolution followed a report, known as The Framework Report (European Parliament, 1985b) written by Wilhelm Hahn MEP (as rapporteur on behalf of the Parliament's Committee on Youth, Culture, Education, Information and Sport). Hahn's authorship has led to The Framework Report sometimes being known, confusingly in view of the existence of Hahn's 1982 report, as the Hahn Report. Hahn's report, and the Parliament's subsequent resolution, constituted the Parliament's response to the rival Commission initiatives on broadcasting which had recently emerged; *Realities and tendencies* and *Television without frontiers*.

The Parliament politely 'welcomed' *Realities and tendencies* and *Television without frontiers* in The Framework Report which, however, emphatically expressed the Parliament's preference for *Realities and tendencies* rather than *Television without frontiers*. The Framework Report referred to the 'increased importance of radio and television for the democratic development of the European Community, the emergence of a European consciousness, and the maintenance of Europe's cultural diversity and identity' (European Parliament, 1985b, p. 6).

The Framework Report (European Parliament, 1985b, p. 13) defined four general contexts for the making of Community broadcasting policy: first, the cultural context (where the primary goal was defined as promoting 'greater cultural exchange between Member States'); second, the information context (where the primary goal was the use of 'new technological capabilities with a view to greater availability of information from domestic and foreign sources'); third, the European context (where the primary goal was to establish 'Community-wide broadcasting of national channels [which] would be the requisite complement to a European television service with a view to achieving European integration'); and finally the economic context (where the primary goal was to establish 'Community-wide broadcasting [which] would provide the large homogeneous internal market that Europe's arts industry requires in order to recoup its investment'). It is interesting to note that The Framework Report put the economic context last.

From these four contexts Hahn defined the goals of Community policy as safeguarding European broadcasting quality and increasing European content in broadcasting. Accordingly the Parliament called for a comprehensive European media policy to include four principal elements:

- Reception of national channels from all member states;
- Establishment of a multilingual European television channel;
- Support for Europe's programme-making industry;
- Harmonization of certain principles of broadcasting law and of technical standards[1].

---

1 The EBU stated that the Parliament's resolution showed that its own lobbying on the Commission's

The conditions for the realization of the first and last of these four recommendations were established with the *Television without frontiers* Directive of 1989 (Council of the European Communities, 1989). The establishment of a multilingual
European television channel was implemented through the Community's support
for the ill-fated Europa channel. The proposals for support for programme making
resulted in resolutions (European Parliament, 1985c and 1985d) proposing a
Community aid scheme for non-documentary cinema and television co-
productions (which were supported by the Commission but which did not receive
the unanimous support in the Council of Ministers necessary for implementation)[1]
and ultimately produced a Council decision to establish the MEDIA 92 (later
MEDIA 95) programme.

The following year, 1985, the Parliament (responding to de Vries' report as
rapporteur for the Committee on Economic and Monetary Affairs and Industrial
Policy) adopted a Resolution on the Economic Aspects of the Common Market for
Broadcasting in the European Community (European Parliament, 1985a). This
Resolution put forward audio-visual policy goals similar to those advocated in The
Framework Resolution on media policy of the same year and strengthened the
dirigiste case for intervention in the audio-visual sector by stating that Community
policy goals could not be achieved within the context of a common market for
broadcasting unless 'accompanied by the simultaneous development of a fully-
fledged European communications industry producing infrastructures and hardware on the one hand and software on the other' (European Parliament, 1987, p.
12). In the same year the Parliament adopted the Addonino report and in consequence 1988 was established as European Film and Television Year.

Both Commission and Parliament continued to press for further support for the
audio-visual sector. In 1986 the Parliament adopted the Baget Bozzo report (European Parliament, 1986) and passed a resolution On the European Community's
Information Policy (European Parliament, 1987a). The Resolution (the Baget
Bozzo Resolution) stated, *inter alia*, that 'the national television and film production capacity of the individual Community Member States cannot compete with
that of the United States (and) the productive cultural forces of Europe therefore
have insufficient opportunity in the mass media to show what they can do' (European Parliament, 1987a, p. 112). It went on to urge the 'creation of a common
European television programme with one picture but in the various national

---

(contd) *Television without frontiers* initiative had had positive results. Notably that 'the cultural aspects
of television programmes has been acknowledged' and the 'value of public broadcasters' programmes
is emphasized' (de Kalbermatten, 1985, p. 1).

1 The Amended proposal for a Council Regulation (EEC) on a Community Aid Scheme for
Non-Documentary Cinema and Television Co-productions (European Parliament, 1985d) is formally
still before the Council. Indeed the Official Journal (OJ C 351/37 31.12.1985) states that the regulation
has been adopted by the Council. Under Community procedures which are now in effect the proposal
would have fallen but, because it was tabled before the promulgation of new procedures in 1987, has
not formally fallen. However action on this proposal is very unlikely, particularly because a scheme to
support co-production, Eurimages, has been achieved through 'variable geometry'.

languages of the Community and hopes that the Commission will support the Europa television experiment so that a programme may be compiled which is of high quality and widely accepted by the people'. The Parliament also called on 'the Council to declare itself in favour of a multilingual television channel' (European Parliament, 1987a, p. 114). This was a striking demand, given the failure of the EBU's Europa multilingual television channel the previous year: a multilingual channel which had received the support of both Commission and Parliament.

Broadcasting vs. the audio-visual: single market or failed market?

From 1986 those who viewed the creation of a single market as the major priority sailed under the colours of 'broadcasting policy'; those who sought the protection and pro-active development of the film and video production industry nailed 'audio-visual policy' to their mast.

The first document issued by the Commission in which the term audio-visual formed part of the title was the information release, The Community's Audio-visual Policy (Commission of the European Communities, 1986b, p.4). The release described the Commission's Draft Directive deriving from the *Television without frontiers* Green Paper of 1984 and set out suggestions for a proposed balancing of the Community audio-visual market. On one hand the market was to be integrated and the 'entangled underwood of national regulatory obstacles to admitting broadcasts from other Member States' swept away on the other pro-active measures to support and shape the film and television industries were to be promulgated. Support should be given, the Commission stated, to the 'strengthening of the technological capacity of the Community's industry in the audio-visual and communications area' (Commission of the European Communities, 1986b, p.3) and for the Europa pan-European satellite television channel (Commission of the European Communities, 1986b, p.4)[1].

---

1 The Committee sketched its vision of the programme content of such a channel and proposed (European Parliament, 1982, p. 15) that: 'The following basic principles should be respected: An additional European channel must provide a full range of programmes such as those transmitted by the national broadcasting companies. It will not be possible to win over viewers by showing only reports on, or broadcasts from, the European Community and the European Parliament. Neither should it be an official European channel produced on behalf of the European institutions. On the contrary, it should express a wide range of political opinions and social and cultural attitudes so as to reflect the rich variety of life in Europe. It is the very diversity of Europe which should be conveyed. Consequently all the Member States and regions must contribute to the channel; The picture should be the same everywhere, but the language adapted to each receiver area. It would be desirable and technically feasible in the future for the viewer to be able to select whether he wishes to see a programme in his own language or in the original language; The criterion of a full range of programmes means that the channel should fulfil the functions of entertainment, information and education. The channel could derive a European character from its origins, subject matter and target audience. European in origin means that as far as possible journalists, film directors, artists, etc. from all the European Member States should participate in the production of programmes. Private producers could also be brought in. The subject matter will be European in that the channel will reflect the European scene, deal with problems affecting all Europeans or provide opportunities for intra-European cultural exchanges. The

The same year the Commission restated its policies (Commission of the European Communities, 1986) responding to the controversy aroused by the draft broadcasting directive (which followed *Television without frontiers*) by downplaying the implications of the Draft Directive ('All that is proposed is a minimum of co-ordination: in regard of advertising, sponsorship and protection of young people' (Commission of the European Communities, 1986, p. 7).

The Commission clearly distinguished between its policies of market integration and harmonization (the *Television without frontiers* initiative and through promotion of the common MAC transmission standard) and those directed towards the development of the audio-visual production industry. 'Satellites, cables, and common technical and legal standards are all very well, but what of the programmes themselves?' was the question the Commission asked (Commission of the European Communities, 1986, p. 8). The active programme of support for the audio-visual software sector which the Commission proposed (and which later resulted in the establishment of MEDIA) was justified both of the economic importance of the European audio-visual sector and the importance of the cultural challenge from outside which, the Commission judged, was 'as urgent as the technological and economic ones' (Commission of the European Communities, 1986, p. 8).

In 1989 the Parliament put forward a fresh rationale for an interventionist Community audio-visual policy and identified three principal factors which, in its judgement, necessitated and legitimized intervention:

> Technological change – which has expanded and internationalized distribution (notably through satellite television) and demands new production practices (notably HDTV);[1]
> Liberalization of markets which have both eased entry for new actors and permitted a growing consolidation of private oligopolies;
> The Americanization of European audio-visual markets, particularly those for fiction films and television programmes.

The Parliament's case for intervention echoed similar arguments from DG X and testifies to the close alliance between the Parliament's Committee on Youth, Culture, Education the Media and Sport and DG X. The alliance was cemented through close personal associations between key members of each institution. The Chairman of the Parliament's Committee, Roberto Barzanti, had Matteo Maggiore

---

(contd) target audience would be the same as for the national channels except that it would include viewers in other countries'.

1 The EBU, drawing on RAI's experience with HDTV, concurred with the Parliament's judgement that HDTV productions would require more resources than conventional television productions. RAI found that HDTV required 'more time spent on rehearsals, lighting to take account of all shadow areas with their various nuances, need to work more often in real surroundings and construct larger studios outside traditional TV production centres, necessity to adapt the training of directors, cameramen, sound and light engineers, etc, all these elements resulting in a considerable increase in costs' (CA 2060 SPG 4967 9.5.1990, p. 17).

(the son of Mariano Maggiore, then Deputy Head of the Audio-visual Unit of DG X) and the author of the Commission's publication *Audio-visual production in the single market* [Maggiore, 1990]) as his factotum.

The Parliament's Committee on Youth, Culture, Education the Media and Sport and DG X (the Commission's Directorate charged with audio-visual policy, see Chapter One) both judged Community audio-visual markets to have failed[1]. They had failed because they had not allocated sufficient resources to the development of a new communication technology, HDTV (which, it was believed, would stimulate and protect sections of the Community's electronics industry)[2]. Moreover, the single market policy had also, in the eyes of DG X and the Parliament's Committee on Youth, Culture, Education the Media and Sport, failed because it had facilitated consolidation of private media oligopolies (the Parliament's and DG X's concerns have focused on *private* oligopolies, not the *public* service broadcasting oligopolies which exercised DG IV). And, most important, the single market had also failed in that too much American, and insufficient European programming, filled European cinema and television screens.

The Parliament therefore argued for Community intervention in film and television production, distribution and finance to compensate for the perceived failures of the European audio-visual market. Overall the Parliament judged that 'Economies of scale and cost are an important reason for this European decline' (European Parliament, 1989, p. 12). However, *dirigistes* in the Commission, whilst often supporting the Parliament's viewpoint, have acknowledged that the economies of scale (to which the Parliament attributed US success in European audio-visual markets) are not a complete explanation of the United States' dominance in world audio-visual markets. Scale economies, the Commission stated, do not explain 'why other countries such as Australia, Brazil and Japan (as regards cartoons) have been able to establish themselves in this market' (Commission of the European Communities, 1990, p. 8). Latterly the Commission argued that 'a stockpile of ready-to-go programmes and an efficient marketing structure which are the prerequisites for success on world markets' (Commission of the European Communities, 1990, p. 8) and that the structure of European film and television industries are not well fitted to the international market because it lacks both.

1 DG X's statement on *European Community audio-visual policy* (Commission of the European Communities, 1992c) advocates promotion of the programme production industry (Commission of the European Communities, 1992c, p. 6), expansion of support measures for technologically advanced television (Commission of the European Communities, 1992c, p. 10), and (whilst dutifully describing the Community's principal broadcasting initiative, the creation of the single Community television market) identifies 'the problems of amalgamating media and maintaining pluralism' as meriting assessment of 'the need for action at Community level' (Commission of the European Communities, 1992c, p. 6).

2 HDTV would also create a demand for European television programming and (because it was based on a distinctive European technical standard) keep out exogenous software. Hence both the Parliament and Commission supported subsidy for the D2- MAC/HDTV development programme.

The role of the United Kingdom

> Apart from the United Kingdom, on account of language factors, the European industry does not have the necessary economic capacity to finance a massive production of expensive high-quality programmes (Charter of the Association of Commercial Television in Europe).

It is interesting that the success of the United Kingdom's audio-visual sector was not taken into account in the Parliament or the Commission's deliberations. In many respects the UK's record suggests that its audio-visual production sector has been well adapted to the international market. Certainly, in comparison to other Community Member States, the UK's audio- visual sector has enjoyed success. During the 1980s it consistently returned a positive balance on its international trade account (see CSO, 1991, p. 1),[1] and the OECD (OECD, 1986 pp 23 and 25) estimated the UK to be the world's second largest exporter of telefilms. Maggiore, for the Commission of the European Communities, estimated (Maggiore, 1990, p. 45) that the UK accounted for 68.5 per cent of community audio visual exports in 1985 (the latest year for which comprehensive comparative statistics were available)[2].

The Commission's neglect of the UK industry is surprising given the UK's success and the Commission's recognition that language is a powerful competitive factor in world audio-visual markets. Indeed the Commission stated 'the capacity to overcome linguistic and cultural barriers should be an asset to the European audio-visual industry in conquering world markets, especially since languages other than English are still very widespread (German in Eastern Europe, French in Africa, Spanish and Portuguese in Latin America' (Commission of the European Communities, 1990, p. 11). However it did not comment on the advantages enjoyed by English language producers, although these have been explicitly recognized by other European institutions.

The ACT (Association of Commercial Television in Europe) in its Charter recognized both the distinctive differences between the UK and other Community audio-visual markets and the importance of the factor of language in advantaging UK producers. 'Apart from specific national markets like the United Kingdom' it stated 'the programme market in Europe is extremely small' and 'the root of the

---

1 However in 1991 the UK overseas trade account in film and television programmes went into deficit (CSO, 1992).

2 Others stress the *weakness* of the UK audio-visual industry. Prescott (1991, p. 1) suggests that the UK has fewer feature film productions per head of population than does any of 17 other western film producing states and that investment in UK films including investment by US producers has fallen in the latter half of the 1980s (Prescott, 1991, p. 2). Moreover the surplus formerly enjoyed by UK television companies on the overseas trade account became a deficit in 1990 (CSO, 1991) [but see Collins, 1991]. However all such judgements must be treated with some scepticism for there are major discrepancies in the data on which these judgements are made. For example the UK Central Statistical Office stated that the UK's receipts from overseas transactions in respect of film and television material in 1985 was £370m whereas Maggiore stated that the UK exported 335m ECU worth of audio-visual products (CSO, 1992, p. 2 and Maggiore, 1990, p. 45).

problem of the audio-visual industry in Europe is the inability of market structures to encourage production at European level and the export of programmes to the world market', whereas 'Apart from the United Kingdom, on account of language factors, the European industry does not have the necessary economic capacity to finance a massive production of expensive high-quality programmes' (cited in Maggiore, 1990, p. 202–3).

If the ACT recognized the strength of the UK sector of the Community's audio-visual industry why did the Commission not also do so? Why was there no mention of Community anglophone states and their pre-eminent linguistic competitive advantages in the Commission's flagship policy document on audio-visual policy – its Communication from the Commission to the Council and the Parliament on audio-visual policy (Commission of the European Communities, 1990)?

Explanation must include several factors. First, none of the UK's MEPs on the Parliament's Committee on Youth, Culture, Education, the Media and Sport has the media (still less the audio-visual sector) as a particular interest and none have been lobbied by the UK audio-visual sector (interviews by the author November 1991). Thus UK interests are unlikely to have been represented as vigorously as the interests of other sectors of the Community's audio-visual industries.

Second, the UK Government has eschewed involvement with Community audio-visual policy. Indeed its 'ultra liberalism' has made it antipathetic to virtually all demands for pro-active audio-visual policies[1]. Thus interventionist Community policies have developed in opposition to the UK's perspective, interests and experience rather than in harmony with it. The evidence given to the House of Lords Select Committee on the European Communities' enquiries into the *Television without frontiers* Green Paper and on European Broadcasting (Great Britain. Parliament. House of Lords, 1985 and 1987) by UK broadcasters and government departments testifies eloquently to the virtually unanimous opposition of UK interests to the Commission's initiatives.

Third, the majority of Community member states do not have, and have not had, the broadly positive experience of the UK's audio-visual sector. The UK has long been second only to the United States as an exporter of television programmes and, throughout the 1980s, had a broadly positive balance in international trade in film and television programmes. By contrast, France, although second to the United States as an exporter of cinema films (OECD, 1986) and the only Community state to remotely rival the UK in the importance of its audio-visual sector was, in 1989, Europe's biggest purchaser of American television programmes and had a negative balance in international trade on the audio-visual account.

---

1 A striking case in point is the UK's veto of Community subventions for development of HDTV which led to charges that the UK reneged on a deal to support development of HDTV concluded at the Edinburgh meeting of the Community's Council of Ministers. The UK's decision to block a support programme endorsed by the other eleven Community Member States was reported to have been perceived as mendacious by EC officials and other Community Member States. The *Financial Times* (17.12.1992, p. 2) headlined its report 'Major "misled EC partners over HDTV".'

Fourth, other Community Member States, and pre-eminently France, have been very active (and very successful) in setting the agenda for European Community audio-visual policy. Thus it has been France's viewpoint, interests and experience, rather than the UK's, which has influenced the formation of European Community audio-visual policy and, as might be expected, France's policies and perspectives have reflected what Fumaroli provocatively named the 'gout incurable des français pour le dirigisme d'Etat' (Fumaroli, 1990, p. 427) a *dirigisme* which was anathema to the 'ultra liberal' UK.

Fifth, recognition of the strengths of UK production (and the competitive advantages of anglophone producers) could not easily be reconciled with either of the two superordinate rationales under which the Community's pro-active audio-visual policies have been legitimized.

The UK was, as George (1990) felicitously put it, an awkward partner in the development of a collective European identity because the strength of its audio-visual sector and language meant that any collective European cultural project might have been swamped by anglophone influence. A doubly troubling prospect given the close ties between the UK (and Ireland) and extra-European anglophone states. And, in respect of the second goal of diversity, the *dirigistes'* view was that it was rampant English language media which constituted the Community's problem and that other European audio-visual industries and cultures required support in their struggle against anglophone media. Clearly the UK could not be enlisted in this programme yet, equally clearly, Community policies could only be formulated with difficulty when their goal was to discriminate against a Community member. The strength of the UK threatened to make a Community policy directed towards European cultural union a vehicle for UK media dominance in Europe, and its strength made a Community policy directed towards European cultural diversity similarly difficult to realize since the elements which constitute European cultural diversity are so patently unequal.

The first of the rationales for Community broadcasting and audio-visual policy, the use of television to foster and develop a collective European identity, was prominent in the early and mid 1980s. The second, the need for pro-active intervention in broadcasting and audio-visual markets to countervail the reduction in cultural diversity which was thought to follow market integration, has been uppermost in the late 1980s and early 1990s. At first a single Community broadcasting market was advocated for its integrative effects in the political and cultural, as well as economic, domains. The *Television without frontiers* Green Paper cited the celebrated syllogism of the Hahn Resolution to legitimize its advocacy of a single market:

> European unification will only be achieved if Europeans want it. Europeans will only want it if there is such a thing as a European identity. A European identity will only develop if Europeans are adequately informed. At present,

information via the mass media is controlled at national level (Commission of the European Communities, 1984a, p. 28).

But later, as the prospect of a single market loomed, *dirigistes* gave priority to intervention in order to maintain cultural diversity. As Mariano Maggiore[1], the Deputy Head of DG X's Audio-visual Directorate said (interview with author 11.11.1991) 'We have no interest in promoting a melting pot. We want to preserve European identities.' Maggiore stressed the importance of the MEDIA programme (notably EFDO) in promoting the circulation of works produced in one Community location to consumers in others.

Diversity over unity

The Hahn Report of 1982, from which the birth of Community broadcasting policy is usually dated, is best known for its advocacy of pan-European television and the use of television as an instrument of European union. The Hahn Report, however, also warned explicitly against broadcasting becoming 'an article of merchandise in the framework of the Common Market' (European Parliament, 1982, p. 23) and foresaw a possibility of satellite television *threatening* a broadcasting war in which European culture would be annihilated as well as *promising* to be a vehicle for European integration. It is this latter perspective (with its consequential emphasis on regulation and political intervention in markets) which proponents of an interventionist Community audio-visual policy increasingly now put forward. Hahn is now more often cited to legitimize intervention to ensure diversity than, as formerly, to ensure unity. It is Clause 6 of the Resolution on Radio and Television Broadcasting in the European Community (European Parliament, 1982a) and the Parliament's statement that the essence of European culture is 'diversity in unity', to which interventionists now have recourse.

The stress on diversity in contemporary Community policy reflects the failure of transnational broadcasting by satellite in the 1980s and the consequential recognition that Europe was culturally and linguistically diverse. It also reflects the threat that the single market appeared to pose to national audio-visual and broadcasting markets (and thus to national media industries): a threat which was mainly perceived to come from anglophone services and productions. Roberto Barzanti (formerly President of the European Parliament Committee on Youth, Culture, Education, Media and Sport) eloquently resumed the arguments of the interventionists in a publication of DG X. Barzanti argued that, without compensatory action by the Community, the single market would be fatal to the audio-visual sector in Europe.

---

1 Maggiore was the Commission official principally responsible for the Commission's liaison with pan-European ventures such as Eurikon – which he described as 'a very bold attempt' – and Europa. He described Europa as 'the proof that pan-European television did not succeed' (interview with author 11.11.1991). However Maggiore argued that Euronews (a pan-European television news service which began service in 1993 and established in Lyons by a Consortium of EBU members) was 'evidence that the efforts and resources devoted to Eurikon and Europa were not wasted'.

Unless there is solid support from the outset, the audio-visual industry of all European countries will be thrown into the Single Market like a Christian to the lions in the arena (Barzanti, 1990, p. 1).

Like Maggiore, Barzanti judged that the threat came from anglophone media. However he believed that the lion to which the Community's audio-visual industry would be thrown was dressed in the Stars and Stripes. Barzanti believed that only the film and television industries of the USA (and perhaps Japan) were organized on a sufficiently large scale to benefit from the single market[1]. Barzanti's comment testifies eloquently to the extent and manner of the changes in Community sentiment – from unity to diversity – since Beumer's (a predecessor to Barzanti as Chairman of the European Parliament's Committee responsible for the media and therefore for audio-visual and broadcasting policy) advocacy of a Community melting pot.

In consequence of the threat posed by open and integrated audio-visual markets to Community cultural diversity (a threat perceived to come from the United States *outside* the Community and from the United Kingdom, thanks to the single market, *within* the Community) there has been a steady growth of intervention in the Community's audio-visual and broadcasting markets in order to redress the undesirable effects of the single market. Of these initiatives the MEDIA programme is the most important. Although described by Wangermee[2] as 'useful but inadequate' (Wangermee, 1989, p. 2) and by Moeglin (1991, p. 48) as 'notoirement insuffisantes',[3] MEDIA is an excellent example of the contemporary emphasis on diversity, rather than unity, in Community policy.

---

1 The President of France, Francois Mitterand, made a similar point at the Assises de l'audiovisual; 'American pictures combined with Japanese technology today overwhelm the European market' (Assises, 1989, p. 16).

2 Chairman of the Walloon Conseil Superieur de l'Audiovisuel Communaute Francaise and formerly an eminent Belgian broadcaster.

3 Several Member States have voiced disquiet over the MEDIA programme. A UK official interviewed 10.2.1992) stated that the policy of the UK Government on MEDIA was 'to close it down', and Germany noted that it 'regrets that this matter has not, moreover, been the subject of a political decision of the 'joint' type. The MEDIA programme clearly also has cultural implications and consequently touches on an area which is the prerogative of the Member States' (Note from the General Secretariat of the Council of Ministers to the Council 20.12.1990 10927/90 ADD 1).

6

Dirigiste initiatives

'The commitment of citizens to the European idea depends on positive measures being taken to enhance and promote European culture in its richness and diversity. In this context the European Council considers it essential to consolidate recent achievements and capitalize on the guidelines which emerged from the Audio-visual Conference in order to develop Europe's audio-visual capacity: Directive on the free movement of televised programmes and competition policy. It hopes that the efforts to produce the European HDTV system will be stepped up, that the Community action programme extending MEDIA will receive the necessary financial support and that the necessary synergy with audio-visual Eureka will be ensured' (Conclusion of the Presidency. European Council, Strasbourg, 8 and 9 December, 1989).

MEDIA 92 and MEDIA 95

The European Parliament and the Commission of the European Communities proposed measures to support the Community's audio-visual and broadcasting sectors throughout the 1980s[1]. These proposals were realized in the MEDIA[2] programme the pilot phase of which was established by DG X in 1986 (see Commission of the European Communities, 1986d). The programme was to support production, distribution and financing of film and television especially:

As regards production: Development of European projects; Improvement of production methods; Introduction of new technologies; Exploitation of audio-visual archives;

---

1 See, *inter alia*, the Pruvot and Arfé Reports of the European Parliament (in 1983 and 1984) and the Commission's proposals *Trends in broadcasting in Europe* of 1983, *Towards a European television policy* of 1984, *Television and the audio-visual sector: towards a European policy* of 1986 (and its Communication on Audio-visual Policy of 1990).
2 MEDIA is an acronym for Measures to Encourage the Development of the Industry of Audio-visual Production.

As regards distribution: Development of multilingual media software; Improvement of distribution structures; Tax harmonization;

As regards financing: Search for new credit structures at Community and national level (Commission of the European Communities, 1986d, p. 4).

The pilot phase of the MEDIA Programme was established using the Commission's 'own resources' and did not require approval by the Council of Ministers. The pilot phase, known as MEDIA 92, was reviewed in 1990 by a Committee of Experts[1], often known as *Les Sages*, appointed by the Commission and chaired by Sir Ian Trethowan[2]. The Committee of Experts stated that it was generally 'impressed by the efficiency and realism of the small MEDIA Programme central unit and most of the project teams' (MEDIA, 1990, p. 380) and stated:

> ... we attach great importance to the underlying financial philosophy of MEDIA 92. It is ...'not a subsidy machine'. On the contrary ... over a five years action programme, [MEDIA 92 aims] to bring their operations to financial autonomy ... the administrative costs of the MEDIA 92 projects ... are usually paid partly by the Commission and partly by the host country. We feel these should be borne in their entirety by MEDIA 92, and should be regarded as repayable loans (MEDIA, 1990, p. 379).

The Committee of Experts encouraged MEDIA to extend its remit and its geographical area of operations. They foresaw that 'by the end of its five year term MEDIA 92 might be providing an umbrella for audio-visual co-operation from the Atlantic to the Urals' (MEDIA, 1990, p. 400).

The favourable report of *Les Sages* led to confirmation of the programme by the Council of the European Communities in December 1990 when MEDIA 92 was granted 200m ECU for a period of five years commencing on 1.1.1991 (Council of the European Communities, 1990) of which 84m were to be allocated in 1991 and 1992[3]. The Council's decision required the Commission to report (to the Council, the Parliament and to the Economic and Social Committee) on the MEDIA programme after two years. The Council's decision to support MEDIA (Council of the European Communities, 1990) reflected interventionist assumptions and interests and confirmed the *dirigiste* view that structural change in the European audio-visual market was required in order to enable European producers to benefit from 'economies of scale'. The Council advocated the use of 'new forms of technology,

---

1   The members were: Sir Ian Trethowan (UK) Bo Christensen (Denmark) Enrique de las Casas (Spain) Massimo Fichera (Italy) and Hans Tijssen (Netherlands).

2   *Les Sages*' report (and DG X's own report on the activities of its initiative) during the pilot phase of MEDIA 92 is in MEDIA, 1990.

3   Barzanti (1990) stated that the 250m ECU which Delors had committed to the audio-visual sector at the Assises de l'audiovisuel (Maggiore, 1990 p. 199) was insufficient. The Council's decision reduced this already inadequate sum by 20 per cent (although the 250m ECU had already been endorsed by the Economic and Social Committee of the Community). Two hundred million ECU allocated to MEDIA for five years for the whole audio-visual sector (annual sterling equivalent £26.3m) compares unfavourably with the estimated £2,099m spent on programming by UK television in 1990 (Knowledge Research, 1990).

particularly European forms, including high definition television' to promote development of the audio-visual sector. Following the Council decision MEDIA 92 was renamed MEDIA 95 and its remit expanded. Participation in the MEDIA programme is open to EFTA[1] member states and 'may be extended to most Central and East European countries' (Commission of the European Communities, 1992c, p. 6) because 'European culture has no frontiers' (Commission of the European Communities, 1992c, p. 6).

Extensively, if ungenerously, funded though MEDIA's initiatives are, MEDIA (unlike the Council of Europe's EURIMAGES scheme) is limited to funding pre- and post-production of films and television programmes. The Commission of the European Communities funds up to 50 per cent of the operational costs of each initiative established under the MEDIA Programme. MEDIA does not support production as such. It has fostered cultural pluralism within the Community by supporting the circulation of Community productions, particularly those made in minority languages. MEDIA 92 was mandated to promote: 'the production and dissemination of audio-visual works throughout the Community' (OJ C 115 29.4.91, p. 18) and to promote 'training, pre-production, multilingualism of programmes, use of nex (sic) technologies, distribution and commercial promotion, the creation of a 'second market' and easier access to venture capital' (Council of the European Communities, 1990, p. 174). The Commission described the goals of the MEDIA programme as:

– Remove the barriers from national markets and initiate cross-frontier co-operation so that those concerned can expand their operations through economies of scale;

– Assist the reorganization of the audio-visual industry by giving priority to small and medium-sized operators and by giving support to all audio-visual sectors since they are interdependent;

– Maintain proper regard for national differences and cultural identities, avoiding any cultural uniformatization and paying especial attention to the needs of smaller countries and less widely spoken languages (Commission of the European Communities, 1992c, p. 7).

The pilot phase of the MEDIA programme: MEDIA 92

During the pilot phase of MEDIA 92 projects were launched to support different activities within the European audio-visual sector. These included; the European Film Distribution Office (EFDO) the Espace Video Européen (EVE) Broadcasting Across the Barriers of European Language (BABEL) the European Organization for an Audio-visual Independent Market (EUROAIM) Support for Creative Inde-

---

1 European Free Trade Area.

pendent[1] Production Talent (SCRIPT) Association Européene du Film d'Animation (CARTOON) the Media Investment Club (MIC) Les Entrepreneurs de l'Audiovisuel Européene (EAVE), Media Guarantee and Media Venture.

Les Sages recommended increased support for EFDO (and proposed that EVE should be merged with EFDO) CARTOON, BABEL and SCRIPT. Qualified support was given to EAVE, EUROAIM and the Media Investment Club (support for the last two initiatives was made conditional on review and revision of their financial arrangements). However *Les Sages* recommended withdrawal from Media Venture.

Support for distribution

EFDO is based in Hamburg and has become the most important MEDIA initiative. In 1990 EFDO disbursed 1,171,649.74 ECU, and will account for a 40 per cent share of future MEDIA 92 expenditure. The Committee of Experts (*Les Sages*) stated that EFDO should be considered one of the central projects of the MEDIA 92 programme (MEDIA, 1990, p. 384). EFDO (MEDIA, 1990, p. 9) assisted 37 films and 154 distribution projects (of 88 different distribution companies) for the expenditure of 3.6m ECU during the two year pilot phase of the MEDIA programme. EFDO gave priority to 'the "classical" low budget film' (MEDIA, 1990, p. 22) and assisted projects in all Community Member States and also in Austria and Switzerland[2].

EVE aims to improve returns to producers from exploitation of their properties via video distribution 'throughout the internal market ... to help cover the costs and contribute to the financing of European audio-visual production' (MEDIA, 1990, p. 91) and to increase the share 'held by European films of a video market that is constantly changing and growing' (MEDIA, 1990, p. 95). EVE grants loans (of not more than 20,000 ECU and up to 40 per cent of budgeted costs) to publishers of videos produced by a European Community company and by a producer whose 'cultural affiliation' is European (MEDIA, 1990, p. 96). EVE favours projects produced by, or distributed in, small Community countries and joint production and distribution video ventures in which not less than three Community member

---

1   DG X commissioned Booz Allen to report on the status of independent production in the Community and to make recommendations on a definition of independent production and an independent producer. Booz Allen proposed that not more than 60 per cent of an independent producer's output could be for a single broadcaster, no more than 25 per cent of ownership of a producer could be by a single broadcaster and not more than 50 per cent by broadcasters.

2   MEDIA assistance to audio-visual projects in non-member states was officially sanctioned in the Council decision of 21.12.1990 (Council of the European Communities, 1990 p. 39). This decision authorized the promotion of 'co-operation with professionals in the audio-visual industry in Central and East European countries'. Co-operation with Austria and Switzerland offers significant benefits to German (and to a lesser extent French and Italian) language producers and Austria and Switzerland have participated in several European audio-visual initiatives such as Eurikon and the European Co-production Association (see, *inter alia*, Collins, 1990a, p. 202/4). French projects received circa 23.6 per cent of EFDO support, the UK 7.4 per cent, the Netherlands received least support, Dutch projects received 1.2 per cent of EFDO support (Derived from MEDIA, 1990, Table 5 Ibid. p. 25).

states have participated and which 'yield economic and cultural worth to the business of each of the partners' (MEDIA, 1990, p. 104).

EUROAIM was established in 1988 as a 'service and promotion organization for independent European production' to establish 'a truly European Market, making full use of the creative diversity of its different peoples, demanding the right to different standards and tastes than its US counterparts, and promoting the broadcasting of European programmes' (MEDIA, 1990, p. 120). According to EU-ROAIM, realization of these goals requires commitment and will. The goals are 'culturally *and* economically possible. What we need to add to this is conviction, the refusal to accept the colonization of our screens' (MEDIA, 1990, p. 119). EU-ROAIM provides 'umbrella' services to independent producers at trade fairs such as MIP-TV (for a UK view of EUROAIM in action see Kelly, 1991). During the pilot phase of the MEDIA programme 14.5 per cent of EUROAIM's clients were UK companies; in this respect the UK was second to France (which accounted for 23.75 per cent of EUROAIM's clients)[1]. Membership of EUROAIM is not confined to European Community Member States (Switzerland is a member and EUROAIM has also assisted clients in Sweden, Israel, Poland and Venezuela).

The MEDIA programme exemplifies several important motifs in the Community's *dirigiste* audio-visual policies. Cultural goals are paramount (hence the emphasis on small countries, whose audio-visual cultures are perceived to be threatened by the single market). European culture is defined very permissively and seems to have one key distinguishing principle; it is not American. A further theme in the MEDIA programme (albeit subordinate to the major concern of maintaining the distinctiveness of European cultures by support for small countries and opposition to the United States) is promotion of European co-operation and collaboration. EVE, for example, favours works with participation from partners in more than two Community Member States as do programmes in MEDIA's portfolio of production support initiatives (such as BABEL and Club D'Investissement Media).

Support for production[2]

BABEL[3] was launched in 1988 as a joint venture by the EBU and MEDIA 92[4]. In the two years of the pilot phase of MEDIA 92 (from 1988 to 1990) BABEL disbursed 500,000 ECU. BABEL supports post-production linguistic re-presentation (such as dubbing and subtitling) and in the pilot phase of MEDIA 92, BABEL supported '... 50 works representing 100 transmissions in 12 European languages ...' (MEDIA, 1990, p. 137) made by EBU members (including member

---

1 *Producer News* reported that Euroaim's 'bank account has been frozen following dismissal of secretary general Rudi Barnet and allegations of misuse of funds in Spain' (*Producer News*, 1991, p. 5).
2 MEDIA is not permitted to finance production directly. It assists pre-production, such as SCRIPT, and post-production, such as BABEL, initiatives.
3 Sometimes referred to as FEMA – Fonds européen pour la production multilingue (see Melich, 1990, p. 125).
4 See Naef, 1990 for an account of the EBU's part in BABEL.

broadcasters in non-European Community states). Priority was given to 'projects involving less widely spoken languages, to pilots for TV series, to works of fiction, to European animation films for young viewers, and to transfrontier magazines' (MEDIA, 1990, p. 137).

Club d'Investissement Media (Media Investment Club) was established by INA (the French Institut nationale de l' audiovisuel) and the MEDIA 92 programme in 1988. The objective of the Media Investment Club is to promote 'the creation and production of audio-visual programmes made by means of advanced technology' (MEDIA, 1990, p. 149). It has nine members (from France, the UK, Spain, the Netherlands and Italy) in addition to MEDIA 92 and INA. The Club supports the management of projects in order to maximize synergies, facilitate joint ventures, and provide information on technological developments to interested parties. It has (to June 1990) supported 6 of the 91 projects which have been proposed to it.

MEDIA GUARANTEE guarantees bank loans for European co-productions established by partners from at least three European countries.

SCRIPT supports the writing side of the audio-visual industry. During the pilot phase of the MEDIA Programme SCRIPT disposed of 2m ECU per year in loans for script development. Applicants from Switzerland, as well as from EC Member States, are eligible for SCRIPT support. 50 per cent of the administrative costs of SCRIPT are defrayed by UK institutions (including the Shell-UK/BAFTA venture, the BFI, BBC, Channel 4 and ITVA) the balance of funding for SCRIPT comes from the media programme. Of 1450 applications, in the pilot phase of MEDIA 92, 129 secured SCRIPT development loans. SCRIPT criteria for awarding development loans are: '... a good story with likely appeal to European audiences; the story may play in several countries, or it may be entirely indigenous, and should preferably be innovative and original; the project should have a good chance of being produced' (MEDIA, 1990, p. 162).

CARTOON was established as a joint venture in 1988 by MEDIA 92 and the Ministry of the French Speaking Community in Belgium. It aims to stimulate European production of animated films and to substitute European works for imported animated films[1]. CARTOON supports production by augmenting the flow of skilled workers, supporting creative initiatives (with loans along lines similar to SCRIPT) assisting co-productions and modernizing the production infrastructure (MEDIA, 1990, pp. 192–193). Production of animated films is, MEDIA reports, booming in Europe in consequence of 'national co-production policies' and/or 'real political will', particularly in the UK and in France. However, production in formerly well-established, centres of animated films (such as Belgium and Italy) is in decline.

EAVE (European Audio-visual Entrepreneurs) is dedicated to (a) developing production projects, (b) developing entrepreneurially minded European producers,

---

1 MEDIA 92 states that 70 per cent of animations screened in Europe are of non-European origin and that Europe accounts for only 8 per cent of world production of animations (MEDIA, 1990, p. 196).

(c) developing a network of independent producers in Europe and (d) disseminating information on best production practice (MEDIA, 1990, p. 284). EAVE's particular concern is training, particularly in pre-production, where the European industry (with the partial exception of the UK) was thought to be particularly deficient (MEDIA, 1990, p. 289).

MEDIA VENTURE is a venture capital fund 'specializing in productions with high commercial potential and world appeal' (MEDIA, 1990, p. 318). It emphasizes high budget productions (in which it will invest up to 25 per cent of the anticipated production costs) and judges that 'the most profitable type of film has production costs in excess of US 12 million dollars, corresponding in Europe to expenditure in excess of 8 million ECU' (MEDIA, 1990, p. 321) and co-production (with American partners) of television series budgeted at between 500,000 and 1m ECU.

MEDIA's production support initiatives, like those established to support distribution, have prioritized cultural considerations, pan-European joint ventures and import substitution. *Les Sages'* refusal to recommend continuing support for Media Venture which emphasised co-ventures with US, rather than strictly European, partners is consistent with MEDIA's emphasis on European collaboration, on content and support for small countries, and on minority languages and cultures.

MEDIA 95

Following the Council of Ministers' extension of the pilot phase of the MEDIA programme to 1995, MEDIA 92 was renamed MEDIA 95. Several new initiatives were then established in 1991 (See Commission of the European Communities, 1991a). The most notable were; GRECO (Groupement Européen pour la Circulation des Oeuvres) MAP TV (Memory, Archives, Programmes) and MCD (MEDIA project for Creative Documentaries). Further programmes were later established including the Media Business School (MBS), the European Film Academy (EFA), SCALE (Small Countries improve their Audio-visual Level), LUMIERE (which fostered Europe's film heritage through support for archives and libraries etc.) and MEDIA SALLES/Media Theatres.

GRECO assists distribution of independent fiction television productions by offering a loan of up to 12.5 per cent of project budget to co-ventures which involve at least three European broadcasters from three different linguistic zones. The definitions of 'European' and 'Independent' used by GRECO are similar to those used by other MEDIA 95 programmes. Its European content criteria[1] are similar to

---

1 The points system used by MEDIA for definition of European content was first canvassed at the Audiovisual Eureka and is based on that used by Telefilm Canada for definition of Canadian content. To be eligible for support a production must score 11 European content points. Two points are scored for a European director, 2 for a European author, 2 if 50 per cent or more of the other wage earners are European, 2 if a European and an international marketing plan is presented, 1 if one of the two best paid actors is European, 1 for a European Director of Photography, 1 for a European composer, 1 for a European editor and 1 if the project is supported by SCRIPT (Commission of the European Communities, 1991a, p. 187).

those used by CARTOON. GRECO also uses the EFDO's criteria to determine eligibility for aid[1].

MAP TV (Memory, Archives, Programmes) assists co-productions of archive based creative programmes which have partners from at least three European countries and at least 51 per cent of resources originating in EC states. MAP offers support of up to 7.5 per cent of budget to projects which include a 20 per cent minimum of archive footage and are 'in keeping with the hope of bringing together the peoples of Europe in the long term; as well as with a European view of world events and culture' (Commission of the European Communities, 1991a, p. 120).

MCD (MEDIA project for Creative Documentaries) offers assistance of up to 50 per cent of budgeted costs to the pre-production research and post-production promotion and packaging of independently produced creative documentary projects.

MEDIA 95 was given a budget of ECU 200m by the Council of Ministers' Decision (Council of the European Communities, 1990) of which an indicative budget (in the Annexes to the Decision) allocated 85m ECU to distribution (of which 40m was allocated to EFDO, 10m to EAVE, 10m to BABEL and 25m to EUROAIM). Pre-production was allocated 85m ECU (of which SCRIPT received 23m, CARTOON 23m, Media Investment Club 20m and MAP 9m; finance, notably MEDIA VENTURE, received 10m ECU). Training received 15m ECU (EAVE 3m, Media Business School 12m) and SCALE was to receive 15m ECU. MEDIA 95 gave augmented support and an extension of remit to several initiatives established under MEDIA 92, notably to EFDO. Henceforth EFDO will distribute medium and high budget as well as low budget productions[2]. Moreover, 'Priority will be given to co-operation with professionals from Central and East European countries' (MEDIA, 1990a, p. 3). Thus the MEDIA programme was 'widened' as well as 'deepened' as a consequence of the Council of Ministers' decision. In 1992 MEDIA's budget for 1992 was 45.8m ECU. 5m ECU was spent on administration and promotion, 5.5m on HDTV and CD-I under the auspices of the Media Investment Club, 14m ECU on production (CARTOON, SCRIPT, GRECO) and 11.5m ECU on distribution (EFDO, EVE, EUROAIM) and 8.5m ECU on MEDIA's smaller initiatives (Media Policy Review No. 4, 1992, p. 11).

---

1 Independent producers from member states of the EC and/or states which are signatories to the Audiovisual Eureka.

2 In 1990 the British Screen Advisory Council (BSAC) organized a seminar on European film and television in the 1990s. Participants were drawn from eight countries and from all sides of the UK industry. The seminar report commented on MEDIA 92 'Its impact has been skewed towards low-budget productions. There is a general feeling that MEDIA should become more involved in the commercial side of the industry' (BSAC undated, p. 15). Moreover the BSAC seminar suggested that 'Europe may be producing too many films. It may be spreading its resources too thinly. Instead of producing a large number of low-budget films it may be better advised to produce a smaller number of more expensive films' (ibid., p. 4). Overall however the seminar (and thus, in so far as the participants were representative of the UK industry, the UK industry) was supportive of MEDIA 92. BSAC emphasized that UK priorities were establishment of a single market and development of the UK dubbing industry.

Evaluation of the MEDIA programme

In 1992 DG X awarded a contract for evaluation of the MEDIA Programme. At the time of writing the evaluation had not yet been completed or published. However, Mariano Maggiore, the official in charge of DG X's audio-visual policy, judged that MEDIA is 'still a success story but not all of its projects were equally successful' (interview 11.11.1991). Maggiore indicated that revisions to CARTOON and EAVE might be anticipated but expressed satisfaction with EFDO, BABEL and SCRIPT. Overall, he stated 'the value of the MEDIA programme has been positive. One of the dangers is that certain projects are propelled because of political reasons, because of lobbying by certain countries'.

The MEDIA Programme has consistently been strongly supported by the European Parliament's Committee on Youth, Culture, Education, the Media and Sport. In 1992 its Vice-Chairman (sic) Mary Banotti stated that 'The Committee's attitude to the MEDIA Programme is extremely positive. It has proved to be of enormous advantage particularly to the smaller countries such as the Republic of Ireland' (Banotti, 1992, p. 7). The Committee's report (European Parliament, 1990) on Community audio-visual policy (and the MEDIA programme in particular) – the Barzanti Report – strongly supported the Commission's proposals for MEDIA[1] and Jacques Delors' commitment (made at the Assises de l' audiovisuel in 1989) to allocate 250m ECU to the MEDIA programme[2].

The Barzanti Report echoed that prepared for the Parliament's Committee on Economic and Monetary affairs and Industrial Policy (the de Vries Report) which was published in 1989 (European Parliament, 1989). Both reports identified the dominance of non-European (United States) distributors and the growing preponderance of non-European productions on European screens as the principal problems facing the Community[3]. Both recommended measures to redress the disparities in the resources enjoyed by the audio-visual sectors in small and large Community Member States. Barzanti referred to 'weak regions' and de Vries identified the strengths of 'the FRG, France, Italy, Spain and the UK [which] possess, for both cinema and television, production resources incomparably better than those in the other seven Member States. These disparities must be taken into account in developing Community policy' (European Parliament, 1989, p. 16). Barzanti and de Vries agreed that existing Community measures to support the audio-visual sector were inadequate and that, in de Vries' words, 'considerably more needs to be done' (European Parliament, 1989, p. 18).

---

1 Janey Buchan was the UK representative on the committee which produced the report. However Lyndon Harrison acted as substitute for her in connection with the report.

2 As stated above Delors' commitment of 250m ECU was reduced to 200m ECU by the Council.

3 de Vries stated that '40 per cent of all world trade in audiovisual products consists of European purchases of American programmes' and that 'European dependence on imported American films has grown dramatically ... more than 70 per cent of all fiction (films and series) shown on Member States television is imported and over half comes from the United States' (European Parliament, 1989, p. 10).

Although emphasizing different elements in the audio-visual landscape (the Barzanti report placed its emphasis on the cinema and the de Vries report on television)[1] both European Parliament reports advocated Community action to support the audio-visual sector, though de Vries was careful to remind the Commission that its 'approach should be 'enabling' not 'interventionist' (European Parliament, 1989, p. 7). Both de Vries and Barzanti argued for an expansion of the boundaries within which Community audio-visual policy and 'enabling' was to take place: for 'widening' and for 'deepening'. de Vries stated that the problems facing the European film and television industry are wider than those currently tackled by the MEDIA Programme, and that there should be a more comprehensive Community programme to meet cultural, industrial, fiscal, internal market, competition and trade policy objectives (European Parliament, 1989, p. 5).

The Barzanti report concurred and argued for extension of the bounds of Community audio-visual policy to embrace Eastern Europe and western European states which had not yet become members of the Community (European Parliament, 1990, p. 26). Barzanti advocated linking the MEDIA programme with Eurimages, the Audio-visual Eureka and with European initiatives on HDTV, notably the Vision 1250 EEIG[2] (European Parliament, 1990, p. 32).

The Barzanti report also stressed the complexity of the audio-visual sector, and the relevance of both cultural and economic considerations to policy making. It advocated measures to 'boost the competitiveness of European production on the world market' and to 'improve the cohesion[3] of the European audio-visual industry. Carefully considered measures must be devised, it stated, for 'weak regions'' (European Parliament, 1990, p. 24). Barzanti also stressed the importance of improving the distribution of Community audio-visual productions within the Community (European Parliament, 1990, p. 27) and strongly endorsed the work of EFDO.

In spite of the MEDIA Programme, as Mariano Maggiore recognized, Community support, as it stands, is unlikely to be sufficient to enable audio-visual industries to survive in small Community countries. Such countries, Maggiore stated (interview 11.11.1991) must be the destination for Community subventions. The use of the same criteria to allocate Community resources to big countries as to small 'ends up ... with ridiculous injustices'. Selective aid to national initiatives and industries (notably to the small countries) is, however, incompatible with a single market and

---

1 de Vries stated that 'the main outlet for films is now television not the cinema' whereas the Barzanti report stated that whilst 'Television may act as the driving force or the locomotive of the sector ... cinematographic production must not be determined solely by the parameters of television' (European Parliament, 1990, p. 28).
2 European Economic Interest Group.
3 'Cohesion' is jargon for the transfer of resources from Community states with GDP per head in excess of 75 per cent of the Community average to states with GDP per head less than 75 per cent of the Community average. The 'cohesion' states (i.e. the beneficiaries of cohesion policies) at the time of writing are Greece, Ireland, Portugal and Spain.

with the 'supply specialization' (Commission of the European Communities, 1984a, p. 38) to which *Television without frontiers* referred.

MEDIA emphasizes small countries and minority languages because anglophone producers are powerfully advantaged in competition with producers in other languages. Mariano Maggiore recognized this when he stated (interview with the author 11.11.1991) 'we don't want to leave the audio-visual to the English language media'. Although the success of anglophones will be limited (the 'cultural screens' which separate European audio-visual consumers are only partly permeable) limits will be set in the single market by consumers rather than by national rule making, and the limits set by consumer preferences are likely to disadvantage non-anglophone producers. It is clear that more producers in more Community member states are likely to lose by unity in broadcasting and audio-visual markets than are likely to gain from it[1]. Hence the shift in emphasis in Community policy from unity to diversity and the customary isolation of the United Kingdom in respect of audio-visual policy.

The UK perspective

The UK's interests are different from those of the majority of its Community partners. Yet again, in respect of the audio-visual sector as in other policy arenas, the UK appears to be the 'awkward partner' (George, 1990). Not surprising therefore that the UK Government's policy on the MEDIA programme was described by one UK official (interviewed 10.2.1992) as 'to close it down'. However another UK official, in a different Ministry, described the MEDIA programme as 'well thought out and with services matching the needs of the UK industry' (interview 6.3.1992) and that there were no major rifts in the Community over the MEDIA programme!

The disparity in views between UK officials, both with significant responsibilities for the UK's relationship to the MEDIA programme, reflects the historical division between the UK Ministries charged with responsibility for different areas of the audio-visual sector. The Home Office was formerly responsible for broadcasting and the Department of Trade and Industry for film (both these responsibilities were transferred to the Department for National Heritage in 1992). These Departments of State, however, not only took different attitudes towards UK participation in the European Community's audio-visual initiatives but also towards the role of regulation in the broadcasting and audio-visual sectors. No less than in the European Community itself, therefore, were there divisions and differences in emphasis to be found in the outlook and policies of UK Departments of State. The United Kingdom's European audio-visual and cultural policy had been further compli-

---

1 However the interventionists in and outside the Commission of the European Communities have not yet succeeded in establishing a large scale programme of support for audio-visual production under a Community roof. The opposition of the UK (and Germany) has thus far inhibited it. In consequence advocates of interventionist policies have established programmes, such as Eurimages under the Council of Europe and the Audiovisual Eureka, outside the Community.

cated in consequence of the Office of Arts and Libraries' lead role in respect of cultural policy. The Office of Arts and Libraries, not the Home Office or the Department of Trade and Industry, led negotiations on the content (and very existence) of Article 128 in the Maastricht Treaty.

In spite of the satisfaction with the MEDIA Programme of at least one UK official the fact is that the UK had vigorously attempted to prevent establishment of the MEDIA programme. However, as with the similar case of the inclusion of Article 128 in the Maastricht Treaty, the UK did not veto either MEDIA or Article 128. The lead Ministries were advised by the Foreign and Commonwealth Office that the UK veto should not be exercised over comparatively trivial issues! Once Community cultural support programmes (such as the MEDIA programme) have been established the UK's policy has been to limit damage. As one UK official stated 'we never wanted the MEDIA programme but we are trying to keep it on sensible lines'. In general the UK has traded off concurrence with pro-active Community financial support for the audio-visual sector against increased harmonization and integration of Community audio-visual markets, whereas the policy of other Community Members, such as France, has been the reverse. They have reluctantly concurred with the liberal *Television without frontiers* and have pressed for augmented *dirigiste* Community initiatives of which the MEDIA programme is the most important.

The UK's concern, that money should not be wasted in the MEDIA programme, was shared by other Member States, notably by Germany (see the statement by the German Delegation to the Council of Ministers of 20.12.1990 Document 10927/90 ADD 1). The UK/Germany alliance, however, has not held good for all broadcasting and audio-visual issues. Alliances are often issue-specific and the UK and Germany were on opposite sides in respect of renewal of the satellite television transmission standards directive (the MAC directive) in 1992.

The Community's pro-active policies have not been developed for the UK's needs nor are they well adapted to the needs of the UK's audio-visual sector. As Ken Maidment, former President of the British Film and Television Producers Association, stated in a letter to the Home Secretary, Leon Brittan (later Vice-President of the Commission of the European Communities and in charge of Competition Policy) about the Commission of the European Communities' proposal to establish a European co-production fund for film and television 'The proposals ... seem intended to favour those member countries with smaller film and television production industries' (Maidment, 1988, p. 1).

7

The technological conundrum

Implementation of common technical specifications simplifies the broadcasting of television programmes in all countries of the Community and makes a significant contribution to European unification and to the development of a true European identity (Council of the European Communities, 1986).

The Directive on Satellite Television Transmission Standards

Following the European Parliament's second Hahn Resolution, also known as the Framework Resolution (European Parliament, 1985) and the Parliament's earlier resolution (European Parliament, 1983) calling for a common technical standard for Community television, the Commission proposed a Directive on satellite television transmission standards. The draft Directive was published in 1986 (Commission of the European Communities, 1986c) and was followed by the final Directive the same year (Council of the European Communities, 1986).

The Directive on Satellite Television Standards (Council of the European Communities, 1986) was intended to serve both cultural and economic policy goals. Sections of the Commission and the Parliament believed that European cultural integration and the Community's electronics industry had been ill served by the plurality of television transmission standards used in the European Community. Industry had been disadvantaged by the self-inflicted wounds which denied it economies of scale; European cultural integration had been frustrated because the common technological standard necessary to establish a pan-European television service did not exist (see Commission of the European Communities, 1983 and 1984a). A common television transmission standard would, its proponents argued, remedy both disadvantages.

The separation of the European electronics sector into small, quasi-national industries was attributed to the adoption of different, and incompatible, television transmission and encoding standards at the post-war rebirth of European televi-

sion. The United Kingdom, France and Germany had adopted different transmission standards: the UK 405 lines, France 819 lines and Germany 625 lines[1].
Introduction of colour television to Europe in the 1960s saw a reprise of the
choices of the 1940s and 1950s: France adopted its distinctive SECAM colour
encoding system, whereas most other European states adopted versions of the
German PAL system[2]. Adoption of a co-ordinated incremental approach to a
Community standard for High Definition Television (HDTV) would, it was
thought, lead to the establishment of a single market for a vital new communications technology and thereby assist European electronics firms.

Technological and cultural determinism

The broadcasting and audio-visual policy of the European Community in the early
nineteen eighties was governed by two related presumptions which were consistently reiterated and which underpinned the regulations on satellite television
transmission standards embodied in the Directive (Council of the European Communities, 1986). First, that new communication technologies would profoundly
affect market structures and the social and cultural relationships which derived
from them. Second, that the changed cultural relationships and identities which, it
was presumed, would follow changes in audio-visual and broadcasting markets
would have adverse political and social consequences. These presumptions can be
characterized as technological and cultural determinism. In 1986 the Commission
described the audio-visual policy field in this way:

> At the end of 1986 the whole European television scene will be transformed
> by the appearance of Europe's first direct television satellites ... The choice
> is clear: Either a strengthening of exchanges within Europe and a deepening
> of Community co-operation to promote the identity of our continent in all
> its diversity; or a surrender to powerful competitors and their cultural
> models, be it the Americans today, or the Japanese tomorrow (Commission
> of the European Communities, 1986, p. 3).

More recently Matteo Maggiore[3] has advanced a strong version of a similar,
technologically determinist, argument: 'suddenly, technological progress in broadcasting and telecommunications turned television into a media that is not only
dominant, but will also represent in the very near future the alpha and omega of
social communication. Interactive audio-visual services and thematic TV stations
will replace sheets of paper with screens as broad-band telecommunications via

---

1 In 1948 Francois Mitterand, the Secretary of State for Information, sponsored France's adoption of
   the 819 line standard.
2 European terrestrial television transmission systems use either PAL (Phase Alternation Line) or
   SECAM (Sequence Couleur à Mémoire) transmission standards. However both the PAL and SECAM
   systems are further sub-divided, France uses a different version of SECAM to that used by Greece,
   Germany a different PAL system to that used by the UK.
3 Latterly secretary to Roberto Barzanti, the former chair of the European Parliament's Committee on
   Youth, Culture, Education, the Media and Sport.

cable and/or satellite will make even private audio-visual transmission possible' (Maggiore, 1990, p. 38). Maggiore restates, albeit in dramatic terms, a long established conviction in Community circles that New Communication Technologies are decisively reshaping Europe's media and therefore Europe itself. His statement echoes, in greater length and detail, the fundamental contention of the first *Hahn Report* (European Parliament, 1982, p. 7) from which development of Community broadcasting and audio-visual policy can be said to date, that new technology is bringing about a fundamental change in our whole media system.

The MAC standard

The Directive on Satellite Television Broadcasting Standards (Council of the European Communities, 1986) expired on 31.12.1991. However, between 1986 and 1991 all satellite television broadcasters in the European Community were formally required to use a common, MAC (Multiplexed Analogue Component) transmission standard (although the Community's requirements were honoured more in the breach than the observance). The Directive was badly drafted and the major Community satellite television initiatives were able to escape the requirements enshrined therein. Those services which fell under the Directive's jurisdiction were, on the other hand, competitively disadvantaged, a most unfortunate situation. The balance of advantage and disadvantage entailed by different standards was evident in the rivalry between Sky and BSB over the UK satellite television market.

The most important European satellite television system, Luxembourg's Astra satellite, from which Sky was transmitted (and BSkyB is transmitted) used and uses the PAL standard for television transmission and not the MAC standard mandated by the Community's Directive. Use of PAL standards kept the cost of receiving equipment for Astra signals relatively low, because many of the patents which governed the components used in PAL satellite (and terrestrial) receivers have expired. 'Generic' components can therefore be used and costs reduced. In contrast, the UK BSB satellite television system was required to use MAC standard equipment; it, therefore, incurred consequentially higher costs and was thus competitively disadvantaged. The well proven, low cost PAL system adopted by Sky proved very advantageous to Sky in its lethal rivalry with BSB.

The MAC transmission system required in the 1986 Directive was developed in the UK by the IBA and had been used experimentally since 1981. Proponents of MAC claimed that it offered:

- A common video standard for the whole of Europe;
- A clearer picture than PAL;
- Upward compatibility with future development of HDTV standards; suitability for the bandwidths allocated for satellite broadcasting.

Any common standard, and not necessarily MAC, would give the benefit of a common video standard for whole of Europe (although a common encryption system standard, on which the Community has no policy, is increasingly required if a single satellite television market is to be established for the whole of the Community). Systems other than MAC offer clearer pictures than PAL (e.g. PAL-Plus and digital standards) and upward compatibility. PAL-Plus has the added advantage of offering downwards compatibility so that the existing PAL receiver population does not become obsolete but this advantage to consumers is disadvantageous to electronics manufacturers seeking to stimulate the market with a new generation of products.

A variety of different MAC systems were developed in which a common video transmission standard was coupled with a variety of sound transmission systems: A-MAC was unsuited to distribution via cable and incompatible with established terrestrial broadcasting systems, it was not used operationally; B-MAC inserted sound channels into the video vertical blanking interval and was used for television transmissions by AUSSAT (in Australia) and by the United States for satellite distribution of television signals to the US military forces in Europe; C-MAC used time division multiplexing to combine a MAC analogue video signal with digital sound and was regarded as the best system from the engineering point of view (and was heavily backed by the IBA and other agencies) but it had the disadvantage of requiring greater bandwidth than D-MAC. Although C-MAC was widely regarded as the optimal transmission standard for satellite broadcasting, new generations of MAC standards, D-MAC and D2-MAC, displaced it in the 1990s because they were better fitted to the needs of cable distribution networks.

C-MAC and D-MAC standards differ in their audio channel characteristics. C-MAC offered eight mono sound channels (or four stereo or two stereo with eight commentary channels) D-MAC offered six mono channels (or two stereo or two stereo with four commentary channels) D2-MAC offered four mono channels (or two stereo channels or one stereo channel with four commentary channels). D2-MAC can be distributed over narrowband cable networks, D-MAC over broadband cable networks whereas C-MAC is poorly suited to cable distribution. However, although D-MAC is superior to D2-MAC (though demanding too much bandwidth to be distributed over some European cable networks) its seeming disadvantage of fewer sound channels in D2-MAC than in other MAC standards in fact recommended D2-MAC to many policy makers. For, although the paucity of sound channels in D2-MAC make the standard ill fitted to development of a pan-European television service, this characteristic of D2-MAC offers protection to those national broadcasters and language communities which perceived themselves to be threatened by, either or both, English language or pan-European television. The UK (supported by Denmark) advocated adoption of D-MAC as the Community standard, whereas D-MAC was opposed and the D2-MAC standard was backed by France and Germany.

In 1986 the Community issued a Directive requiring the use of the MAC standard for television transmissions from Community direct broadcast satellites (Council of the European Communities, 1986). The MAC standard was required for all transmissions from Community television satellites, that is, from satellites which transmitted signals at 65dBW or more – the transmitter power level which the Community adopted in its Directive following the WARC[1] definition (formulated in 1977) of a television satellite. However in the decade between the 1977 WARC and the launch of the Astra[2] series of satellites (which transmit at less than 65dBW power) from which the major English and German language European satellite television services are transmitted, the technology of satellite television changed. By the time of the Astra launch in 1988, satisfactory reception could be achieved using smaller receiving antennae and less powerful satellites than WARC (and the Community) anticipated. The drafting of the Community Directive meant that its provisions did not apply to the major satellite television services which came to be established in the Community.

General adoption of MAC as a transmission standard would have meant that the existing Community television receiver population using PAL and SECAM standards would have become obsolete. It was for this reason that broadcasting interests (rather than electronics industry lobbyists) such as the BBC, advocated that E-PAL (extended PAL) be adopted as a transmission standard so as to ensure backward compatibility with the established PAL receiver population[3]. However, MAC, rather than a standard such as E-PAL, was adopted by the European Community for reasons of electronics industrial policy in spite of its disadvantages, notably because MAC, unlike PAL, offered an incremental route to a European HDTV standard.

HDTV

The Commission planned that D2-MAC transmissions in standard 4:3 picture size ratio would be generally established in Europe, and would be followed by 16:9 D2-MAC transmissions and then by 16:9 HD-MAC. The European HDTV standard would in turn provide a defensive screen behind which the Community's electronics industries could shelter from Japanese (and United States) competition and give them early, and protected, access to what was believed would become a very large market[4]. This large market would in turn, it was hoped, provide the basis from which HD-MAC could become a world-wide standard.

HDTV was described by the *Financial Times* as the flagship of EC industrial policy (*Financial Times* 9.2.1993, p. 16) and has been a 'favourite child' of *dirigistes* in the Community policy community. Its proponents have argued for development of

---

1 World Administrative Radio Conference.
2 Astra is the name of the series of satellites owned by the Luxembourg company, Société Européenne des Satellites, from which many of the best known and most watched of satellite television channels are transmitted.
3 E-PAL would have offered no advantages to SECAM receiver users.
4 Moeglin (1991, p. 47) states that the value of the HDTV market in 2000 is estimated at 13.5 billion dollars and that the estimated cumulative value of the HDTV market between 1990 and 2010 is 300 billion dollars.

HDTV as a core, generic technology, the impact of which was thought likely to extend far beyond its immediate application in broadcast television.

Inevitably the HDTV question became a major focus of disagreement and antagonism between the UK and other Member States (notably France and the Netherlands the domiciles of the two lead enterprises, Thomson and Philips, in the development of HDTV). The UK (the 'ultra-liberal' Member State) argued against both a Community industrial strategy which aimed at 'picking winners' and the specific, analogue, HDTV standard chosen by the Community. The UK, however, was not the only opponent of the Community's HDTV strategy. Powerful voices in the EBU argued for a world HDTV standard (see *inter alia* Waters, 1982) although the EBU collaborated closely with Philips and Thomson in implementing MAC based widescreen and HDTV experiments. Events have supported the UK's position.

Four Committees of the European Parliament have interests in HDTV and one of the Parliament's most powerful committees, the Economic and Monetary Affairs Committee, took the lead on HDTV policy[1]. A UK MEP stated (interview 1.11.1991) that commitment to maintaining a strong European presence in advanced technologies was close to universal among Parliamentarians and that, therefore, the HDTV policy had enjoyed widespread support. However the Committee on Youth, Culture, Education, the Media and Sport had, in the words of its former Chairman Roberto Barzanti, not been a major supporter of HDTV. Rather the Committee has been concerned to ensure that introduction of HDTV would not deprive owners of non-HDTV television receivers of access to television services, and that HDTV programme production should become an integral part of Community HDTV policy. As a UK MEP stated 'Programme quality is the most important thing; programme diversity is also important' (interview 1.11.1991).

The chief competitor to the European Community's HDTV standard, Japan's HDTV service Hi-Vision, went live in October 1991 and transmits eight hours of HDTV daily. The first experimental transmissions of the European HDTV system took place in connection with the 1992 Winter Olympics and the 1992 Summer Olympic Games. Considerable technical difficulties remain to be solved before HDTV receivers can combine high resolution with images of brightness comparable to conventional television receivers. Cost is another problem. It will be some time before HDTV receivers can be retailed at prices which will promote the establishment of a large market. HDTV receiving sets (which, in 1992, were on sale only in Japan) remain very expensive; circa £15,000 per unit.

Moreover there is no universal agreement that either the European or Japanese paths to HDTV (based on analogue encoding techniques) are appropriate. Indeed it is widely expected that the United States will adopt a *digital* HDTV standard. The

---

1 A UK Labour MEP (interview 7.11.1991) commented on the characteristic diffusion of power and responsibility between different institutional actors in the European Community of which the divided Parliamentary responsibility for HDTV is representative.

UK opposed the MAC path to HDTV advocated by other Community Member States (and by the Commission itself) on the grounds that analogue systems are likely to be displaced rapidly by digital systems. The MAC standard has also been opposed by many Community broadcasters, by sections of the electronics industry including those (such as Amstrad) with a base in PAL standard manufacturing, and by the few (rather weak) consumer interest groups which have commented on this seemingly recondite aspect of Community policy.

As events unfolded the Community's requirement that satellite broadcasters use MAC for television transmissions was of little relevance. The overwhelming majority of Community viewers who received satellite television signals did so from satellites formally designated as fixed service satellites (FSS) – telecommunication satellites – and to which the provisions of the MAC Directive did not apply. Most satellites transmitting television signals to Community citizens use a lower power than that specified in the Directive. Thus the Directive did not apply to the Astra based services (which were able to use PAL transmission standards) and Astra-based services came to dominate Community satellite television services. PAL enabled Astra broadcasters to establish service on a lower cost base than was possible for competitors such as BSB which, as explained above, was required to use the more costly MAC standard.

The Commission argued that a common Community technical standard for satellite television transmission would materially assist the development of a single European broadcasting market:

> Through technology, direct broadcasting satellites are creating a *de facto* European market for television (Office for Official Publications of the European Communities, 1988, p. 13).

Others argued, however, that adoption of the D2-MAC standard, and development of a community-wide HDTV regime as proposed by the Commission (16:9 format production and true HDTV) would have crippling effects on the cost structure of the European television programme industry. It would, in the words of the Chief Executive of Canal Plus, André Rousselet, 'contribute to making Europe an American colony' (cited in *Media Policy Review* No. 3. July 1992, p. 2). Even though adoption of a common transmission standard did seem to promote a single community broadcasting market the D2-MAC standard, which was *de facto* that chosen (the only standard capable of being used for both satellite and cable services)[1] made establishment of multilingual services, capable of crossing borders and serving audiences from different language communities, more difficult than would have been the case if either C-MAC or D-MAC had been adopted[2].

---

1 The Directive also stated that 'in the case of redistribution by cable of these programmes, the MAC cable system corresponding to the satellite broadcasting system should be preferred'.

2 On the other hand if C-MAC or D-MAC had been adopted signals encoded in those standards could not have been distributed on many European cable networks.

The new directive

The Satellite Television Transmission Standard Directive promulgated in 1986 expired on 31.12.1991. Political agreement on a new Directive was reached at the Council of Ministers' meeting on 27.1.1992. The sponsoring Commissioner (Signor Filipo Maria Pandolfi then responsible for DG XIII) attempted to win support for a new Directive which would establish D2-MAC as a mandatory standard for television satellite transmissions in the Community. On 26 June 1991 the Commission issued a Draft Directive which, as an interim measure, permitted 'grandfathering' of established PAL and SECAM channels. New channels were, however to transmit in MAC from 1992. The effect of the Draft Directive's proposals, if adopted, would be to advantage established channels (because they would be receivable by the established population of European satellite television viewers whereas new, MAC channels would not). The Draft Directive would, therefore, not establish a 'single market' for satellite television within the Community.

New entrants were to be required either, or both, to transmit to a smaller receiver population and/or incur higher costs of services by simulcasting in D2-MAC and, either or both, PAL and SECAM. Moreover simulcasting, if generally adopted, would create a further distortion of the broadcasting market because there is insufficient transponder capacity currently installed to permit all established channels to simulcast. Not only would a barrier to entry be created but some established services would be seriously disadvantaged. Thus the goal of establishing a well functioning *broadcasting market*, open to new entrants and with all service providers competing on equal terms, is not easily reconciled with the goal of promoting the D2-MAC standard in order to support the MAC and HDTV technology.

The Draft Directive was opposed by a wide range of broadcasters supported by some Community member states (and some sectors of the European electronics industry). Objections centred on the costs which the new standard would impose on broadcasters and viewers although other factors, such as doubt as to whether D2-MAC is an appropriate standard, also applied. The Commission proposed several compromises, all of which sought to ensure that new satellite broadcasters must transmit in D2-MAC but they also conceded, to varying degrees, exemptions to established services. D2-MAC standard would trade off the interests of a major part of the Community's electronics manufacturing sector against those of new entrants to the broadcasting market.

Successive revisions of the Draft Directive weakened the requirement to use MAC and, eventually, political agreement was reached in the Council of Ministers on a 'common position' to be enshrined in a new Directive. The 'common position' provided only for a rhetorical, formal, commitment to the MAC route to the establishment of a single Community standard for satellite transmission and conditional access equipment. Indeed the 'common position' of the new Directive opened the door, hitherto closed, to a non-MAC, digital route to HDTV and authorized use of PAL (or SECAM) transmission standards. It provides only that new services must, from 1995, use the MAC transmission standard (however new services are permitted to simulcast in PAL and/or SECAM). Mandatory use of HD-MAC, as a standard for non-digital services, was made conditional on unanimity in the Council of Ministers (thus giving any single member state the power to veto establishment of a single HDTV transmission standard). Incentives for programme production in MAC and the 16:9 ratio are proposed but are also conditional on the assent of the Council of Ministers acting unanimously.

On 11 May 1992 the Council of the European Communities adopted a new Directive (Council of the European Communities, 1992) on satellite television broadcasting standards. The Directive requires that:

- Only the HD-MAC standard may be used for any HDTV transmission that is not completely digital;
- Only the D2-MAC standard may be used for any not completely digital satellite transmission of a 625-line and 16:9 service;
- All 16:9 television sets must be equipped with a D2-MAC decoder and all other television sets must be equipped with a standard socket permitting an open interface standard;
- Use of the D2-MAC standard will also be compulsory for 16:9 services launched after 1 January 1995, provided that the Council adopts a Commission proposal on financial support for such services;
- Periodic monitoring of market trends is planned to ensure that the various instruments, whether regulatory or containing incentives, are adapted to current needs at all times (Commission of the European Communities, 1992c, p. 9).

To sum up, the new Directive lacks teeth because it permits continuance of non-MAC satellite television services, opens up the possibility of digital, rather than MAC services and makes the use of MAC standards by new services conditional on Council approval for a subsidy. In addition, the Council's approval can only be given if there is unanimous support for the subsidy measures proposed by the Commission. This all pleases 'ultra liberal' interests.

A UK official interviewed by the author on 10.2.1992 expressed satisfaction at the outcome and commented 'the UK did very well' in the negotiations about the content of the new Directive. The UK, with Denmark, Spain and Ireland, successfully established a blocking minority against the efforts of France, Germany[1] and the Netherlands to re-establish Community requirements for the exclusive use of MAC satellite television transmission standards.

Thus, the Directives on television transmission standards and on a single market in television (the *Television without frontiers* Directive only came into effect in 1991) express the dominant assumptions in the Community of the early and mid 1980s;

---

1 Latterly Germany's opposition to subsidy for 16:9 production and for establishment of D2-MAC services has hardened as German terrestrial broadcasters have come under increasing financial pressure.

that a single broadcasting market would unify the Community culturally (and therefore politically) and would assist the development of the Community's audio-visual hardware and software industries. However neither Directive established the single market which they were conceived to implement.

The debates around the MAC standard Directive illustrate how some Community policy goals are mutually exclusive. The creation of a well functioning competitive Community broadcasting market was, and is, inimical to the achievement of other Community goals, notably technological development. The Community is subject to pressures from different political and economic interest groups and from advocates of rival theoretical systems. This has caused it to follow neither a consistently *dirigiste* nor a consistently competitive strategy.

Support for audio-visual production for High Definition Television (HDTV)

The Commission's development initiatives for HDTV centred in DG XIII and, in consequence, support for the technological development of HDTV standards, research and manufacturing had been emphasized. Belatedly the Commission presented a Communication on encouraging audio-visual production in the context of the strategy for high definition television (Commission of the European Communities, 1991b) to the Council and Parliament in order to stimulate production of HDTV programmes. The Commission proposed to use the MEDIA programme to 'promote access to and use of the new communications technologies ... in the production and distribution of audio-visual material' (Commission of the European Communities, 1991b, p. 2) and support HDTV programme production by further supplementing the investment already committed to HDTV.

The Community contributed to the creation of a pool of HDTV production equipment and to the establishment of a Media Investment Club initiative – HD MEDIA. HD MEDIA will contribute production funding, either as a co-producer or as a loan, to qualifying projects (5 or 6 per year in 1991 and 1992) which use HDTV as an integral part of their creative strategy[1]. In April 1992 the Commission proposed an HDTV action plan (published as COM (92) 154 final on 11.5.1992) based on the renewed satellite television transmission standards Directive. This included a commitment to the use of D2-MAC on cable networks and a proposed subsidy programme to assist the establishment of HDTV services and productions. The Commission envisaged committing 850m ECU to assist the development and establishment of HDTV services in the Community and later proposed that beneficiaries should specify their plans and sign a declaration of intent so as to become eligible for Community support (*Financial Times* 5.6.1992, p. 4). However implementation of this plan is conditional on support from the Council of Ministers and the European Parliament. This support was not forthcoming during the UK's

---

1 *Media Policy Review* (No. 3, July 1992, p. 2) reported that the German HDTV production centre, initially equipped with European equipment manufactured by Philips, has been re-equipped with Sony production equipment.

Presidency of the European Community (the last six months of 1992) and the UK occasioned considerable opprobrium in December 1992 by using its powers in the Council of Ministers to veto Community subventions to HDTV.

Satellite communications

In 1990 the Commission published its Green Paper on a Common Approach in the Field of Satellite Communications in the European Community (Commission of the European Communities, 1990e) which surveyed satellite communication in (and outside) the Community. The Green Paper testified to the Community's recognition of the importance of satellite communication[1] and to its advocacy of market liberalization[2]. However, whilst notionally a policy initiative concerned with telecommunications, the Green Paper has important consequences for television. It observed that television distribution is the principal application of European communication satellites and that 'Television via satellites to cable TV head-ends and, more recently, directly to businesses and homes has developed into a major application of satellites in Europe' (Commission of the European Communities, 1990e, p. 7). The Green Paper states (Commission of the European Communities, 1990e, p. 43) that television accounts for 80 per cent of European satellite usage and that 'EUTELSAT now derives nearly 75 per cent of its revenues from television distribution' (Commission of the European Communities, 1990e, p. 14)[3].

Since EUTELSAT (European Telecommunications Satellite Organization)[4] is officially a provider of telecommunications, and not television satellite services, such a high level of satellite usage for television is particularly remarkable. Between 44 per

1 'Since satellite communications represent by far the largest commercial application for satellite technology, they will determine, to a large extent, the commercial success of Europe's effort to gain a strategic and future proof position in space. They have developed into an essential element of the common European audio-visual space, which is a central precondition for Europe's future political and cultural identity and coherence' (Commission of the European Communities, 1990 p. 2).

2 'Only with a lifting of restrictive national regulations within the Community, thereby allowing the implementation of Europe wide satellite terminal networks, can the European Community play a full role in meeting the emerging satellite communication needs of its Eastern neighbours. Otherwise Central and Eastern Europe's satellite technology and equipment needs are likely to be met by suppliers from third countries who can build on the existence of major satellite terminal networks already implemented in their home countries due to their more liberal regulatory regime' (Commission of the European Communities, 1990, p. 2).

3 With the exception of the EBU, which is empowered to deal directly with EUTELSAT, potential users of EUTELSAT must contract with their national signatory to the Eutelsat agreements (in the UK British Telecom). The Green Paper argues (Commission of the European Communities, 1990e, p. 32) that television services have developed more rapidly than telecommunication services as a satellite application because, at least in part, telecommunications have been regulated more onerously than has television. However the Green Paper also recognizes that (Commission of the European Communities, 1990e, pp. 38–39) satellites have proven more costly (in comparison to rival telecommunication transmission technologies) than was anticipated.

4 EUTELSAT's first satellite was the ECS-1 (used to transmit Europa services). ECS-1 began operation in 1983; it was preceded by the ESA's OTS (used for Eurikon) and four other European experimental communication satellites; France and Germany's two Symphony satellites and Italy's two SIRIO satellites.

cent and 61 per cent of European satellite carrier revenues in 1989 were accounted for by television (Commission of the European Communities, 1990e, p. 45). Moreover in November and December of 1989 satellites were used (Commission of the European Communities, 1990e, p. 42) to transmit 800 hours of television news footage in multipoint to point modes (Satellite News Gathering). The Green Paper shows (in Commission of the European Communities, 1990e, Figure 2, pp. 19–21) that all European civil satellites launched, or scheduled to be launched, up to 1990, had television as either their sole function or one of their designed functions.

Community satellite policy can thus only be successfully developed if the importance of the applications of satellites, notably television, are recognized. As the Commissioner responsible for science and research (Signor Filipo Maria Pandolfi) and for the future of the MAC standard for satellite television transmissions stated 'One can't have a final product which consists only of a set, or a programme, or a satellite signal. It's the combination of all three which allows one to have a product on the market' (*Financial Times* 13.8.1991, p. 12). Accordingly, within a fundamentally liberal policy perspective, the Commission insisted on the importance of regulation and pro-active Community initiatives because 'Satellites play a key role in the Community's audio-visual policy' (Commission of the European Communities, 1990e, p. 63) and 'will play a pivotal role in the creation and diffusion of pan-European programmes and in the development of a true European audio-visual dimension' (Commission of the European Communities, 1990e, pp. 115–116).

Indeed the Green Paper (within an overall perspective of liberalization) concedes that 'Adjustment of regulatory conditions must match the market conditions identified ... and support the Community's policy for a common audio-visual space' (Commission of the European Communities, 1990e, p. 118). The role of satellites in Community audio-visual policy had been well recognized before publication of the Satellite Communications Green Paper. In 1986 the Parliament (Resolution of 11.12.1986) urged support from all Member States for a 'multilingual European television which would form a link between the multitude of European cultures' (European Parliament, 1987, p. 22). The Commission also re-iterated its support for European satellite television as a means of achieving audio-visual policy goals. Satellite television would, the Commission believed, increase secondary demand for audio-visual programming (Commission of the European Communities, 1990, p. 20). Elsewhere the Commission argued that the absence of a secondary market, resembling the US syndication market for television programming, damaged the European audio-visual industry (see Commission of the European Communities, 1990c, p. 2 and Commission of the European Communities, 1990, p. 20). Satellite television, however, promised to establish such a secondary market in Europe.

Policy contradictions: a summing-up

The contradictions in Community audio-visual policy (between promoting a single market and consequential intensification of competition and division of labour within that market, and mercantilist *dirigisme* directed to supporting activities and localities threatened by free trade within, and without, the Community) also characterizes Community policy in other industrial sectors. Margaret Sharp's discussion of Community technology policy states that 'there appears growing conflict between the main objective of the Single European Act – more competition in the internal market – and what have always been seen as the subsidiary objectives, namely the strengthening of the supply-side of the economy' (Sharp in Crouch and Marquand, 1990, p. 118).

Whilst the most important act of Community broadcasting and audio visual policy to date has been the establishment of a single television broadcasting market, the predominant contemporary policy theme concerns the measures required to redress the perceived adverse effects of an integrated market. However, it is cultural and linguistic barriers which have ensured that Community broadcasting and audio-visual markets have remained separate rather than *dirigiste* initiatives in regulation and subsidy. Although *Television without frontiers* assisted a modest increase in trans-border broadcasting and a consequential restratification of broadcasting markets on a linguistic rather than political basis and an increase in competition within individual markets, divisions between different sectors of the electronics industry and between the broadcasting and electronics industries (and between the Member States which are their sponsors) have frustrated the harmonization of transmission standards.

8

Variable geometry: the role of the pan-European institutions

'... the communications sector becomes increasingly internalized. There has also been a tendency to ignore the role of international institutions, that needs to be corrected' (Dyson and Humphreys, 1990, p. x) .

T o understand the principle object of this study, the broadcasting and audio-visual policy of the European Community, the policy and practice of other European, and pan-European, institutions require consideration. The most important of these pan-European institutions are the European Broadcasting Union (EBU) and the Council of Europe. The EBU numbers among its members the public service broadcasters of the Member States of the European Community: the Council of Europe includes all the Member States of the European Community among its members. There are significant interdependencies and cross impacts between the three chief pan-European organizations in the broadcasting and audio-visual policy domain but, of these, there can be no question that the European Community is the most influential.

The European Broadcasting Union

Realities and tendencies represents a high tide of favourable Commission response to the EBU. In it the Commission recommended that the Community follow the European Parliament's recommendation of collaboration with EBU member broadcasters (Commission of the European Communities, 1983, p. 26) and expressed its own willingness to:

> take all the initiatives which may prove necessary in support of the EBU and its members in their efforts to establish a European service (Commission of the European Communities, 1983, p. 32).

The EBU welcomed both *Realities and tendencies* and the European Parliament's

119

Arfé Resolution, the Parliament's response to *Realities and tendencies* (European Parliament, 1984a). The EBU's welcome for the Community's proposals was based on a perception that the Community was indebted to the EBU for many of the basic ideas in the document and that the Resolution and that the proposed initiatives would serve the EBU very well. The Secretary General of the EBU reported to the Union's General Assembly that:

> The Arfé Resolution, adopted by the European parliament, simply reiterated the Union's idea (EBU document SPG 2652 cited in Hjarvard, 1991, p. 15).

The EBU commented that Arfé's (and Hutton's) reports and resolutions were 'bold ideas (which) although they may seem theoretical, are significant of current thinking in European quarters. As such they raise an all-important question of policy for the EBU and its Members'. However the Union pertinently noted that 'financing of these schemes is never mentioned' (CA 1719 SPG 2787 22.11.1984, p. 6). The EBU judged that the Commission's analysis (and recommendations) were, however:

> ... highly optimistic. It does not appear to have sufficient regard for the linguistic and cultural partitioning which is so important in Europe and which imposes strict limits on the actual reception of foreign programmes, even if they are technically receivable. It also appears to ignore the technical obstacles in the way of general reception of all television programmes in Europe (CA 1719 SPG 2787 22.11.1984, p. 3).

The EBU's judgement was shrewd and was informed by its recent experience with the Eurikon satellite television experiment. Eurikon had shown that, in addition to the linguistic/cultural and technical obstacles which stood in the way of realization of a transnational, European television service, there were formidable financial obstacles to pan-European television which had not been recognized by the Community. The Union commented that nowhere in the Commission's document was there 'any reference to the cost of such a pan-European television undertaking, and this is clearly a serious deficiency' (CA 1719 SPG 2787 22.11.1984, p. 5).

The European Broadcasting Union[1], was established in 1950. It and its Cold War twin, the OIRT, were born out of the International Broadcasting Union (IBU) first established in 1925[2]. The two organizations, OIRT and EBU, which had been created separately as a consequence of cold war political rivalries, reunited on January 1st 1993 under the name of the EBU[3]. At its birth, the EBU had 23 members drawn from Europe and the Mediterranean. By 1990 it had grown to 93 members in 64 countries. Membership is formally open to broadcasting organizations which:

---

1 Also known as the UER after the initial letters of the words Union Européenne de Radiodiffusion.
2 The founding Statutes of the Union Internationale de Radiophonie (IBU) are reproduced in Briggs, 1961, pp. 413–415. The statutes admit to membership 'all societies or associations exploiting public broadcasting enterprises'. The genesis of the IBU is described by Briggs (1961, pp. 308–322).
3 Czechoslovakia, Hungary and Poland joined the EBU in 1990 whilst remaining members of OIRT. They were joined by broadcasters from Belarus, Bulgaria, Estonia, Latvia, Lithuania, Moldova, Romania, the Russian Federation and the Ukraine in 1993.

(1) Are from a country which is an ITU member;

(2) Are authorized by the competent authority to operate a broadcasting service;

(3) Provide a service of national character and importance (from Eugster, 1983, p. 59).

In practice EBU membership is confined to public service broadcasters and to a few commercial broadcasters who have achieved membership in consequence of various anomalies and historical accidents.

The EBU has two classes of member, active members of which there are 39 in the 32 countries of what the ITU defines as the 'European Broadcasting Area' (the 41st parallel divides the European and Asian broadcasting areas) and associate members, of which there are 54 from the rest of the world (source Type[1] 1990). Active members are concentrated in Western Europe and the Mediterranean littoral but have included the former Yugoslavia. (Other former socialist countries of Europe were members of the OIRT). Associate EBU members are to be found as far away from Europe as Australia, Brazil, Korea and Zimbabwe.

The Union's Secretariat (the Permanent Services) is directed by the Secretary General – currently a Swiss national, Jean-Bernard Muench (Muench's predecessor, Regis de Kalbermatten, was also Swiss). The Secretary-General is responsible to the Administrative Council (which is in turn responsible to the General Assembly). The Secretary General supervises five directorates (technical, legal, radio programmes, television programmes and general affairs) the first four of which are linked to committees (technical, legal, radio programmes and television programmes) of the Administrative Council.

The General Assembly meets annually and elects an Administrative Council composed of representatives of 15 of the Active Members, a President and two Vice-presidents[2]. Members of the Administrative Council are elected for a four year term (with a possibility of re-election). Each country represented on the Administrative Council has an 'Administrator' and an 'Alternate' member. Thus the UK's membership has had the BBC as administrator and the IBA as alternate and vice versa. The Council also has an Executive Group to provide for the 'need to take decisions quickly' (interview EBU official 24.2.1992). The General Assembly and the Administrative Council make decisions on the basis of proposals from Committees and Study Groups which are, in turn, supported by the Union's Permanent Services.

The EBU is located in Geneva and in Brussels. Brussels houses the Technical Centre, the headquarters and node of the EBU's networks which are controlled and switched from the Eurovision Control Centre in the Technical Centre. Geneva is the administrative centre of the EBU where the Television Programme Depart-

---

1 Michael Type is head of EBU Data and Reference Centre.
2 Membership of the Council will be expanded to 19 after the Union of the EBU and OIRT.

ment (including the Television News Division) the General Affairs Service, Legal Affairs Department, and Radio Programme Department are housed. The Brussels arm of the EBU is to complete its move to Geneva in 1993.

Although the EBU is best known to European viewers and listeners as the organizer of the Eurovision song contest its chief importance lies in its provision of the Eurovision network of programme exchanges (particularly news exchanges) and acquisition of rights (particularly sports rights) on behalf of its members. In the decade 1982–93 it was the EBU which took the lead in establishing several pan-European satellite television services; notably the experimental Eurikon service in 1982, and its successor Europa in 1985, Eurosport in 1989 and Euronews in 1993. It is here that its work has most clearly impinged on the evolution of broadcasting and audio-visual policy in the Community.

The Council of Europe

The Council of Europe was established in 1949 with 10 members; by 1992 its membership had grown to 25 states and it promises to grow further[1]. The ultimate origins of the Council of Europe can be traced to successive utopian projects for establishing a European Government[2] but the Council itself was born in the late 1940s from the International Committee of the Movement for European Unity which was founded in 1947. This Committee was established following a speech by Winston Churchill in Zurich in 1946. Conservative politicians from the United Kingdom, notably Duncan Sandys, were central figures in the European Movement (as the International Committee of the Movement for European Unity came to be called).

The rationale for the establishment of the Council of Europe advanced by the European Movement was very similar to that advanced by Monnet (and the other founding fathers of the European Communities) in respect of the European Communities. Sponsors of both Council and Communities stressed the inadequate size of national markets in Europe and the need to create political and economic relationships in order to inhibit further European wars. However the founders of the Council of Europe also placed considerable importance on establishment of a supranational European authority to guarantee human rights. Hence the formulation of the European Convention on Human Rights and the early establishment of

---

1   The founder members of the Council were the United Kingdom, France, Belgium, Netherlands, Luxembourg, Sweden, Norway, Denmark, Italy and Ireland. They were followed by Greece and Turkey and then Iceland, Germany, Austria, Cyprus, Switzerland, Malta, Portugal, Spain, Liechtenstein, San Marino, Finland, Hungary and Czechoslovakia. Bulgaria, Poland and Yugoslavia had applications for membership under consideration in 1991.

2   The Council's conception is traced variously to Sully's 'Grand Design' of 1638 for a union of European Christendom and to Penn's 1693 programme of European political union put forward in his 'Essay towards the Present and Future Peace of Europe by the Establishment of a European Diet; Parliament or Estate'.

the European Court of Human Rights under the aegis of the Council of Europe and its Parliamentary Assembly[1].

The European Movement always conceived European culture to be pluralistic, based on democratic traditions and the non-exclusive property of European states. The Brussels Declaration of Political Principles of European Union stated that 'European culture is expressed through that tradition of democracy which is shared by all our nations'; the European Movement stated that 'the richness of European culture depends on its diversity' (European Movement nd, p. 136) and (referring to the major political project of the Movement during the period of its inception) that 'It is very much to be hoped that the fall of Hitler will make possible an ideological reuniting of Germany with the culture of France and England and the United States (European Movement nd, p. 131)'[2].

The inclusion of the United States within the boundaries of European culture was clearly an important factor which differentiated the European Movement and its Council from the European Communities and the cultural policies which were developed in the Community(ies). The European Movement defined European Culture in terms of properties which were not exclusively European. These included; a common morality (derived from Christianity) a political tradition of the rule of law and self-government, and a common, if ill defined, symbolic and intellectual culture (the key characteristic of which was defined as the invention of science by 'the western nations' [European Movement nd, p. 133]).

The structure of the Council of Europe is loose and it is formally held together only by its members' assent to the European Convention on Human Rights. Any measure promulgated by the Council may, or may not, command the adherence of any or all of its members on a voluntary, issue by issue basis. Conventions promulgated by the Council require ratification by seven member states and must be incorporated specifically into the legal codes of individual Member States if they are to take effect. Ministerial Recommendations of the Council of Europe (which have a status comparable to Conventions) require unanimous support from members of the Council's Committee of Ministers (the Ministers of Foreign Affairs of the Member States) and (as do Conventions) specific ratification by the legislatures of Member States if they are to acquire force.

Council decisions are made by the Committee of Ministers, that is by the Ministers of Foreign Affairs of member states. The 192 member Parliamentary Assembly (between 2 and 18 members are appointed from each member country by its parliament) has a consultative status. The Council of Europe has enabled its Members to reach agreements and to develop initiatives which are both weaker

---

1 The membership of the Parliamentary Assembly is drawn from members of the parliaments of the Council's Member States. The Court of Human Rights has one judge from each Member State each of whom are elected by the Parliamentary Assembly to serve the Court for nine years.
2 The role of the Western Occupying Powers in Germany was, of course, to do just that.

and wider than those developed within other institutional contexts such as the European Communities.

Negative freedom

The chief significance of the Council of Europe for broadcasting policy lies in the guarantees of freedom of access to information (and consequential limits on the powers of governments) which the European Convention on Human Rights affords. The Convention's safeguards for 'negative freedom' (the terms 'negative freedom' and 'positive freedom' are drawn from Berlin, 1969) were further affirmed by the Council's Convention on Transfrontier Television, Article 4 of which provides for 'freedom of expression and information ... freedom of reception and ... retransmission ... of programme services' (Council of Europe, 1989) which will come into effect on 1.5.1993. However, the Council has also proved to be an important agency for the realization of initiatives to extend 'positive freedom', in respect of broadcasting and the audio-visual, through the use of European 'variable geometry' (the best instance of which is the Eurimages programme).

Council initiatives, such as Eurimages and the Convention on Transfrontier Television, are examples of the way in which the Council, and the potential it offers to use European 'variable geometry', has enabled Members to achieve objectives in respect of the media which proved impossible to achieve in the context of the European Community because other Community Member States opposed such measures. The Council has also been useful in areas where the European Community lacks jurisdiction and has enabled Members to create rules and agreements in a less binding form than the EC permits (e.g. the Convention on Transfrontier Television). As one Council official stated (interview 17.12.1991) the Council 'gives options for partial agreements'. Thus the Council has enabled Members (notably France and its allies) to develop European policies which support film production which they had been unable to develop within the European Community. It has enabled other Members (such as the United Kingdom and its allies) to establish agreements on transfrontier broadcasting, extending 'negative freedom'[1] of a character different to those possible within the European Community. Indeed the Council is regarded by several Member States of the European Community (Gavin, 1991, p. 20, mentions Belgium, Denmark and Germany) as a more appropriate body for media regulation than the Community itself!

Council resolutions have been passed on a variety of media and cultural matters, including the educational and cultural use of radio and television (Resolution (70) 19). Council Resolutions may, or may not, lead to action (Eurimages, for example, was established in consequence of a Resolution [(88) 15]) but the chief importance of Resolutions is that they pave the way for intergovernmental agreements known as Conventions. Several Conventions relevant to the mass media have derived from

---

1 Though the Convention provides for more stringent measures against pornographic television than does European Community regulation.

Council Resolutions. For example those on television programme exchanges (No. 27 in 1958) and on protection of copyright in television broadcasts (No. 34, 1960).

The most important Convention in respect of the mass media to derive from Council activity is the European Convention on Human Rights (which has been ratified by all the Member States of the European Community as a condition of their membership of the Council of Europe). The European Human Rights Convention guarantees every person freedom to receive and impart information and ideas without interference by public authority, regardless of frontiers. The Convention was signed on 4 November 1950 and entered into force on 3 September 1953[1]. In 1982 (29 April) the Committee of Ministers of the Council of Europe adopted a Declaration on the Freedom of Expression and Information which further affirmed the general principles enunciated in the Convention. Latterly the Convention on Transfrontier Television has been ratified by seven member states of the Council of Europe and came into force on 1.5.1993.

The Human Rights Directorate, through its Steering Committee on the Mass Media (CDMM[2]) and its sub-committees and working parties, was given formal responsibility for media policy within the Council because:

> The proper functioning of free and autonomous media and the availability of a plurality of information sources and of communication links are essential for democracy and international understanding. Freedom of information is not only a fundamental right per se but also facilitates the exercise of other fundamental rights (Council of Europe, 1991b, p. 6).

This formulation expresses the Council's overriding commitment to negative freedom in communications and the status and influence of the CDMM (particularly relative to the CDCC – the Council for Cultural Co-operation) testifies to the strength of the Council's commitments in this respect. The 1980s, when the Council formally took up media issues, were characterized by a Council official (interviewed 18.12.91) as a time of 'tremendous technical change'. At this time

1 Article 10 of the European Convention on Human Rights states:
1. Everyone has the right to freedom of expression. This right shall include freedom to hold opinions and to receive and impart information and ideas without interference by public authority and regardless of frontiers. This Article shall not prevent states from requiring the licensing of broadcasting, television or cinema enterprises.
2. The exercise of these freedoms, since it carries with it duties and responsibilities, may be subject to such formalities, conditions, restrictions or penalties as are prescribed by law and are necessary in a democratic society, in the interests of national security, territorial integrity or public safety, for the prevention of disorder or crime, for the protection of health or morals, for the protection of the reputation or rights of others, for preventing the disclosure of information received in confidence, or for maintaining the authority and impartiality of the judiciary.
2 The CDMM (Comité directeur des moyens de communication de masse) comprises experts from each of the member states of the Council, from the Commission of the European Communities and from the Parliamentary Assembly. Other organizations, including the Audiovisual Eureka, the EBU and the Association of Commercial Television in Europe, have observer status on CDMM. The membership of CDMM (and the sub-committees MM-JU, Committee of Legal Experts in the Media Field, and MM-R-PD, Select Committee of Experts on the Production, Distribution and Marketing of European audio-visual works) is specified in Council of Europe, 1991b pp. 130–131.

members of the Council had become alarmed by the development of doctrines which they believed to threaten freedom of expression and communication, for example, the doctrines of 'prior consent' for reception of satellite television signals and licensing of journalists which were then espoused by UNESCO. Publication of the UNESCO sponsored MacBride report *Many voices, one world* in 1980 (UNESCO, 1980) focused these concerns. In 1981 the Parliamentary Assembly of the Council of Europe adopted a recommendation (No. 926) on 'Questions raised by cable television and by direct satellite broadcasts'. The recommendation welcomed satellite television and affirmed that policy for these new media must be based on a recognition of 'freedom of the press and television, as a fundamental component of freedom of expression' (Council of Europe, 1991d, p. 34) and urged 'concrete legal co-operation, possibly in the form of a convention' (Council of Europe, 1991d, p. 37).

The Declaration on the Freedom of Expression and Information (Council of Europe, 1991a, p. 63) was grounded in Article 19 of the Universal Declaration of Human Rights and Article 10 of the European Convention on Human Rights. The 1982 Declaration (sometimes known as the European Media Charter) included explicit commitments to free flows of information across borders and the 'protection of the right of everyone, regardless of frontiers, to express himself, to seek and receive information and ideas, whatever their source'. The Declaration also specifically rejected 'arbitrary controls or constraints on participants in the information process'. The twenty one (as the membership of the Council then was) members of the Council of Europe therefore unequivocally rejected the central propositions advanced by the MacBride Report (UNESCO, 1980). It was in this context that the Council's Steering Committee on the Mass Media was established within the Council's Directorate of Human Rights.

The Convention on Transfrontier Television

The Council's draft Convention on Transfrontier Television was signed on 5.5.89 by Austria, Liechtenstein, Luxembourg, the Netherlands, Norway, San Marino, Spain, Sweden, Switzerland and the UK. Subsequently Greece, Hungary, Italy, Poland, Portugal and Yugoslavia have added their signatures. For implementation the Convention requires ratification by the parliaments of at least seven signatories. The seventh member state, the Holy See, adhered to the Convention in late 1992. The Convention emanated from the Council's Steering Committee on mass communications, the CDMM, in response to concern among member states about the implications of the development of satellite television[1]:

> The aim of the Convention is to provide an international framework for the unhindered transfrontier circulation of television programme services. It ... lays down a set of minimum rules in ... the essential aspects of transfrontier broadcasting, such as the protection of certain individual rights, the respon-

---

1 See Council of Europe, 1990 for an account of the background to the drafting of the Convention.

sibility of broadcasters in regard to programming matters, the European content of programming, advertising and sponsorship ... the Convention sets out to secure the harmonious development of transfrontier television services, guaranteeing freedom of reception and laying down the principle of unrestricted retransmission of services which comply with the common minimum rules (Council of Europe, 1991b, p. 20).

The fundamental proposition on which the Convention is based is freedom of reception. Viewers are not to be denied access to transfrontier television services, whether by direct reception or via retransmission[1]. However the Convention does not prohibit signatory states from promulgating stricter regulation over television signals which originate within their jurisdiction than is exercised over foreign signals. The Convention establishes common minimum rules for the protection of viewers and requires that 'wherever practicable and by appropriate means' broadcasters reserve a majority of their transmission time for European works.

The Convention does not specify what is meant by European[2], nor requires that the European content regulation apply to each channel of a broadcaster's output or that European content be transmitted at any particular time. Thus a broadcaster transmitting two channels could satisfy the requirements of the Convention by transmitting 24 hours of European content on one channel and 23 hours 59 minutes of non-European content on the other per day. The European content requirement could be also be satisfied by the transmission of European content between the hours of 2am and 2.01pm and non-European content from 2.01pm to 2am. A European company could be established and owned by a non-European and the works it produced would count as European for the purposes of the Convention. The European content regulations prescribed in the Convention are, therefore, minimal when compared to the rigorous requirements and specific definitions of Canada or Australia on content.

Some articles in the Convention and in the European Community's *Television without frontiers* Directive (Council of the European Communities, 1989) are identical. Thus accession by non-member states of the European Community[3] to the

1 The Council comments: 'the use of cable distribution systems cannot simply be equated with "reception" and that the distribution of programmes by cable is subject to obligations arising out of copyright' (Council of Europe, 1991b, p. 25).
2 A senior Council of Europe official (interviewed 18.12.1991) stated that there was no formal definitions of 'European' for the purposes of the Convention. The text of the Explanatory report on the Convention (Council of Europe, 1990, p. 17) states that 'a creative work is considered to be European...if its production or co-production is controlled by European natural or legal persons'. Clearly that definition is rather loose, however the official stated that there 'was a broad consensus that what was meant was Europe in the cultural sense but not in the geo-political sense'. Thus some component parts of the former Soviet Union would be regarded as European (as would of course all members of the Council of Europe) but others would not. Nor would states of the southern Mediterranean littoral be regarded as European. The, elastic boundaries of Europe therefore seem to extend east from Iceland to somewhere in Russia and south from Siberia to Turkey and Cyprus.
3 Indeed it is open to the European Community itself to accede to the Council of Europe's Convention on Transfrontier Television.

Convention on Transfrontier Television will serve to extend the rules of the European Community's single broadcasting market beyond the territorial limits of the Community. Indeed the Community's Directive (Article 6) refers to the Convention as a means of defining whether works may count as European. Works originating from states which are parties to the Convention are recognized, for the purposes of the Directive, as European: a Television without Frontiers indeed.

However it would be misleading to emphasize the similarities between the Council and the European Community although the interdependence of the Convention and the *Television without frontiers* Directive in respect of European content regulation is very important. More striking are the differences. The EBU defined some of the most salient differences between the Council and the Community:

> It is important to stress that the Council of Europe's approach differs completely from the EEC's. Not only do its recommendations lack the legal force of EEC directives, but the national experts and the EBU (as observer) are closely associated in preparing and drafting these documents. Finally, the Council of Europe appears to set greater store by the defence of public service values than does the EEC (CA 1802 SPG 3304 14.5.1986, p. 3).

In addition, although there are similarities and complementarities between the Council's Convention and the Community's Directive (which have been discussed above) it is important to recognize that there are significant differences between the two documents. For example, the Convention (Article 5) regards the point of origin of transmissions to be the locus of jurisdiction whereas the Directive (Article 2) designates the site of service control as the locus of jurisdiction. (For discussion of the provisions of the Convention and Directive and their implications for broadcasters see EBU, 1990.)

Today the dominant concerns within the Council of Europe, in respect of the mass media and cultural policy, is for 'negative freedom' including freedom for legal, as well as natural persons. Clause 2 of Resolution 428 of 1970 of the Consultative Assembly (Parliamentary Assembly) of the Council of Europe states that 'The right to freedom of expression shall apply to mass communication media', that is corporate speech is protected. However Clause 7 of the same resolution states that 'The independence of the mass media should be protected against the dangers of monopolies'. This clause, and provisions of other Council of Europe resolutions (such as Clause 4 in Recommendation 747 of 1975 on press concentrations which states; 'Diversity of the press, as a fundamental component of freedom of expression is a prerequisite for a democratic political system') can be interpreted as requiring active political intervention if the goals they enshrine are to be realized. They can therefore be interpreted as mandating action to realize 'positive freedom'.

Positive freedom

Gavin has argued that reference to the Council of Europe's Convention on Transfrontier Television and to the European Convention on Human Rights in the preamble to the European Community's Television Directive (Council of the European Communities, 1989) indicates that 'by this admission the Commission bowed to the superior status assigned to the Council of Europe in cultural matters' (Gavin, 1991, p. 42). Gavin's proposition is extravagant (though Eurimages lends some support to her contention); the inclusion of Article 128 (the 'culture article') in the Maastricht Treaty, suggests that, even if it were once true, the European Community no longer cedes primacy to the Council of Europe in cultural matters.

Latterly, however, the Council has fostered pro-active initiatives designed to augment 'positive freedom' in the broadcasting and audio-visual arena. These have taken place outside the institutional context and jurisdiction of the Directorate on Human Rights (although the Directorate remains the most important locus of Council of Europe jurisdiction in respect of the media and a bastion for defence of 'negative freedom'). 'Positive Freedom' initiatives have centred on the Council's Directorate of Education, Culture and Sport which has grown in importance in respect of the mass media. The Directorate of Education, Culture and Sport is responsible for Eurimages and is the sponsoring Directorate for an emerging Council Convention on multinational co-productions. Indeed one of the 'three main aims' of the Council, that is 'to promote the emergence of a genuine European cultural identity' (Council of Europe, 1991 np) falls within the jurisdiction of this Directorate[1] and the CDCC (the Council for Cultural Co-operation).

The CDCC has unequivocally asserted its interest in television and in the development of Council media policy. It stated 'Culture is one of the basic components of the Council of Europe's action to achieve a "closer union" between member states'. Television undoubtedly exerts a cultural influence, of whatever sort. It is part of our daily lives, and to some extent shapes them – for better or worse' (Council of Europe, 1991c, p. 2).

The development of a pro-active, interventionist 'positive freedom' emphasis in the Council of Europe's work on broadcasting, the audio-visual and the mass media, and the growing importance of the CDCC, is associated with the themes articulated by Council members at the succession of Council Ministerial Conferences on Mass Media Policy. The Council's pro-active stance has also been used by Member States (notably France) of the European Community to achieve, by 'variable geometry' and intergovernmental agreement within the Council, what could not be achieved under the umbrella of the Community, notably a European film and television co-production programme; Eurimages.

---

1 Elsewhere Council documents state similar, but not identical, goals. For example 'the aim of the Council of Europe is the achievement of greater unity between its members for the purpose of safeguarding and realizing the ideals which are their common heritage' (Council of Europe, 1991a, p. 23). The other two aims of the Council are 'to protect and strengthen pluralist democracy and human rights' and 'to seek solutions to the problems facing society' (Council of Europe, 1991 np).

Eurimages

Just as the audio-visual and broadcasting policy of the European Communities combines, often uneasily, commitments to reducing obstacles to the effective operation of markets and to redressing those effects of the operation of markets which are deemed to be undesirable, so too does the audio-visual and broadcasting policy of the Council of Europe. The Council's commitment to freedom of expression and the free flow of information and ideas (see the Declaration on the Freedom of Expression and Information of 29.4.1982 in Council of Europe, 1991b, pp. 36–37) underpins the Council's approach to media questions and has thus led the Council to oppose restrictions on the operation of information markets. However, on the other hand, the Council's policy also incorporates strongly pro-active elements designed to redress the effects of the operation of markets perceived to be undesirable. Again, as with the European Communities so with the Council of Europe, a *dirigiste* approach is associated with one (or more) administrative unity within the organization and a liberal approach with an other(s). In the Council the CDMM customarily adopts a liberal approach whereas the CDCC tends to be more *dirigiste*..

The Council's Recommendation On Aid for Artistic Creation of 1985 (Council of Europe, 1991a, p. 27) – which falls under the responsibilities of the CDCC – refers to the support, maintenance and development of 'certain artistic forms which are indicative of a country's cultural identity and are experiencing difficulty in gaining access to, or surviving in, the commercial circuit'. It refers (Council of Europe, 1991a, p. 29) 'to providing appropriate resources for keeping cinema (sic) in operation, reopening those which have closed for economic reasons', and to 'the need ... to protect traditional activities [i.e. in the cultural sector RC threatened by technological developments' (Council of Europe, 1991a, p. 38).

The European Support Fund for the Co-production and distribution of Creative Cinematographic and Audiovisual works (Eurimages) was established (following an initiative of France) on 26.10.1988 in order to develop European cinematographic and audio-visual production (Resolution (88) 15 modified by Resolution (89) 6 of the Committee of Ministers of the Council of Europe). The initial budget (1989) for Eurimages was 56m FF (in 1991 its budget amounted to ca. 90 m FF). France contributes the largest share of Eurimages' budget.

The establishment of Eurimages followed a succession of Council Resolutions which affirmed the importance of the audio-visual sector to the fostering of European culture and identity[1]. Of these prior resolutions the one on promotion of audio-visual production in Europe (R (86) 3) was the most significant. Its

---

1 See, *inter alia*, recommendation R (85) 6 On Aid for Artistic Creation (sometimes known as the resolution on European Cultural Identity) R (85) 8 On the Conservation of the European Film Heritage, R (86) 3 On the Promotion of Audiovisual Production in Europe, R (86) 9 On Copyright and Cultural Policy, and especially R (87) 7 On Film Distribution in Europe (all in Council of Europe, 1991a).

purpose was described by the Council (Council of Europe, 1991b, p. 17) as the achievement:

> ... of a genuine and diversified European audio-visual production capable of meeting the needs of television viewers and of encouraging closer unity between peoples as well as the mutual enrichment of cultures ... Without increased and competitive audio-visual production, there is a real risk that the new channels will be fed by re-broadcasts of existing programmes or extra-European programmes[1].

Eurimages began operations on 1.1.1989 and is well established in the Council; its President, Gaetano Adinolfi, is Deputy Secretary General of the Council. Adinolfi was described as personally committed to Eurimages (by Ryclef Rienstra, Executive Secretary of Eurimages, interviewed 17.12.1991). The founding members of Eurimages included all EC states (except Ireland and the UK)[2], and Cyprus and Sweden. Subsequently Austria, Finland, Hungary, Iceland, Norway, Poland, Turkey and Switzerland joined Eurimages. The fund was established to:

> ... encourage the co-production and distribution of creative cinematographic and audio-visual works originating in the member states of the fund, particularly by helping to finance the co-production of such works and by partly financing the cost of dubbing and subtitling (Council of Europe, 1988, p. 2).

The rationale for Eurimages was threefold; to develop the programme industries, 'take advantage of the new communications techniques and meet the cultural and economic challenges arising from their development', and promote Europe's cultural identity (Council of Europe, 1988, p. 1). Aid is granted to projects which originate in a member state of the fund (though co-productions which involve a share of 30 per cent or less of a non-member state are eligible for support)[3] and involve at least three co-producers from member states, none of which may contribute more than 60 per cent of project costs[4]. Eurimages support for co-produc-

---

1 This formulation well illustrates the contradiction between the exploitation of the economies of mechanical and electronic reproduction of information – which permit and promote the integration of information markets over time and space and the reuse of existing information products – and the achievement of goals external (and hostile) to the operation of markets to realize these economies. That is maintenance and growth of levels of employment in the information sector, support for European production and prioritization of works which exhibit the character of established, endogenous European cultures.

2 In 1991 the UK Prime Minister, Margaret Thatcher, established a European co-production fund of £5m over three years to promote collaboration between feature film producers in the UK and other European Community Member States. Part of this fund (33 per cent in 1991/2 and 25 per cent in each of the years 1992/3 and 1993/4) is earmarked as a contribution to Eurimages. However the Government's contribution to Eurimages was conditional on the UK film and television industry contributing to the membership fee required for UK membership of Eurimages. The UK joined Eurimages on 1.4.1993. Ireland joined Eurimages in late 1992.

3 Peter Greenaway's UK films *Prospero's Books* and *Darwin* have qualified for Eurimages distribution and production support, and for Eurimages production support respectively, under these provisions.

4 Detailed regulations devised for the Eurimages scheme (beyond those defined in the Committee of Ministers' resolution) provide that no minority co-producer may have less than a 10 per cent share in a project, that the principal language must be the language of one of the co-producers originating

tion and distribution places particular emphasis on financial assistance to co-productions and subtitling and dubbing (to overcome what Rienstra [interview 17.12.1991] described as 'the terrible language barrier') and has focused its activities on fiction feature films and creative documentaries. Thus far (1992) Eurimages support has been confined to cinematographic works.

The Eurimages board of management stated that it would take into account 'the quality of the work' and 'whether it is apt to reflect and to promote the contribution of the diverse national components to Europe's cultural identity' (Council of Europe, 1988, p. 3) in granting assistance to eligible projects. Latterly the board of management has specified that it will 'take into account the quality of the work concerned and ascertains whether the work is capable of reflecting and promoting the contribution of the various national components to Europe's cultural identity' (Eurimages, 1991, p. 5).

Ryclef Rienstra, the Executive Secretary of Eurimages explained (interview 17.12.1991) that Eurimages was established because of lack of success in establishing a co-production support scheme as part of the MEDIA programme. The abortive European Community initiative was opposed by Germany (in consequence of the Lander sensitivity over loss of cultural sovereignty) by Greece and Denmark (both of which were troubled by the growth of the European Commission's jurisdiction in the audio-visual sector) and by the UK (which opposed extension of Community activity into the cultural domain). France took the lead in establishing Eurimages in the Council of Europe through the Council's Cinema Export Committee. As Rienstra stated:

> The French are the most concerned with national cultural identity – in that sense they are very European in their thinking (interview 17.12.1991).

Indeed Rienstra (interview 17.12.1991) described Eurimages as driven 'more by a cultural than by an industrial point of view'.

In its first two years of operation (1989-90) Eurimages has supported the co-production of 55 fiction films and four documentaries. Its Executive Secretary stated (17.12.1991) 'it should develop towards TV, especially European high level drama'.

(contd) from a member state, key personnel must be European and productions originating from small countries will be given 'particular attention'. There are further provisions, differing from scheme to scheme, for each of the two Eurimages production schemes. That for Creative Documentaries requires producers to be independent of broadcasters and to have a presale agreement from a broadcaster or distributor and limits support to 15 per cent of project costs. The scheme for Feature Length Fiction Films provides that support will not exceed 20 per cent of costs or 5m FF. Production support takes the form of a repayable advance. Distribution support is available for works which broadly satisfy the criteria defined for production support and which are given theatrical distribution in at least three member states *excluding* the country of origin of the work (unless the country of origin is not an EFDO member, i.e. films from non-EC states such as Cyprus, Turkey, Iceland, Finland, Hungary and Norway may be eligible for exemption under this provision). Eligible films are ones which received Eurimages production support, were co-produced with East European states, or are distributed in three states of which two are Eastern European. Distribution support is limited to 50 per cent of the costs of release prints and internegative, subtitling and the dubbing of children's and creative documentary films up to 150,000 FF per distributor (derived from Eurimages, 1990).

Eurimages' contribution of 133m FF (in advances on receipts – interest free loans which are repayable only if projects are financially successful) accounted for 12.3 per cent of the total production value of the production projects supported. Thus far France has been the most active co-production partner and principal recipient of Eurimages support (interview Ryclef Rienstra 17.12.1991). By mid-1991 France had participated in 59 Eurimages projects (in 23 of which it was the dominant partner) Germany in 28, Switzerland in 21, Spain in 20, Italy in 20, Belgium in 17, no other Eurimages member had participated in more than 10 projects. Eurimages has supported the distribution of 5 films.

Eurimages is thus an exemplary instance of successful use of 'European variable geometry', that is, the use of European institutions outside the European community by a Member State of the Community, to achieve goals unachievable through the institutions of the Community. France sought to establish a film and television subsidy programme and to foster pan-European co-productions. Its aspirations were frustrated by other Community Member States able to use the blocking powers they possessed in respect of initiatives developed under Article 235 of the Treaty of Rome. However, the Council of Europe provided a forum for successful development of the initiative which had hitherto been frustrated and for securing the eventual adherence of all Member States of the European Community to Eurimages.

9

The battle of images

'... pour reprendre la formule de Jacques Delors, le risque devient serieux de voir à terme les téléspectateurs européens ne plus regarder sur des téléviseurs japonais que des séries americaines' (Decaux, 1989, p. 8[1]).

Une offensive mondiale de l'audiovisuel français

Community policies have evolved in ways inimical to the desires and interests of the United Kingdom in consequence of the reluctance of the United Kingdom (both Government and broadcasters) to participate actively in European ventures and policy formation. In consequence, Community policy has more closely reflected the interests of France which, unlike the UK, has consistently involved itself in Community audio-visual policy making.

The Commission dates the official birth of the Community's audio-visual policy from 1988[2], when the European Council first made a formal testimony, at its Rhodes meeting, to the importance of 'co-operation to develop Europe's audio-visual capacity' in order to 'contribute to a substantial strengthening of a European cultural identity' (in Commission of the European Communities, 1990b, p. 7)[3]. At Rhodes the Council also acknowledged the importance of the French Government in developing the Community's audio-visual policy, in particular, the part France had played in orchestrating, in Paris in 1989, the meeting variously known as the Audio-visual Eureka or the Assises de l'audiovisuel (see below).

France's vision of the European audio-visual landscape was eloquently sketched out in a report submitted to the Prime Minister of France by the Minister for La

---

1 '... to adopt Jacques Delors' terms, the risk of European television viewers only being able to see American series on Japanese televisions is becoming serious.'
2 If 1988, and the Rhodes Council meeting, constitute the birth of the Community's audio-visual policy, then the Hahn Report and Resolution of 1982 constitute its conception.
3 The Council reaffirmed its commitments at its Madrid and Strasbourg meetings in 1989 (see Commission of the European Communities, 1990b, pp. 8–9).

Francophonie, Alain Decaux, entitled *La politique televisuelle exterieure de la France* (Decaux, 1989). In the preface to the report Decaux wrote:

> J'ai écrit à Michel Rocard [the Prime Minister]: il faudrait que, dès mainten-ant, tous les ministères concernés commencent à travailler ... sur une des plus considérables remises en cause culturelles qu'un pays aura su genérer: une offensive mondiale de l'audiovisuel francais (Decaux, 1989, p. 7)[1].

Military metaphor suffuses Decaux's analysis. Not only does he refer to 'une offensive mondiale', but elsewhere the report refers (Decaux, 1989, p. 8) to 'La bataille mondiale des images'; a battle which France had been fighting long before the publication of Decaux's report and in which it sought common cause with the Commission of the European Communities. The Decaux report was both cause and consequence of a remarkable series of French initiatives in respect of the audio-visual during the late 1980s, during which France cemented important alliances with the Commission of the European Communities and with other European states.

Story states 'French diplomacy regularly takes the lead in Brussels as champion of protectionist stances in international trade negotiations' (Story in Crouch and Marquand, 1990, p. 5). The French approach developed under the 'ever closer union' provision in the 1957 Rome Treaty; a provision which has often been used to legitimize the engrenage whereby Community jurisdiction and authority have expanded.

France has successfully set the *dirigiste* policy agenda. The French emphasized that both Europe and France faced the problem of 'la tres forte preponderance anglo-saxonne', to which the solution was 'européaniser la production télévisuelle' (De-caux, 1989 pp. 23 and 40). As early as February 1987, nine Community Member States, led by France had undertaken to support European Co-productions on an intergovernmental basis rather than under the umbrella of the Community. This was the short-lived Plan Léotard, to which Eurimages owes its origins. However, France has also sponsored other initiatives outside the Community, notably, the Paris 'Symposium International sur l'Identité Culturelle Européene' in 1988 and the 'Assises de l'audiovisuel' (also held in Paris and jointly sponsored by the Government of France and The Commission of the European Communities) in 1989. The Assises (also known as the Audio-visual Eureka) was endorsed by the European Council in 1988 which characterized the Assises as seeking to encourage the emergence of a truly European audio-visual market. French audio-visual policy provides a text book example of the way 'variable geometry' has been used to achieve European policy goals.

---

1 'I wrote to Michel Rocard: all the relevant ministries should immediately begin to work on one of the most important national cultural questions: a global offensive by the French audio-visual sector.'

The Assises de l' audiovisuel and the Audio-visual Eureka

The Assises européennes de l' audiovisuel (also known as the Audio-visual Eureka) were held in Paris between 30 September and 2 October 1989. They were organized by the French Ministry of Foreign Affairs led by Bernard Miyet[1] later the Chairman of the Audio-visual Eureka Co-ordinators' Committee – and the Commission of the European Communities which was represented by the President of the Commission, Jacques Delors, and officials from DG III, DG X, and DG XIII (see Miyet, 1990). Although the Assises, and the Audio-visual Eureka programme which it established, were not official programmes of the European Community Delors' presence at the Assises, the status of the Commission of the European Communities as joint organizer of the Assises, and the consistently reiterated support of the Community's Council of Ministers for the Assises, demonstrates the strength of the commitment of major sections of the European Community to the Assises, and thus to a *dirigiste* policy and programme for the European audio-visual sector.

The 26 countries[2] represented at the Assises in Paris signed a declaration which established an Audio-visual Eureka. The Audio-visual Eureka was modelled on the technological Eureka which had been established by France in 1985 as a Europe wide industrial research and development initiative. It was conceived as a complement in 'software' to the 'hardware' emphasis of the technological Eureka. Just as the technological Eureka had been established to foster collaboration between European (including non-members of the EC) electronics and high technology enterprises, so the audio-visual Eureka was established to foster collaboration (act as a 'marriage bureau') between European audio-visual enterprises[3]. High Definition Television (HDTV) has been a common focus of both Eurekas.

Miyet (1990, p. 10) described the Assises as inspired by 'a realization of the existence of structural weaknesses in the production and circulation of European programmes, insufficient capacity, especially in drama, Europe's marginal position on world markets, imbalance in exchanges, political mobilization still confined to a few isolated concerted actions'. His remarks echo the rationale for the technological Eureka, which was to be the locomotive of a high technology European renaissance in response to the United States' 'Star Wars' research and development

---

1 Miyet later became a senior official in cultural affairs in the Commission of the European Communities, he was formerly Chef du Cabinet to Georges Fillioud, when Minister of Communications, and became President of SOFIRAD before taking up his position in Brussels.

2 Austria, Belgium, Cyprus, Denmark, Finland, France, Germany (W) Greece, Hungary, Iceland, Ireland, Italy, Liechtenstein, Luxembourg, Malta, Netherlands, Norway, Poland, Portugal, Spain, Sweden, Switzerland, Turkey, United Kingdom, USSR, Yugoslavia. The Commission of the European Communities had the status of an official delegate to the Assises, the Council of Europe the status of an observer.

3 The Audio-visual Eureka and Eureka work in similar ways. Sharp (in Crouch and Marquand, 1990, p. 115) describes Eureka as 'an umbrella mechanism for encouraging firm-to-firm collaboration'. A senior European Commission official concerned with the audio-visual sector (interviewed 8.11.1991) referred to the Audio-visual Eureka as a 'marriage bureau'. However a BBC official (interviewed 9.12.1991) was less generous and described the Audio-visual Eureka as a 'mirage'.

programme. Both Eurekas were conceived as responses to perceived threats from the USA and Japan.

The legitimization of Community audio-visual policy

Before 1988 only the Commission and Parliament had made commitments to development of the audio-visual sector. However, once the Council had recognized its importance a major obstacle to the implementation of Community audio-visual policies had been removed. Following the Council's formal commitment to a Community audio-visual policy the Commission transmitted a Communication to the Council and the Parliament on audio-visual policy (Commission of the European Communities, 1990). The Communication proposed a co-ordinated development of the Community's 'audio-visual *triptych*'. The three elements of the triptych were the rules of the game, the programme industries, and new technologies (Commission of the European Communities, 1990, p. 3). The Commission stated that its proposals had been informed by discussions at the Assises de l' audiovisuel: the Community's audio-visual policy in the 1990s began, therefore, from the foundations laid by the Government of France.

In its Communication to the Council and Parliament the Commission compared the structure of the European audio-visual market unfavourably to that of the United States. In Europe, it argued, there was scant incentive for broadcasters to produce programmes for secondary markets nor to market them vigorously. Moreover a plurality of producers were faced with a few powerful, monopsonistic, distributors. Yet, in spite of the supposed dominance of monopsonistic distributors, Europe had too few distributors 'capable of bringing out a film or videocassette in all European countries at the same time with adequate promotion budgets'. Accordingly the Commission proposed that 'promoting the emergence of ... distributors must become one of the priorities of Europe's audio-visual sector' (Commission of the European Communities, 1990, p. 18).

Market failure

The Commission viewed the European audio-visual market as a failed market which required intervention in order to redress its deficiencies. Like the world market, the European market was 'dominated by American and Japanese firms' and vitiated by 'structural constraints'. Accordingly (in respect of 'rules of the game') the Commission proposed to build on the basis of *Television without frontiers* and further reduce constraints. The measures it proposed included harmonization of national copyright laws, ensuring pluralism in the European audio-visual sector and developing a secondary market for films and television programmes (Commission of the European Communities, 1990, pp. 3–4). In respect of the programme industries, it advocated continued development of the MEDIA programme and a preferential allocation of support to SMEs (Small and Medium Sized Enterprises). This support, the Commission believed, would contribute 'to the restructuring of the audio-visual industry and....promote a balance between the large and small national industries' (Commission of the European Communities, 1990, p. 4). The Commission also foreshadowed a new Directive on satellite television transmission standards and a programme for the development of HDTV.

Latterly, the Community has sought to ensure that the audio-visual sector is not developed at the expense of pluralism but, on the contrary, that it helps to strengthen it by encouraging 'the diversity of the programmes offered to the public' (Commission of the European Communities, 1990, p. 21). Clearly, the Commission reasoned, even modest steps towards re-circulation of 'the 90 per cent of European products – all types together [which] never go beyond their country of origin' (Commission of the European Communities, 1990c, p. 2) would assist pluralism in programme supply, as well as redress the 'conspicuous mismatch between supply and demand' (Commission of the European Communities, 1990c, p. 1) in the audio-visual programmes industry.

However this seemingly attractive policy begs the question of why established distributors have not already recycled and recirculated such programmes. One peculiar economic characteristic of information, including film and television programmes, is its inexhaustibility in consumption. Further, there are characteristically low marginal costs involved in enabling an additional consumer (viewer) to consume audio-visual products. Thus there are powerful incentives to rights holders and broadcasters to extend markets and serve as many consumers as possible, because so doing will yield returns which are disproportionately higher than costs. In the absence of formal regulatory barriers to the integration of audio-visual markets in the European Community one would expect the market to optimize integration and that the limits to market integration will be set by consumers.

There are at least two possible answers to the lack of a secondary market for recycled programmes in Europe; the first, and the one which *dirigistes* in the Commission support, is that the European audio-visual market is structurally deficient. It lacks a 'secondary' market in which value can be realized from (an unfortunate turn of phrase) 'old and forgotten films from the archives' (Commission of the European Communities, 1990d, p. 1)[1]. The second, non-exclusive, explanation, is that distributors (whether rightly or wrongly) believe that such works are unattractive to viewers. The Commission has therefore attempted to remove the barriers in the way of development of a secondary market by promoting change in copyright[2] regulations (so that audio-visual works may be exploited across the whole of the single market) and by encouraging establishment of new channels (such as satellite, cable and video-cassettes) for the distribution of audio-visual works. However, these initiatives are likely to achieve success only if the

---

1 In 1990 the MEDIA 95 programme established its Lumière project. Lumière is directed to 'the conservation, restoration and valorization of Europe's cinematographic patrimony' (MEDIA Newsletter 10/1991, p. 1).

2 The Green Paper on Copyright, COM (88) 172 final, refers.

underdeveloped secondary market is due to structural problems rather than a mismatch between audience preferences and the characteristics of the European film and television programmes supplied.

Drawing on the declaration of the Assises de l' audiovisuel (and the Conclusions of the European Council's meeting in Strasbourg in December 1989) the Commission drafted its most substantial interventionist audio-visual policy initiative since *Realities and tendencies*: the Communication to the Council and Parliament on audio-visual policy (Commission of the European Communities, 1990). In the Communication the Commission reiterated the *dirigiste* axiom that the Community's audio-visual markets had failed and that intervention was required in order to redress market failure:

> ... the European audio-visual industry is seeking an appropriate development space likely to enable it to take the place it is entitled to claim. Subjected to the pressure of a world market dominated by American and Japanese firms, the structural constraints of the European market are obstacles to be overcome (Commission of the European Communities, 1990, p. 3).

The Commission's Communication to the Council and Parliament on audio-visual policy rejected the single market established by *Television without frontiers* in its euphemistic statement that the single market requires to be supplemented (Commission of the European Communities, 1990, p. 4). The Commission argued that supplementary initiatives should be directed towards harmonization of copyright laws in member states (this proved to be a major battlefield) and to ensuring that 'development of the audio-visual sector is not at the expense of pluralism but, on the contrary, helps to intensify it by promoting, in particular, the diversity of the programmes shown to the general public'. Finally, it argued for supplementary measures to foster independent production (Commission of the European Communities, 1990, pp. 4–5)[1].

The *dirigiste* view

In 1990 the Commission of the European Communities published *Audio-visual production in the single market* (authored by Matteo Maggiore). Although published with a Commission disclaimer[2] Maggiore's book has several claims on readers' attention. It contains useful data and forcefully states the *dirigiste* case for intervention in the Community's audio-visual markets. Although *Audio-visual production in*

---

1 Although independent production is a lynch pin of Community audio-visual policy there is no consistent, Community wide, definition of an independent producer or an independent production. In some jurisdictions the definition of independent is a question of company ownership, in others of contractual relationship. Thus in France a company which is a subsidiary of a broadcaster is not considered an independent producer when it produces for the parent company but is considered an independent producer when it produces for other clients. In the UK a company with such an ownership would not be considered an independent producer.

2 'This publication, designed to contribute to public debate on European integration, was prepared outside the Commission of the European Communities. The views expressed are those of the author alone, and do not necessarily reflect the opinion of the Commission.'

the single market is not an official statement of Commission policy there is much to suggest that the views it puts forward are representative of powerful currents in Commission opinion.

Matteo Maggiore is the son of Mariano Maggiore (formerly Deputy Head of the Audio-visual Directorate of DG X and then responsible for the co-ordination of audio-visual policy) and a member of the 'Cabinet' of Roberto Barzanti (to whom the author, acknowledges a debt of gratitude in his book) formerly the Chairman of the European Parliament's Committee on Youth, Culture, Education, the Media and Sport. Whilst it would be quite wrong to attribute the views advanced in Matteo Maggiore's book to either his father or to Roberto Barzanti the author's personal associations with leading policy makers in the two chief loci of *dirigiste* influence and sentiment within the European Community suggest, to put it no more strongly, that the analysis advanced in *Audio-visual production in the single market* have a representative quality.

Maggiore stresses the importance of new communication technologies in restructuring European audio-visual markets[1]. He states:

> The first effect of the audio-visual revolution is the transborder circulation of programmes and films through broadcasting via cable and satellite. The unification of Europe is an accomplished fact as far as air-time and broadcasting areas are concerned (Maggiore, 1990, p. 12).

Given a belief in the power of new communication technologies to establish European unity through television, a unity which has hitherto proved to be beyond politicians' power to establish at the level of institutions, it follows that:

> Any national policy in the field of audio-visual production is insufficient. The main effort should be displayed on a continental scale, within European Community institutions and the Council of Europe (Maggiore, 1990, p. 11).

Maggiore reiterates his belief that national solutions are insufficient to deal with what he regards as an international problem:

> The inanity of such a regulatory framework [country by country allocation of the orbit/spectrum resource by the WARC. RC] should be perfectly clear. A healthy legal environment for the production and circulation of TV programmes must be developed on a continental scale. In its absence, the perspective is that of the reproduction of the Italian case in European television, i.e. the law of the jungle followed by belated regulatory efforts succeeding only in endorsing the existing situation (Maggiore, 1990, p. 32).

If a successful approach to its broadcasting and audio-visual problems cannot be national, and hence demands co-ordinated action by the Community so too must it embrace more than strictly economic considerations because:

---

1   He goes so far as to state that 'National DBS programmes ... are definitely pointless! The only reasonable perspective would seem to be that of a pan-European second generation of direct broadcasting satellites' (Maggiore, 1990, pp. 25–26).

Culture, economics and industrial production all represent aspects fundamental to audio-visual production. They cannot be separated and none of them may be forgotten or left behind. No cultural activity was ever in the past as conditioned by industrial and economic factors, and no industrial activity has ever depended so much upon its cultural content and mission. As a single sector, audio-visual production is new in the sense that the activities involved in it are undergoing such changes as to alter their nature and mould them into something new (Maggiore, 1990, p. 11).

Yet, Maggiore argues, the Commission of the European Communities has been unable to establish effective audio-visual policies because its competence has, thus far, been exclusively economic (in accordance with the provisions of the Treaty of Rome):

... there is no institution that can explicitly deal with the cultural aspect of this development. The European Community is still dominated by an economistic approach: the only European institutions have, on the basis of the Rome Treaties, purely economic competencies. The Community is still under the spell of major setbacks in its attempts, in the 1950s, to become a real community, i.e. political (Maggiore, 1990, p. 37).

Nonetheless 'In spite of the EC's weak role in cultural affairs, its institutions seem to be the most convenient framework for the development of an audio-visual policy' (Maggiore, 1990, p. 132). Ironically the chief Community broadcasting and audio-visual policy achievement, the establishment of the single market in television, a *Television without frontiers*, is perceived by many to be the Community's chief audio-visual policy problem. For Maggiore (and here his analysis is widely echoed) Japan and the USA are likely to be the chief beneficiaries of the newly integrated Community market: the Americans will dominate the software market and Japan the hardware market.

In respect of software, Maggiore suggests that:

To American distributors, Europe already is a single market for products whose costs are wholly recouped on the world and domestic market before they arrive on the old continent. The European programme production could virtually disappear and leave the continent with no ink with which to write (Maggiore, 1990, p. 41).

Free competition on the unified market four years from now will mean competition between the United States and the individual European countries. This is something the Americans do not fail to grasp when they point out that a European culture as such does not exist and that the cultures in Europe are the French, the Italian, the Spanish, etc, coming to the conclusion that, the motive for any quota is the protection of an industry and not the defence of culture (Maggiore, 1990, p. 38).

Maggiore eloquently states the analysis which underpins the Community's two chief audio-visual interventionist initiatives; establishment of an electronics sector industrial policy designed to establish a European HDTV standard and industry and a programme of subsidy and protection for the European film and television programme production industry. In respect of software, the crisis Maggiore foresees is highly specific: it is a crisis of fiction programming. For of all kinds of programmes fiction is by far the most expensive. Yet it is, at the same time, the most attractive to audiences and the one for which the demand is highest (Maggiore, 1990, p. 43).

And, Maggiore claims:

> ... as television becomes the main distribution outlet for fiction, the invasion of American television productions (serials, films, sitcoms, etc.) threatens the very survival of European film production. While investment in broadcasting enjoys a more mobile and transborder status because of its economic quality, fiction production is rooted in national cultures. From this point of view, not only does a European single market not yet exist, but the very idea faces opposition in most EC countries. Therefore, in the European Community there exists a nearly unified television channel market and 12 single, separate and relatively small production-offering markets (Maggiore, 1990, pp. 46–47).

For an appropriate European response to the threats posed by Japan and the United States to be formulated political intervention in audio-visual hardware and software markets is required. However the intervention necessary cannot, Maggiore believes, be limited to European programme content quotas which he describes as 'particularly clumsy'. (Maggiore, 1990, p. 38)[1]. Moreover Member States have found it difficult to agree on national (or European) television (and cinema) content quotas[2]. Thus, rather than quotas and regulatory and legislative inhibitions, Maggiore advocates pro-active policies of subsidy and incentives for both software and hardware sectors.

> The financing of European productions must go beyond the occasional accumulation of resources that remain separate and national in nature. It has to be continental in scale. It must have constant, unchanging European dimensions and a European working range. It must also become substantial: fiction production needs as much resource investment as the broadcasting and electronic component segments of the audio-visual industry (Maggiore, 1990, p. 62).

Without increased production finance for European film and television fiction

---

1   Elsewhere Maggiore lauds quotas as 'an asset to guarantee real freedom of choice on the part of the "consumer" ' (Maggiore, 1990, p. 39).

2   Maggiore notes that the EBU has opposed Community software quotas (Maggiore, 1990, p. 109) and interventionist Community hardware policies too. He states that 'The EBU initially supported quite strongly the Japanese [HDTV] system' (Maggiore, 1990, p. 125). Here too Maggiore's viewpoint is representative. Whereas in the early 1980s the Commission perceived EBU to be a 'good European' (see *inter alia* Commission of the European Communities, 1983) latterly the EBU has been regarded as a problem by both *dirigiste* and liberal forces within the Commission. The *dirigistes*, like Maggiore, regard the EBU as too liberal and the liberals (see extensive discussion of the EBU's adversarial relations with the Competition Directorate) see the EBU as an anti-competitive club of monopolists.

growth in television distribution capacity (and consequential change in reception relations) delivered by satellite television, carries 'the risk of indiscriminate and 'wild' broadcasting, and therefore the danger of ... loss of quality in services; loss of cultural identity for entire continents' (Maggiore, 1990, p. 113). Maggiore's apocalyptic conclusion is that 'The European audio-visual single market cannot wait until 1993. Progress unfolds itself with the blind inertia and the speed of an avalanche. Unless choices are formulated and followed up quickly, there will be no choice left' (Maggiore, 1990, p. 131).

Maggiore's argument can be summarized as:

> The Community should develop political and cultural dimensions as implied in the Treaty of Rome's conception of 'ever closer union';
> The creation of a single Community television market has seriously damaged the Community's ability to shape its own economic and cultural destiny;
> Audio-visual (and broadcasting) policy embraces cultural as well as economic considerations;
> Thus far, the development of a satisfactory Community broadcasting and audio-visual policy has been severely compromised by the Commission's lack of powers in the domain of culture;
> National policies are simply incompetent to deal with the problems facing the Community and that insistence on national prerogatives seriously inhibits the Community's response to the challenges it faces;
> New communication technologies are determining factors in the future economic, political and cultural development of the Community.

These are the fundamental propositions in which interventionist Community policies are grounded and which underpinned the Council of Ministers' decision in December 1990 (Council of the European Communities, 1990) to formally endorse the MEDIA programme, and to promulgate successive Directives on satellite television transmission standards (Council of the European Communities, 1986 and 1992). We now return to the development of the audio-visual and broadcasting policies and practices of the Community's liberals. Policies and practices which, like those of the interventionists, have developed without much participation by UK government, broadcasting or audio-visual interests but the outcomes of which have chimed more harmoniously with UK government tunes than have those played by the interventionists.

10

Television and the marketplace

It makes no kind of political, cultural or economic sense that within the European Community, Community citizens should be unable, even when the technical and economic possibilities exist, to enjoy the television programmes of their neighbours. Television is an economically and socially important service provided by Europeans to Europeans – if the European Community has one central task above any other it is to provide that integration between the states of Europe, that freedom of circulation so conspicuously lacking in the field of television broadcasting (Cockfield, 1986, p. 9).

Competition, liberalism and the single market

The effect of European Community competition law and policy on television has grown in the last decade and has become a major influence on the nature and content of European television services. Indeed, the impact of competition law and regulation on the whole audio-visual sector been remarkable and exemplifies the extent to which Community broadcasting has been shaped by Community officials rather than by either elected members of the European Parliament or by the Council of Ministers. It is an odd feature of Community history that policies to do with competition and market structure have been more important than have overt and explicit broadcasting and audio-visual policies in shaping th audio-visual and broadcasting sectors in the European Community.

The *Television without frontiers* Green Paper published in 1984 (Commission of the European Communities, 1984a) argued that the Treaty of Rome carried out for remuneration, and that this included broadcasting and other cultural activities. The Green Paper (initiated by officials in DG III, the Directorate responsible for the internal market) laid the groundwork for a single European Community broadcasting market, and was rooted in general provisions of Community law rather than in measures specifically drafted for the broadcasting sector. Fundamental changes to European broadcasting thus derived from an initiative of unelected officials unprompted by elected bodies in either the Community or its Member States.

Second only to *Television without frontiers* in its impact on Community broadcasting has been the application of Community competition regulation to the European television market. DG IV (the Competition Directorate) of the Commission of the European Communities has had a major impact on broadcasting in Europe. Its initiatives have derived from general principles of Community law, interpreted and implemented by officials, rather than from regulations specifically enacted for broadcasting by elected representatives of Community citizens.

Competition policy and broadcasting

Between 1984 and 1988 (the period in which the *Television without frontiers* Green Paper and the first Draft Directive on television services was published) DG III was led by a UK Commissioner, Lord Cockfield. At the time when many of the significant decisions on broadcasting and competition were handed down, DG IV was led by another British Commissioner, Sir Leon Brittan. Both Directorates responsible for establishing a single broadcasting market and for ensuring competition were, therefore, at crucial junctures, headed by British Commissioners. This has reinforced a well-established perception that the UK is irrevocably 'ultra liberal' on questions of broadcasting and audio-visual policy.

The impact of DG IV's policies has been particularly controversial. However, the appointment in 1992 of Karel van Miert as the Commissioner responsible for competition policy to succeed Sir Leon Britten, suggests that the rigorous application of the provisions of the Treaty of Rome, associated with Brittan's tenure of office, may be tempered. van Miert has signalled that Competition policy would be exercised 'without ideological preconceptions' over the two years of his stewardship and 'from a philosophical point of view there might be a different attitude on ... how to cope with the rules' (quoted in *Financial Times* 15.1.1993, p. 12) to that which obtained during Britten's term of office.

Time will tell whether or not a new competition Commissioner is a harbinger of changed competition policy but there can be no doubt that DG IV has had a dramatic impact on the Community's audio-visual sector. Indeed it can plausibly be argued that DG IV has been the most important of all the Community's Directorates in respect of the audio-visual sector. Its successful prosecution of cases under Articles 85 and 86 of the Treaty of Rome has not only directly affected broadcasters' conduct but has led them both to organize their activities so as to forestall action by DG IV and to restructure their activities after pre-judicial approaches from DG IV. Moreover the application of Community competition regulations by DG IV has strengthened and encouraged the competition authorities of Community Member States to take action against anti-competitive behaviour by broadcasters. The action by the United Kingdom's Office of Fair Trading against the ITV network in late 1992 is a case in point.

The impact of Community competition law on broadcasters has been particularly strong because, for reasons of national policy and/or the technological regime which prevailed in broadcasting, most European broadcasters were used to working in environments which had minimized competition. Most European broadcasting systems were state monopolies, authorized broadcasters competed neither for programmes nor for funding, and 'pirate' broadcasters were ruthlessly closed down by the authorities. According to the Peacock Report (1986) even in the United Kingdom, one of the few broadcasting environments in which a commercial broadcasting sector (and therefore a degree of competition) existed a 'comfortable' duopoly prevailed. As Hodgson observes (1992, p. vii) at the beginning of the 1980s there were four commercial television broadcasters in Europe, by the beginning of the 1990s there were fifty eight. This growth in 'external' competition was paralleled by a growth in 'internal' competition as vertically integrated broadcasting systems were disaggregated and internal procurement of all manner of goods and services from programming to training were 'externalized'.

Three factors have radically changed the competitive regime under which European broadcasting functions. First, national regimes have been 'deregulated' and have permitted (often indeed encouraged) new entrants to broadcasting markets. Second, the successful establishment of satellite television has permitted transnational, pan-European services to be launched. Third, and probably most important, *Television without frontiers* established a single Community television market wherein television services originating from any Community Member State must be distributed, and re-distributed, in other Member States on the same basis as services originating in that state.

If competition in European Community broadcasting is new so, in some Community jurisdictions, is competition policy itself. The Assises de l'audiovisuel noted that although 'in West Germany, the UK and France competition law is highly developed ... in other countries such as Italy it is practically non-existent' (Assises, 1989, p. 243). Whilst Community competition law does not supersede national law, in the event of conflict between Community and national law Community law prevails. Thus the growth of competition in broadcasting over the last decade has had a striking effect. Broadcasters, regulators and viewers everywhere have had to grapple with new services made possible by Community regulation and a new regulatory order based on the jurisdiction of the Community rather than the Member State. Indeed some Community Member States have had to contend with competition regulation itself for the first time and thus have not only experienced a change in the regulatory order but an unprecedented codification of the terms on which broadcasters (and other enterprises) can operate.

DG III and DG IV

Between 1982 and 1992 responsibility for the structure of Community markets and the conduct of competition policy has been divided between two Directorates of the Commission of the European Communities. DG IV has been responsible for competition and DG III for the internal market. The Directorates have broadly divided their responsibilities so that DG III makes rules and DG IV enforces them (interview DG III official 11.11.1991). However the distinction between market structure and market operation is not clear and categorical. There are areas where DG IV lacks jurisdictional standing and where DG III has enforcement functions and others where DG IV's enforcement of regulations has set standards and thus made rules. DG IV's annual report for 1989 testifies to the extent to which the Competition Directorate has been concerned with the audio-visual sector (and the extent to which its activities and DG III's overlap): 'the Commission has increasingly focused on the audio-visual media in recent years, from the standpoint of competition policy. Its main concern has been to keep markets open and to prevent or reduce barriers to market entry' (Commission of the European Communities, 1990a, p. 51).

The most important interventions made by DG IV, in the audio-visual media concern broadcasters' acquisition of rights to sporting events and cinema films. There have been two particularly important cases[1] where DG IV set the terms on which broadcasters acquired rights to programmes. In both instances DG IV has made new rules rather than enforced already established rules and has successfully exercised jurisdiction over activities which had not formerly been regulated under competition law.

The first of DG IV's important interventions in broadcasting came in overturning the ARD's deal with MGM/United Artists (MGM/UA) whereby the ARD (German television stations as they were named in the judgement) secured exclusive transmission rights in Germany to 1,350 feature films in MGM/UA's archive. The ARD acquired 14 James Bond films, all cartoons in the MGM/UA archive and 416 hours of TV programming from MGM/UA. The ARD also concluded an output deal whereby it gained exclusive rights to all new MGM/UA films between 1984 and 1998 and to all James Bond films made or acquired by MGM/UA (see Decision 15.9.89 in OJ L 284, pp. 36–44 3.10.1989). The ARD paid US$80m for these rights. The Commission objected to the ARD's acquisition of exclusive rights under this agreement because it judged that 'The agreements in question have as their object and effect the restriction of competition' and that the extent and duration of the rights acquired by the ARD did indeed restrict competition. The Commission was able to exercise jurisdiction in this case because the ARD had acquired rights for German speaking regions of Community Member States rather than for Germany alone. In acquiring rights for the German language areas of Italy and Luxembourg (and for the non-Member States Liechtenstein, Switzerland, German Democratic

---

1 Other relevant cases include the intervention of both the UK Office of Fair Trading and the Commission of the European Communities to prohibit London Weekend Television acquiring exclusive rights to the screening of English Football League soccer games and the Commission of the European Communities' intervention in respect of an agreement between the German Sports Federation and the ARD.

Republic and Austria) as well as for the Federal Republic the ARD's agreement was deemed to have affected trade between Member States and thus to have fallen within DG IV's jurisdiction. However, in response to DG IV's action, the ARD restructured the agreement with MGM/UA in such a way that its acquisition of rights satisfied the 'benefit test'[1] applied by the Commission of the European Communities. Commission Decision 89/536/EEC granted the ARD an exemption under Article 85(3) of the EEC Treaty subject to the ARD sublicensing film rights to other broadcasters. The Commission commented 'agreements relating to exclusive television rights can only be exempted if suitable access facilities are made available to third parties'. (Bull. EC 9-1989, p. 25-26).

The second important intervention by DG IV came in the Screensport/EBU Members case (also known as the Eurosport case). The UK company W H Smith Television[2], the principal investor in the satellite television channel Screensport[3], complained under European Community competition law that Eurosport[4] infringed Community competition requirements in that it had preferential access to sports rights (in consequence of its links to the EBU) and that Screensport, its competitor, was thereby disadvantaged.

The Commission upheld Screensport's complaint and found that the 'complex series of agreements' between the EBU Members who formed the Eurosport Consortium and Sky Channel had the 'object and/or effect of restricting or distorting competition' (OJ L 63/40). The Eurosport Consortium argued in its own defence that, the arrangements under which the Eurosport channel was established, were not anti-competitive, as Screensport had alleged and the Commission had found.

However, the Commission found that the agreement between the EBU and Sky Channel had been concluded in order to negate 'the threat that Sky might become a direct competitor as a transnational commercial satellite channel dedicated to sport' (OJ L 63/40) and that the 'terms of the joint venture clearly confer a privileged position' (OJ L 63/41) on the Eurosport partners in that they enjoyed preferential access to the sports programmes acquired by the EBU and distributed through Eurovision and had free access to the Eurovision signal (OJ L 63/42).

---

1 In circumstances where competition is impaired, or is likely to be impaired, exemption from the provisions of Community competition regulation which would otherwise apply can be granted if a 'benefit test' is satisfied. To satisfy the benefit test an agreement must contribute to improving production or distribution or technical and economic progress, it must allow consumers a fair share of benefits, it must not impose restrictions which are not essential to the achievement of benefits and it must not eliminate competition in respect of a substantial part of the product in question.

2 W.H. Smith's holding in Screensport was later acquired by ETN (European Television Networks).

3 Screensport has been variously known as Screen Sport and ScreenSport.

4 A satellite television channel which had established under an agreement between the Eurosport Consortium – a group of EBU member broadcasters including the BBC – and News International's company Sky Television. The Eurosport Consortium Agreement (that is between EBU member broadcasters) was signed on 5.5.88. The 'shareholders' agreement' between Sky Television and the Eurosport Consortium dated from 23.12.88. The Eurosport Channel was first transmitted from the Astra satellite on 5.2.89 for 17 hours daily in English, Dutch and German languages.

Moreover the complementarity between Eurosport and the EBU made the EBU (as the establishment of Eurosport was designed to make it) a more attractive customer for sports rights than it would otherwise have been (OJ L 63/42).

In its defence Eurosport claimed that Sky Television was simply a sub-contractor to the Consortium rather than a partner. Indeed the Consortium maintained that 'Eurosport enjoys the rights of an EBU member' and that the service has a 'public service character' (OJ L 63/38). The Commission rejected these propositions and argued that 'By contrast the viewing public has tended to associate Eurosport more closely with Sky' (OJ L 63/38) than with public service broadcasting. However it also found, in an extremely subtle argument, that a *perception* of the public service status of Eurosport prejudiced cable operators in favour of Eurosport and that this prejudice endowed Eurosport with illegitimate and anti-competitive advantages. Thus the Commission found in favour of Screensport's challenge to Eurosport. It judged that 'The joint venture agreements and all related contractual provisions ... constitute an infringement of Article 85(1) of the EEC treaty' (Decision 19.2.91 recorded in OJ L 63. 9.3.91, p. 32-44). In its XXIst Competition Report (Commission of the European Communities, 1992a, pp. 65–66) the Commission recognized that establishment of Eurosport as a pan-European service had served the public interest but judged that this benefit was outweighed by the damage its specific form of organization had inflicted on a well functioning broadcasting market in the Community.

The ARD/MGM and Screensport cases are the most evident instances of a consistent strategy by officials of DG IV to unscramble long established organizational arrangements in European public service broadcasting and to ensure that incumbent broadcasters (notably public service broadcasters) were not able to disadvantage new entrants to broadcasting markets (notably commercial broadcasters) by reason of their preferential access to attractive programming. Indeed the EBU recognized that the Commission's proposals in the *Television without frontiers* Green Paper foreshadowed a regulatory regime hostile to the EBU's established practices. It anticipated that 'non-voluntary licensing and dismantling of the European Agreement on the protection of Television Broadcasts, as proposed in the Green Paper, might well weaken the position of the public broadcasters and involves a serious threat of undermining European culture' (Great Britain. Parliament. House of Lords. Evidence, 1985, p. 38). The EBU maintained its opposition to the Community's initiative. The EBU's opposition was cited by UK witnesses giving evidence to the House of Lords Enquiry into European Broadcasting (Great Britain. Parliament. House of Lords, 1987) i.e. on the Community's Draft Directive on Broadcasting, in support of their own, almost unanimous opposition to the principle and the specific character of the Commission's proposed intervention in European broadcasting.

Officials in DG IV stated (interview with DG IV officials 11.11.1991) that their concern is to ensure that 'the foreclosure effects of exclusive contracts are limited' and that this is a particularly important issue for Community broadcasting policy because 'new operators find it difficult to get access to attractive programmes', and the success of new entrants depends on access to attractive programming. DG IV states that it remains concerned that other, longer standing, arrangements of the EBU such as Eurovision[1] and joint acquisition of rights by the EBU on behalf of member broadcasters may contravene Community competition policy. DG IV 'fears (that there are) some foreclosure effects which are detrimental to individual channels which are not admitted as members' to the EBU.

The element common to the ARD and Screensport cases, and the Commission's growing adversarial entanglement with the EBU, is the Commission's presumption that public broadcasters have operated arrangements disadvantageous to new commercial entrants to the broadcasting market. Indeed, as the Screensport case demonstrated (OJ L 63/42) the Commission believed that the very identity of public service broadcasters as public service broadcasters endowed them with unfair and anti-competitive advantages. The long established EBU collaborative programme acquisition and sharing arrangements which have permitted broadcasters to share costs (and from which small broadcasters have gained more than have large broadcasters) are, in the eyes of DG IV, abuses of dominant market positions by a public broadcasting cartel. DG IV has also regarded public service broadcasters' attempts (with Eurosport) to strengthen their bargaining power in competition for sports rights (programming which was then to be distributed to viewers of both terrestrial and satellite services free of charge at the point of consumption) as illegitimate. Porter and Hasselbach point out (1991, p. 159) that the criteria which the Commission has applied to public broadcasters, and which have led to successful competition policy actions against them, have not always been applied to privately owned concerns[2]. However, the Commission eventually authorized continuance of the EBU's Eurovision programme sharing arrangements (Commission Decision 93/403/EEC of June 11, 1993).

Public service broadcasting and competition

It is certainly true that public service broadcasters have used the EBU to strengthen their competitive position vis a vis commercial broadcasters and that they have excluded commercial broadcasters from the EBU club. Not only have EBU members benefited from long established co-operative arrangements, notably in respect of collective acquisition of sports rights, news gathering and Eurovision, but they have sought to extend their, putatively anti-competitive, collaboration into new areas. The EBU's policy group on the future of public service broadcasting, the Wangermee Group, proposed, for example, that 'the appearance of Pay-TV, raise(s) in entirely new terms, the question of *collective acquisition of rights* not only

---

1   See OJ C 251/2 of 5.10.1990 for DG IV's intervention to require the EBU to sublicence sports rights.
2   They cite the practices of the film distributor Kirch but elsewhere (Porter and Hasselbach, 1991, p. 140) instance the collective acquisition of European (excluding the UK) rights to the All England Tennis Championship by another Germany company, UFA, in 1989 which, prima facie, raises similar issues to those which have exercised the Commission in respect of the actions of public broadcasters.

for sports events but also for other events broadcast in Eurovision. It must also be asked to what extent EBU Members could unite their efforts in order to acquire *rights for the broadcasting of films* ... If a minimum of caution is not agreed on between EBU Members, there may well be exaggerated competition and an *explosion of the purchase cost of rights*' (AG 551 SPG 2642 June 1984, p. 15). Undoubtedly, there was substance to the Competition Directorate's concerns.

However it is less clear that it was only public service broadcasters which threatened the Competition Directorate's successful efforts 'to keep markets open and to prevent or reduce barriers to entry' (Commission of the European Communities, 1990a, p. 51). It is also open to question whether or not the putative harm experienced by consumers in consequence of public service broadcasters acquisition of rights to attractive programming was outweighed by the benefits which accrued to them as a consequence of the actions of public service broadcasters. The EBU's collective acquisition of rights made it possible for small and poor broadcasters to bring programming to their viewers which otherwise they would have been denied. It can also be argued that the very existence of small public service broadcasters (and thus maintenance of competition between public and commercial broadcasting) was materially assisted by the EBU's long standing programme sharing arrangements. However, whether or not commercial broadcasters were guilty of establishing barriers to market entry, it was public service broadcasters which DG IV put in the dock. Once there, DG IV decided that the benefits which public service broadcasters delivered to viewers and listeners were insufficient to outweigh the harm inflicted on them by the barriers to entry constituted by public service broadcasters' acquisition of programme rights.

Independent of its effect on the relative strengths of European commercial and public service broadcasters the Competition Directorate's interventions have advantaged rights holders in their bargaining with broadcasters. DG IV judged that the ARD's block booking deal with MGM would enable the ARD to acquire film rights more cheaply than would have been the case had the ARD competed with private broadcasters for rights on a film by film basis. It judged that private broadcasters were thereby improperly disadvantaged as they were in respect of Eurosport and the EBU's collective acquisition of rights on behalf of its members. The competition for rights between EBU members and private broadcasters on a market by market basis has had an unfortunate consequence: it has led to an escalation in the price of rights, and a consequential increase in the exclusion of viewers from the consumption of spectacles. Clarke and Riddell give a telling example:

> The EBU paid US$5.95 million for the 1980 Summer Olympics in Moscow and NBC paid US$85 million for the American rights. These figures rose to US$19 million (EBU) and US$225 million (ABC in the US) for Los Angeles in 1984. For Seoul in 1988 the Olympic rights were US$28 million (EBU) and US$300 million (ABC). By 1992 the EBU was forced to bid US$75 million and

NBC US$401 million for the rights to the Barcelona Games (Clarke and Riddell, 1992, p. 203).

The cost of rights rose significantly in the 1980s but the cost of European rights is still considerably less than the cost of North American rights. This suggests that competition between European broadcasters has driven up the costs of rights. However, the residually monopsonistic character of the EBU's acquisition of rights has slowed the transfer of resources from broadcasters (and ultimately viewers and listeners) to rights holders. Price has restricted viewers' access to programmes, particularly sports programmes, to which they had formerly had access under the Eurovision system of collective acquisition of rights. As the EBU rightly stated 'competition ... leads to a growth in production costs, if only because of competition for acquisition of the rights' (AG 551 SPG 2642 June 1984, p. 8). Increased and less imperfect competition has had the effect of excluding viewers from access to goods and services which they were formerly able to enjoy and has transferred resources from viewers to rights holders.

The Community's Competition Directorate has crystallized the conflict between the rival principles of organization on which European broadcasting is to be based: is it public service or the market? Garnham (1990, pp. 104–105) identified 'reinforcement of the market and progressive destruction of public service as the preferred mode for the allocation of cultural resources ... by the formation of a two-tier market divided between the information rich ... and the information poor'. Garnham asserts that this is a fundamental structuring principle of contemporary information and cultural markets. Certainly, DG IV's actions exemplify this process. However DG IV was, and is, insufficiently well staffed to actively and continuously intervene in Community broadcasting and audio-visual markets. The officials responsible for media competition policy are also responsible for consumer electronics policy and have been unable to take up cases which have not already been the subject of complaints to the Commission. Moreover DG IV's jurisdiction extends only to 'enterprises'[1]. Competition issues which concern governments, such as national programme content quotas, are outside the competence of the Competition Directorate.

Nevertheless, the Commission has acted against state aids which favour the nationals of one Community Member State and exclude others. In 1989, for example, the Commission prohibited the Government of Greece's support for Greek language film production being made conditional on the producers being Greek nationals (OJ L208/38 20.7.1989). The Commission did accept that, in countries where a small number of films are produced, state aids may be necessary to maintain and develop the film industry and are therefore permissible under Article 92 (3)(c) of the EEC Treaty (Assises, 1989, p. 247). Clearly the question of what is a

---

1 Articles 85 and 86 of the EEC Treaty refer to 'undertakings'. It is on these articles and the Community's merger regulations that Community competition policy for the broadcasting and audio-visual sectors chiefly rests.

'small number' is of the essence here but, as yet, the Commission has not published guidelines on what constitutes a 'small number'.

It is clear that important areas of broadcasting and audio-visual policy – such as agreements between cinema and television sectors on the release of films to television, royalty rates, licence conditions and fees, co-production agreements, co-ordinated scheduling of programmes, and advertising policy, cross media ownership – all fall within DG IV's jurisdiction. The absence of activity by DG IV on such matters reflects the staff establishment levels of the Directorate rather than an insufficiency of competence or a disinclination to root out those broadcasters' practices which Competition officials deemed to be anti-competitive even when these practices are long established and, *prima facie*, offer benefits to viewers and listeners.

Conclusion

I've despaired of finding a culture – other than that of Barbara Cartland, Batman, Indiana Jones and the Coca-Cola can – which should bring Europe and Asia closer together, so I accept, with no sense of despair at all, a Europe united only in its substructure ... If we wish to speak of a single European culture, we shall find it only in a tolerant liberalism which accepts those impulses which seem to be disruptive. National culture has nothing to do with political nationalism ... We are making an error of logic if we think that political and economic unity automatically signifies cultural unity. Culture is somewhere else (Burgess, 1990, p. 21).

Although the European Community is grammatically singular it will be apparent from the preceding discussion that broadcasting and audio-visual policy in the Community is complex and contradictory and that only by disaggregating the, nominally singular entity, European Community into a plurality of distinct institutions pursuing different goals can sense be made of the convolutions of Community policy. However some enduring continuities can be identified among the baroque intricacies traced by the passage of a plurality of institutional rivalries, the forces of technological change and the marks left by conflicts between advocates of rival visions of the Community and antagonistic conceptions of the role of the cultural industries within it.

The first of the continuities which can be teased out from the history of the Community's broadcasting and audio-visual policy is that the UK is as awkward a partner in the broadcasting and audio-visual domain as George (1990) identified it as being in other Community domains. The UK's interests, and its perception of the future of the Community and the optimal form of the Community, have differed from those of many of its Community partners (and from those of France in particular). Conflicts in the domain of broadcasting and audio-visual policy, which are represented in a particularly pure form in the differences between France and the UK, are paradigmatic of deep-rooted and pervasive divergences in policy outlook and practice in the European Community.

A UK MEP noted that the UK was generally less supportive of Community cultural initiatives than were other European actors and asserted that the UK had exercised scant influence over the Parliament's broadcasting and audio-visual initiatives: 'the UK Government tries to find reasons *not* to do things in the European Community. The UK is generally pretty negative' (interview 6.11.1991). The MEP explained the difference between the perspectives of the UK and its Community partners in terms of the relative positions of the UK and other Community Member States in world audio-visual markets. 'The UK doesn't see pan-European culture as positively as do others and the UK does not have so big a problem with English language television programmes imported from Australia and the United States' (interview 6.11.1991)[1]. Such sentiments are customarily perceived in other quarters of the Community as evidence that the UK is invincibly anti-European (rather than as differently European) for, as the Parliament stated, it is widely believed that:

> European media policy ... is a touchstone for judging whether the Member States, and public broadcasting corporations, are prepared to take European unification seriously and adopt a common policy on the media (European Parliament, 1985b, p. 35).

The course of Community broadcasting and audio-visual policy has been determined by the outcomes of the struggles between two principal rival nexuses: the *dirigiste* and the liberal policy nexuses. These conflicts are no less evident in the relations between Member States of the Community as they are in the rivalry between different institutional power centres within the Community. Just as the UK is paradigmatic of the liberal nexus at the level of the Member States, and France the paradigm of the *dirigiste* nexus at this level, so is DG IV, the Directorate General for Competition the paradigm of liberalism in the Commission of the European Communities and DG X, the Directorate General for the Audio-visual, Information, Communication and Culture, the paradigm of *dirigisme*.

The first decade of the European Community's broadcasting and audio-visual policy, between 1982 and 1992, saw this pervasive 'grand narrative' in the European Community's history articulated in a series of liberal 'wins'. Of course the *dirigistes* had their successes too: they promulgated the satellite television transmission standards directive and established the MEDIA Programme, but these initiatives have been of lesser consequence than have those of the liberals. The successful establishment of a single television market, DG IV's implacable pursuit

---

1   When asked (in November 1991) if they were lobbied by UK industry or government on audio-visual and broadcasting policy none of the four UK members of the European Parliament's Committee on Youth, Culture, Education, the Media and Sport replied in the affirmative. In November 1991, these members were Mrs Janey Buchan, Mr Michael Elliott, Miss Patricia Rawlings and Sir Jack Stewart-Clark. The two Labour members stated that UKREP produced regular briefings on matters of Government policy but they, being members of the party in opposition in Westminster, paid little attention to UKREP's briefings. They said that they were not lobbied by UK industry; whether broadcasting, audio-visual or electronics (one claimed to be well-known as 'unlobbyable'). The two Conservative members made similar claims though one, with a history in the electronics industry, did sometimes seek advice from personal industry contacts.

of European public service broadcasters, and effective use of the Community's 'constitution' to block *dirigiste* gambits must all be scored as liberal successes.

The provisions in the Treaty of Rome (Article 235) requiring unanimity among the Member States for the Community to implement measures in domains – notably the cultural domain – not explicitly within the ambit of the Treaty, has enabled liberals to weaken *dirigiste* measures (such as the establishment of the MEDIA programme and subsidies for the development of HDTV) but has also provoked *dirigistes* to circumvent, and challenge, the constitutional minimalism enshrined in the Treaty of Rome. Establishment of 'Eurimages' under the auspices of the Council of Europe through European 'variable geometry' is a notable instance of a successful circumvention of the veto on subsidy to Community audio-visual pro-duction with which the liberals were endowed under Article 235 of the Treaty of Rome. Latterly the inclusion of the 'culture article', Article 128, in the Maastricht Treaty on European Union represents a potentially most successful gambit (if the Maastricht Treaty is finally ratified) in the *dirigiste* campaign to establish interven-tionist policies for broadcasting and the audio-visual in the European Community.

To a considerable extent therefore the story of European Community broadcasting and audio-visual policy can be written as a tale of international and intra-institu-tional competition between rival interests: represented in its purest form between France and the UK on the international level and between DG IV and DG X of the Commission of the European Communities on the intra-institutional level. How-ever the story is also one of a conflict between two different visions of the Community, between the European Community as a *Europe des Patries*; of separate states bound together in pragmatic arrangements (such as a customs union) for mutual benefit; and a pan-European state bound together by a culture shared by its citizens and supranational political institutions. These 'minimalist' and 'maximal-ist' visions of Europe correlate with different conceptions of how societies hold together and consequentially different conceptions of the role of film and televi-sion in the European polity. Broadly speaking the maximalist, European unionist, vision of the European Community is rooted in classically nationalist conceptions of the relationship between polity and culture and a presumption that the exist-ence of the desired European political institutions is conditional on their iso-morphism with a sentiment of collective European identity shared by European citizens. Whereas the minimalist, pragmatic association, vision of the European Community is rooted in functionalist notions of political community. The latter vision, it is worth stating explicitly, neither necessarily denigrates the importance of culture nor camouflages a Europeanism of bad faith, whereby participation in the European Community is simply a covert surrogate for the ruthless pursuit of national self interest in a zero sum game. Rather it proposes (rather as does Burgess in the citation which heads this chapter) that politics and culture are not linked as nationalists assert.

Functionalist political theory places considerably less emphasis than do nationalist theories on the necessary congruence of polity and culture in the construction of stable, popular and legitimate political arrangements. Indeed functionalists, who emphasize the establishment of practical mechanisms of co-operation and collaboration for the realization of mutual interests as the primary motor of developing political unions, customarily regard the harmonization of culture (perceived by nationalists as a necessary condition of enduring political unions) as an obstacle to the realization of practical, enduring and union-building political arrangements. Indeed the 'father' of functionalism, Mitrany, developed his theory (or what he modestly described as an uncovering and clarification of 'the relation of things' [Mitrany, 1975, p. 17]) in response to what he saw as the blight of nationalism; a doctrine which he characterized as a 'ruthless political stress for uniformity' (Mitrany, 1975, p. 143). From this point of view the 'harmonization' (the equivalent German term *gleichshaltung* carries the right connotations) of culture and polity (regarded as necessary by nationalists) may be an *obstacle* rather than an aid to the establishment of stable and robust political institutions.

Curiously, given the pervasive citation by *dirigistes* of Monnet's comments on the role of culture in the development of the European Community, a powerful case can be made for Monnet as a functionalist. Indeed Monnet was rather contemptuous of the pursuit of the chimera of European identity supposed by European unionists to be the *sine qua non* of successful establishment of a robust European Community. He wrote 'While fifty-five countries were meeting in Lome or Brussels to seek their common interests, our diplomats were holding pointless debates about a "European identity" ' (Monnet, 1978, p. 499). It is clear that radically different policies for the film and television industries follow from the different, nationalist and functionalist, models of coherence for the European Community (and that proponents of political intervention to favour the film and television industries are likely to find more fertile soil for their advocacy in nationalist rather than functionalist theory). Broadcasting and audio-visual policy in the European Community is, thus, inevitably bound up in debates about the structure, organization and future of the Community itself.

There is no single consistent European Community vision of policy for the broadcasting and audio-visual sectors. However, not only are there rival, and exclusive, visions of how best the political institutions of the Community are to survive and prosper (on the one hand a 'nationalist' vision of a close relationship between culture and polity and on the other a 'functionalist' vision of loose and pluralistic associations between polity and culture) but there have also been important temporal changes to the dynamics of European Community policy. An account of Community policy, which explained events in terms of an enduring opposition between liberals and *dirigistes* with *dirigistes* espousing a 'nationalist' vision of European union and liberals a 'functionalist' vision of pragmatic institution building which eschewed interventions which cut across long established cultural identities, would serve very well to characterize the period from, say, the early to the mid 1980s but not that which succeeded it.

The Satellite Television Directive (Council of the European Communities, 1986) which sought to establish a common European satellite television transmission standard to lay the foundations both for a Community industrial policy for the electronics industry and to permit the development of pan-European television services, and the policy report *Realities and tendencies* (Commission of the European Communities, 1983) both combined unionist and interventionist policies. However the homology between unionist ends and interventionist means evident in both these interventions started to unravel with *Television without frontiers*. The 'supply specialization' which the Green Paper threatened, or promised, foreshadowed an integration of European audio-visual production and television markets on terms which the unionist/*dirigiste* nexus found profoundly uncomfortable.

Publication of the *Television without frontiers* Green Paper (Commission of the European Communities, 1984a) followed by promulgation of the *Television without frontiers* Directive (Council of the European Communities, 1989) produced something analogous to a polarity change in European Community policy circuits. Thereafter *dirigistes* advocated intervention to secure cultural *diversity* rather than a *common* European culture and in pursuit of diversity (rather than the unity which they had formerly sought) succeeded in establishing the MEDIA Programme inside the European Community and Eurimages outside it. Whereas liberals, commanding a powerful base in the Competition Directorate, DG IV, pursued policies which were perceived by *dirigistes* to threaten both cultural diversity and European culture (in that they were judged to serve the interests of English language products and services – notably those from the United States) in the name of a unified competitive single audio-visual market. Henceforward *dirigisme* and diversity (including opposition to concentration of private ownership in the mass media) ran together in opposition to unity and liberalism.

The consequences of European Community broadcasting and audio-visual policy have ranged from the profound impact which the policies of the liberals have had on public service broadcasting (which has been brutally buffeted by the hostility of DG IV to the EBU and the accustomed practices of public service broadcasters and by the collapse of public service broadcasting monopolies in consequence of technological change and *Television without frontiers*) to a nominal increase in the supply and circulation across the Community of feature films of European origin achieved by the *dirigistes*. In general *dirigiste* initiatives have had less effect than have those of the liberals. MEDIA 92 and 95, coupled with Eurimages, have granted modest subventions to European distributors and producers of films and television programmes of European origin. And no more than MEDIA has the satellite television transmission standards directive of 1986 had a profound impact on the Community's broadcasting and audio-visual sectors. Albeit the requirement to use MAC transmission standards, which the directive imposed, contributed to the demise of the UK DBS channel BSB in the face of competition from a Sky Television unencumbered by the necessity to conform to a standard conceived to protect some sectors of the European electronics industry from Japanese and American competition. Whereas *Television without frontiers* and the vigorous actions of DG IV have been relentlessly hostile to public service broadcasters. The liberal policy nexus has eroded both the accustomed privileges of European public service broadcasters and national sovereignty over broadcasting.

The future of broadcasting and audio-visual policy in the European Community will depend, as does so much of the Community's affairs, on the future of the Maastricht Treaty on European Union and on the degree to which the Treaty's provisions are implemented (if, that is, the Treaty is ratified by all Member States). The importance of the Maastricht Treaty for the cultural industries chiefly resides in its 'culture article', Article 128. The Treaty provides for the first time grounds for the Commission to exercise jurisdiction in the cultural domain. It has been welcomed by prominent members of the *dirigiste* camp and one of these, Roberto Barzanti formerly the Chair of the European Parliament's Committee on Youth, Culture, Education, the Media and Sport, made it clear that the inclusion of culture within a revised Rome Treaty (i.e. the Maastricht Treaty) was necessary to ensure that Community initiatives in the audio-visual sector were effective. He stated: 'Il faut qu'initiatives comme le programme MEDIA, constamment menacé par les atteintes pendantes portées à la faiblesse de ses bases juridiques, deviennent l'esprit même de l'action communautaires dans le secteur (Barzanti, 1990a, p. 36)[1].

Not surprisingly Article 128 has been firmly opposed by the UK. The minutes of a meeting of UK officials in September 1991[2] (in preparation for negotiations on the Maastricht Treaty) recorded that the UK government 'was not convinced of the need for a new Treaty article ... effective cultural co-operation already existed and the addition of a cultural article extending Community competence would mean increased Community expenditure. Any increased UK contribution would be at the expense of OAL's domestic spend ... we were concerned about the scope of 'artistic and literary creation'; about the inclusion of audiovisual; and heritage' (Source: note of meeting to discuss European Cultural Co-operation, Office of Arts and Libraries 17.9.1991).

The UK did not succeed in excluding the Culture Article from the Treaty but did succeed in limiting its scope. The text of Article 128 confines the Community's competence in the audio-visual to 'artistic and literary creation, including *in* (my emphasis) the audio-visual area' rather than opening the whole of the audio-visual sector to Community intervention. Moreover Article 128 provides that Council decisions in cultural matters should be taken unanimously, rather than by qualified majority voting. Thus, although the Maastricht Treaty will permit more powerful interventionist initiatives by the Commission in the broadcasting and audio-visual sectors in spite of UK negotiators' successful insertion of the preposition 'in' in the final sentence of clause two of Article 128[3] and the agreement that unanimous,

---

1 'Programmes like MEDIA, although always vulnerable to hostile forces in consequence of their fragile legal basis must become the essence of Community actions in the audio-visual sector'.
2 Representatives from the Foreign and Commonwealth Office, the Office of Arts and Libraries and various UK cultural quangos.
3 Thus limiting Commission powers to the audio-visual sector only insofar as it is a vehicle for 'artistic

rather than majority, decision making is required in respect of Council decisions in respect of culture, the UK (the 'ultra liberal' Member State par excellence) achieved a significant success by maintaining a single state veto over Community cultural initiatives.

Article 128 of the Treaty on European Union reads:

> 1. The Community shall contribute to the flowering of the culture of the Member States, while respecting their national and regional diversity and at the same time bringing the common cultural heritage to the fore.
>
> 2. Action by the Community shall be aimed at encouraging co-operation between Member States and, if necessary, supporting and supplementing their action in the following areas:
>
> - improvement of the knowledge and dissemination of the culture and history of the European peoples;
> - conservation and safeguarding of cultural heritage of European significance;
> - non-commercial cultural exchange;
> - artistic and literary creation, including in the audio-visual sector.
>
> 3. The Community and the Member States shall foster co-operation with third countries and the competent international organizations in the sphere of culture, in particular the Council of Europe.
>
> 4. The Community shall take cultural aspects into account in its action under other provisions of this Treaty.
>
> 5. In order to contribute to the achievement of the objectives referred to in this Article, the Council:
>
> - acting in accordance with the procedure referred to in Article 189b and after consulting the Committee of the Regions, shall adopt incentive measures, excluding any harmonization of the laws and regulations of the Member States. The Council shall act unanimously throughout the procedures referred to in Article 189b;
> - acting unanimously on a proposal from the Commission shall adopt recommendations (Treaty on European Union. Article 128).

Although the UK had sought to forestall inclusion of a Culture Article in the Treaty both Conservative and Labour UK MEPs on the European Parliament's Committee on Youth, Culture, Education, the Media and Sport (interviewed in November 1991) joined their colleagues on the Committee in supporting the inclusion of Article 128 in the Maastricht Treaty. Indeed a Conservative MEP, Miss Patricia Rawlings, wrote the Committee on Youth, Culture, Education, the Media and Sport's official Opinion (sent to the Parliament's Committee on Institutional Affairs) on the matter. Rawlings' Opinion stated the Committee's support for 'a

---

(contd) and literary creation' rather than establishing the audio-visual sector itself as an authentic locus of artistic and literary creation.

paragraph on cultural affairs [being] included in the revised Treaty of Rome' (European Parliament, 1991, p. 3). The Opinion began with Matthew Arnold's celebrated definition of culture in *Culture and anarchy* (Arnold, 1963) as 'the best that has been known and said in the world'. It identified two distinct meanings of culture. 'Firstly ... an artistic concept, which includes all the arts ... Secondly as a social concept. This is the broader definition incorporating the socio-culture of individual countries, their food, language, attitudes, philosophy and behaviour' (European Parliament, 1991, p. 3). Culture is, the Opinion states, 'at the very foundation of Europe. It reflects each country's individuality, as well as being a means of communication and integration between Member States' (European Parliament, 1991, p. 3).

The Committee, through its amanuensis Miss Rawlings, stressed that 'we are not suggesting the harmonization of European culture into some kind of 'Euro-culture' ... Diversity must be safeguarded at all costs' (European Parliament, 1991, p. 3). However, later in the Opinion, the Committee referred to it being 'essential to specify a cultural common denominator.' For, the Committee believed, 'the Community as is (sic) stands today is held back by the very limited nature of its cultural dimension ... Business prosperity and economic freedom are vital, but alone they will not convince the European people of the value of the Community. But, culture will.' (European Parliament, 1991, p. 5). 'Culture is' the Committee believed 'the human face of the Community, it is the face which all people understand and can identify with. It is therefore the cement which will bind the Community together and enable us to promote further integration in Europe' (European Parliament, 1991, p. 7).

The Committee on Youth, Culture, Education, the Media and Sport, like other Community institutions, was unable to do more than rhetorically reconcile the contradictory imperatives of cultural diversity and cultural unity in weasel words such as 'unity in diversity', which now appear promiscuously in Community documents. Unsurprising perhaps that UK MEPs spoke in similar terms. When interviewed one stated: 'If you have movement towards political and economic union you need to have cultural exchange. You must respect national cultures but must respect culture as such'. However this respondent also stated, and was not alone in doing so, some reservations and said: 'Whilst cultural exchange was good and that therefore bringing culture within the treaty merited a sceptical yes, one had to ask what was meant by culture' (interview 6.11.1991). Unfortunately the Committee's Opinion did not do so, it covered its bases by citing T.S. Eliot's formulation that culture is 'the characteristic activities and interests of a people' (Eliot, 1948, p. 31) as well as Arnold's better known Pollyanna-ish formulae.

However Miss Rawlings' intervention, in the meeting of the Parliament's Committee on Youth, Culture, Education, the Media and Sport on 7 November 1991, suggests that although able to agree on rhetorical formulae the motives of proponents of greater powers for the Community in the audio-visual domain in the Parliament's Committee on the media were not identical. Miss Rawlings' assertions that the principle of subsidiarity should not apply to the regulation of satellite television and that the content of satellite television required regulation by the European Community (and that national regulation of satellite television was meaningless) did not express a concern with European culture (still less with the economic viability of the European cultural industries) but about what she perceived to be unregulated flows of pornographic television programming in the Community.

The concepts 'community' and 'market' are among the most troubled categories in the social sciences. Not surprising therefore that there is no consensus in the European Community about the nature and effects of a single broadcasting market. Indeed in important respects the single market does not exist. Certainly any Community enterprise has right of establishment in any Community state, goods and services which originate in any Community state may circulate in any other Community state and national ownership of broadcasters can no longer be required. But establishment of a single market has been at the level of the enterprise rather than the viewer. The technological and regulatory changes which European television has experienced over the last decade may have been necessary to the creation of a single market but they have not been sufficient.

Linguistic and cultural differences between Community citizens have left the notionally single market an agglomeration of barely overlapping distinct markets. This is not to say that nothing has changed, only that the changes (at the level of the viewers' experience) have, *grosso modo*, been ones *within* established 'national' markets rather than the creation of a single European market. Thus competition has increased within national markets, UK viewers watch BSkyB, German RTL Plus and national regulatory structures have lost power, Belgian and Dutch cable networks can no longer be required to exclude signals from other Community states and the UK cable regulator can no longer require the naughty bits on RTL Plus to be denied (or put on the 'top shelf') to UK viewers. Although European regulation has eroded the basis on which national broadcasting and audio-visual policies were and will be made European film and television viewers remain obdurately national, rather than European, in their consumption habits. Profound though the changes to European Community broadcasting and audio-visual regimes have been in the decade between 1982 and 1992 from another point of view – that of the viewers rather than the producers – what is most striking is how little, rather than how much, has altered. Consumption, even if not regulation, remains obdurately national.

Over the decade in which the European Community's audiovisual and broadcasting policies have evolved the superordinate values to which policy makers tend to appeal in order to legitimize their preferred courses of action have changed. Formerly unity was the superordinate value to which both interventionists and liberals referred. Latterly diversity has become the dominant superordinate value for interventionists in the software realm. In respect of hardware interventionists continue to espouse a single Community standard, a single Community electronics market and Community unity. Whereas in the early 1980s intervention was principally directed towards the construction and dissemination of a single European culture and identity latterly it has been directed towards ensuring that the Community remains culturally diversified.

Unity is the value to which those in the Community who are confident[1] (or who hope to be) of dominance appeal. Diversity is the value which those who fear domination invoke. The UK has backed diversity in hardware (a loose satellite transmission standard) for fear of the effects on its electronics industry of domination by the Philips/Thomson/Siemens D2/MAC nexus. In software it has backed unity (the single market and inhibition of the subsidies for audiovisual production threatened by the supply specialization likely to favour anglophone and UK based producers).

However Community broadcasting and audiovisual policy has been governed by a fundamental paradox, the Community has lacked power in the cultural domain and has therefore had to make its broadcasting and audiovisual policies using the, fundamentally economic, powers granted under the Treaty of Rome. The Treaty gave the Community power to develop economic policies for cultural industries which are growing in economic importance but, because these industries are *cultural* industries on which the political future of the Community is deemed by many to depend, the Community's policies have been opposed for cultural and political reasons by powerful interests. The bargaining between the interest groups has resulted in curious conjunctures such as establishment of Community programmes (MEDIA) to countervail the effects of Community regulations (*Television without Frontiers*). But because the Community's powers remain fundamentally economic, *cultural* initiatives have tended either to develop outside the Community (via 'variable geometry') or under the Commission's powers to use its 'own resources' (MEDIA 95). But these initiatives have lacked the solid economic base necessary to effective action. Consequently the Community has been unable to develop a policy framework that meets the cultural, political or economic needs of Europe, and its audio-visual and broadcasting policy satisfies none of the principal actors or interest groups within the Community.

Moreover, although both the liberal and *dirigiste* policy camps have set in motion processes with significant political consequences, neither interventionists nor liberals have been subject to effective democratic political control (although the alliance between DG X and the Parliament's Committee on Youth, Culture, Education, the Media and Sport has lent interventionism a more plausible appearance of

---

1 Here the generalizations which convention demand be made in a conclusion become very dangersou. For the 'unity' initiative to establish the D2/MAC satellite television standard followed the fear of Japanese and United States competition (domination) of influential sectors of the Community's electronics industry. Moreover, whilst the UK's policy stance is, I believe, rational from a macro-economic point of view, there is a consequential risk of political isolation and thus of UK industry having to respond to compelling Community political agendas which have been set to meet the needs of the weak rather than the strong.

political accountability than has covered liberalism). Audio-visual policies, whether explicitly directed towards the achievement of political goals (whether the promotion 'ever closer union' or the maintenance of media pluralism) or presented as politics free restructuring of markets have evolved through Community procedures that are acknowledged to be democratically deficient (Commission of the European Communities and European Parliament, 1990, p. 6).

The Community's 'democratic deficit'; the dissatisfaction of Member States endowed with strong and with weak audiovisual sectors with the Community audiovisual and broadcasting regime; the unsatisfactory articulation between the Community's hardware and software sectors under the established policy regime; and widespread belief that the cultural industries are both vitally important to the economic future of the European Community (entering a post-industrial, information society, stage of development) and to its very political integrity (because polity and culture must, many believe, be congruent if political institutions are to survive) mean that we can anticipate that European Community audiovisual and broadcasting policy will continue to develop. However, although its importance is likely to remain undiminished, its structure will remain complex and the objectives of policy makers will continue to be contradictory. Television (and its pendant audio-visual sector) has been the first of the Community's cultural industries to have had explicit Community policies made for it. As the most important of the cultural industries television has thrown into view the plethora of contradictory interests and presumptions which have informed the making of the European Community's first cultural policies and first policies for the cultural industries. The themes present in the story of the first decade of the European Community's audio-visual and broadcasting policy are likely to endure and to recur over the next decade. A decade in which the story of European broadcasting and audio-visual policy will continue to unfold and in which other cultural industries and the cultural industries of other countries are brought into the inescapable embrace of ever closer European union.

Appendix 1

Resolution on Radio and Television Broadcasting in the European Community

The European Parliament,

– having regard to the motion for a resolution by Mr Pedini, Mr Hahn and others on radio and television broadcasting in the European Community (Doc. 1409 80) the motion for a resolution by Mr Schinzel and others on the threat to diversity of opinion posed by commercialization of the new media (Doc.1-422/80) and the European Parliament's resolution of 16 January 1981 on the information policy of the European Community, of the Commission of the European Communities and of the European Parliament,

– having regard to the report of the Committee on Youth, Culture, Education, Information and Sport and the opinions of the Political Affairs Committee and the Legal Affairs Committee (Doc. 1-1013/81),

– convinced of the need for all citizens of the Member States to receive authentic information on Community policy and thus to be given a share in the political responsibility,

– whereas adequate and expert information is essential to the development of a sense of common responsibility and willingness to take joint political action,

– whereas radio and television are today the chief media for informing and shaping public opinion,

– whereas reporting of European Community problems in the past has been inadequate and in many cases negative,

– having regard to the public opinion polls recently conducted among the citizens of Europe, which show an alarming disappointment with the development of the Community and at the same time, a lack of information as to what is actually going on,

– having regard to the unsatisfactory results of the latest European Council summit with regard to the solution of existing urgent problems,

– whereas the introduction of transmission by satellite, which may be expected in the years ahead as a result of new technologies, and the different cable systems, will vastly increase broadcasting capacity via the additional channels and make it possible to reach all regions of Europe simultaneously,

– whereas the anticipated media revolution in the Member States is causing increasing discussion of the reorganization of television broadcasting and whereas a large number of different proposals have been made on the use of the new facilities and in some cases far-reaching decisions are about to be taken,

– concerned that if the European Community and its institutions do not participate in this decision-making process, developments might take place which would not be in the interests of the Community,

– convinced that the timely intervention of the European Community in the decision-making process will help to achieve an appropriate solution,

– convinced that the role and involvement of publicly controlled broadcasting corporations in the Member States is of paramount importance in ensuring the development of appropriate policies and initiatives in the interests of the people of the Community:

> 1. Calls on the Commission to submit within six months a report on the media giving assistance to the Community institutions in preparing the decisions to be taken by them in this field and containing in particular the information mentioned in paragraph 8 of the explanatory statement and, on the basis of this report, to create the political and legal basis for the realization of a European television channel;

> 2. Regards it as essential for the European Community to encourage the national television companies and the European Broadcasting Union in their plans to establish a European television channel and for it to take part in the related discussions and decisions;

> 3. Considers close co-operation with the European Broadcasting Union to be imperative;

> 4. Calls on the Community institutions to ensure that the Member States make the fifth channels of the national satellites available for a European channel, or to see that one channel of the L-satellites to be launched by the European Space Agency in 1986 is reserved for this purpose;

> 5. Proposes that the European television channel should provide a full range of programmes, covering news, politics, education, culture, entertainment and sport and that it should be European in origin, transmission range, target audience and subject matter;

> 6. Expects that equal weight will be given to all regions of the European Community to increase European awareness and recommends that account

be taken of the essence of European culture, namely diversity in unity; and that initiatives will be undertaken to ensure the involvement of people in the regions concerned and their organizations in the preparation of appropriate programmes;

7. Considers that outline rules should be drawn up on European radio and television broadcasting *inter alia* with a view to protecting young people and establishing a code of practice for advertising at Community level;

8. Instructs its own television service to make available all technical facilities possible for Eurovision broadcasts, and urges the Commission to do likewise;

9. Instructs its President to forward this resolution and the report of its committee to the Council and the Commission (European Parliament, 1982a).

Bibliography

In this work, I have referred to documents published in the Official Journal of the European Communities and to internal documents of the European Broadcasting Union and have used the standard referencing conventions of the European Community and the EBU to identify these documents.

Arnold, M. (1963 [1869]): *Culture and Anarchy*. Cambridge University Press, Cambridge.

Assises Européennes de l'audiovisuel. Projet Eureka audiovisuel (1989): Ministère des affaires étrangères. République Francaise and Commission of the European Communities, Paris.

Banotti, M. (1992): Interview in *Media Policy Review*. No. 4. pp. 6–7.

Barzanti, R. (1990): 'Audiovisual Opportunities in the Single Market' in *MEDIA 92 Newsletter of the MEDIA 92 Programme*. 09/1990, p. 1. Brussels.

Barzanti, R. (1990a): La culture, paramètre vital de la 'société européenne'. In *Coherence in diversity: the challenge for European television*. European Institute for the Media, Manchester.

Bell, D. (1976 [1973]): *The coming of post-industrial society*. Penguin, Harmondsworth.

BBC [British Broadcasting Corporation] (1992): *Extending choice. The BBC's role in the new broadcasting age*. BBC, London.

Berlin, I. (1969): *Four essays on liberty*. Oxford University Press, Oxford.

Boekwijt, M. (1989): Directive on transfrontier television in Danger. *Media Bulletin* Vol. 6 No. 3, pp. 4–5.

Booz Allen and Hamilton (1991): Study to establish a Methodology for the Interpretation of article 4 (2) and (4) of Council Directive 89/552/EC. Brussels, September (cited in Media Policy Review No. 3, July 1992, p. 12).

Briggs, A. (1961): *The History of Broadcasting in the United Kingdom*. Oxford University Press, Oxford.

Bruhann, U. (1985): Untitled address to the IBA Television without Frontiers conference 30.4.1985.

BSAC. British Screen Advisory Council (undated but 1990): The European Initiative. The

Business of Television and Film in the 1990s. British Screen Advisory Council mimeo, London.

Burgess, A. (1990): European culture: does it exist? *European Broadcasting Union Review Programmes Administration Law*, V XLI N 2 March, pp. 17–21

Burgleman, J.-P. and C. Pauwels (1991): La Convergence de l'Audiovisuel et des Télécommunications en Europe. La Politique des Communautes Européennes. CSNMIT. Free University of Brussels, Mimeo.

Clarke, N. and E. Riddell (1992): *The Sky Barons*. Methuen, London.

Cockfield, the Lord (1986): The future of television in Europe. *European Broadcasting Union Review. Programmes Administration Law* Vol XXXVII No 6 November, pp. 8–13.

Collins, R. (1990): *Satellite television in Western Europe*. John Libbey, London.

Collins, R. (1990a): *Television: policy and culture*. Unwin Hyman, London.

Collins, R. (1991): Programme trade off balance. *Broadcast* 13.12.1991, p. 30. London.

Collins, R. (1993): Public service broadcasting by satellite in Europe: Eurikon and Europa. *Screen* Vol. 34 No. 2, pp. 162–175.

Commission of the European Communities (1983): Interim Report. *Realities and Tendencies in European television: perspectives and options*. COM(83) 229 final. 25.5.83. Brussels.

Commission of the European Communities (1984): *Towards a European television policy*. European File 19/84. Commission of the European Communities, Brussels.

Commission of the European Communities (1984a): *Television without frontiers*. Green paper on the establishment of the Common Market for broadcasting especially by satellite and cable. COM (84) 300 final. Office for Official Publications of the European Communities, Luxembourg.

Commission of the European Communities (1986): *Television and the audio-visual sector: towards a European policy*. European File 14/86. Office for Official Publications of the European Communities, Luxembourg.

Commission of the European Communities (1986a): The Community's broadcasting policy. Proposal for a Council Directive concerning broadcasting activities. Bulletin of the European Communities Supplement 5/86. Office for Official Publications of the European Communities, Luxembourg.

Commission of the European Communities (1986b): The Community's audiovisual policy. Information Memo P-26, March, COM (86) 146 Brussels.

Commission of the European Communities (1986c): Proposal for a Directive on common technical specifications of the MAC/packet family of standards for direct satellite television broadcasting (COM (86) 1 final 22.1.1986. Office for Official Publications of the European Communities, Luxembourg.

Commission of the European Communities (1986d): The MEDIA programme. Commission of the European Communities, Brussels.

Commission of the European Communities (1988): Green Paper on copyright and the challenge of technology. (COM (88) 172 Final. July.) Office for Official Publications of the European Communities, Luxembourg.

169

Commission of the European Communities (1990): Communication by the Commission to the Council and to the European Parliament on audio-visual policy. COM(90) 78, 21/02/1990. (Also in Commission of the European Communities, 1990b).

Commission of the European Communities (1990a): XIXth Report on Competition Policy, 1989. Office for Official Publications of the European Communities, Luxembourg.

Commission of the European Communities (1990b): The European Community Policy in the audiovisual field. Legal and political texts. Office for Official Publications of the European Communities, Luxembourg.

Commission of the European Communities (1990c): Commission communication to the Council accompanied by two proposals for Council decisions relating to an action programme to promote the development of a European audiovisual industry 'MEDIA', 1991-1995. COM(90)132 final. (Also in Commission of the European Communities, 1990b).

Commission of the European Communities (1990d): Background report. The Commission's audiovisual policy. ISEC/B11/90. 9.3.90.

Commission of the European Communities (1990e): Green Paper on a common approach in the field of satellite communications in the European Community. COM (90) 490 final. Office for Official Publications of the European Communities, Luxembourg.

Commission of the European Communities (1990f): European unification: the origins and growth of the European Community. Office for Official Publications of the European Community, Luxembourg.

Commission of the European Communities (1991): Proposal for a Council Directive on the coordination of certain rules concerning copyright and neighbouring rights applicable to satellite broadcasting and cable retransmission. COM (91) 276 final -SYN 358. Office for Official Publications of the European Communities, Luxembourg.

Commission of the European Communities (1991a): *MEDIA guide for the audiovisual industry. Edition 6*. Commission of the European Communities, Brussels.

Commission of the European Communities (1991b): Communication to Parliament and the Council on encouraging audio visual production in the context of the strategy for high definition television. SEC (91) 1470 final. Commission of the European Communities, Brussels.

Commission of the European Communities (1991c): *A Community of twelve: Key figures*. Commission of the European Communities, Brussels.

Commission of the European Communities (1991d): Follow up to the Green Paper. Working programme of the Commission in the field of copyright and neighbouring rights. COM (90) 584 final. Office for Official Publications of the European Communities, Luxembourg.

Commission of the European Communities (1991e): Proposal for a Council Decision concerning the accession of Member States to the Berne Convention for the Protection of Literary and Artistic Works, as revised by the Paris Act of 24.7.1971 and the International Convention for the Protection of Performers, Producers of Phonograms and Broadcasting Organisations of 26.10.1961. COM (90) 582 final. Office for Official Publications of the European Communities, Luxembourg.

Commission of the European Communities (1991f): Proposal for a Council Directive on rental right, lending right, and on certain rights related to copyright. COM (90) 586 final -SYN 319. Office for Official Publications of the European Communities, Luxembourg.

Commission of the European Communities (1991g): Public Opinion in the European Community. *Eurobarometer* No. 35, June, Brussels.

Commission of the European Communities (1992): From the Single Act to Maastricht and beyond: the means to match our ambitions. COM (92) 2000. Office for Official Publications of the European Communities, Luxembourg.

Commission of the European Communities (1992a): XXIst Report on competition policy, 1991. Office for Official Publications of the European Communities, Luxembourg.

Commission of the European Communities (1992b): From Single Market to European union. Office for Official Publications of the European Communities, Luxembourg.

Commission of the European Communities (1992c): European Community audiovisual policy. European File 6/1992. Office for Official Publications of the European Communities, Luxembourg.

Commission of the European Communities (1992d): Proposal for a Council Directive harmonising the term of protection of copyright and certain related rights. COM (92) 33 final. Office for Official Publications of the European Communities, Luxembourg.

Commission of the European Communities (1992e): Amended Proposal for a Council Directive on rental rights, lending right and on certain rights related to copyright in the field of intellectual property. COM (92) 159 final. Office for Official Publications of the European Communities, Luxembourg.

Commission of the European Communities (1992f): Amended Proposal for a Council Decision concerning the accession of Member States to the Berne Convention for the Protection of Literary and Artistic Works, as revised by the Paris Act of 24.7.1971 and the International Convention for the Protection of Performers, Producers of Phonograms and Broadcasting Organisations of 26.10.1961. COM (92) 10 final. Office for Official Publications of the European Communities, Luxembourg.

Commission of the European Communities (1992g): Pluralism and media concentration in the internal market. COM (92) 480 final. Office for Official Publications of the European Communities, Luxembourg.

Commission of the European Communities and the European Parliament (1990): Europe, our future. The Institutions of the European Community. Office for Official Publications of the European Communities, Luxembourg.

Congdon, T. *et al.* (1992): *Paying for Broadcasting. The Handbook.* Routledge, London.

Council of Europe (1988): Resolution (88) 15. Setting up a European support fund for the co-production and distribution of creative cinematographic and audiovisual works (Eurimages) Strasbourg.

Council of Europe (1989): European Convention on transfrontier television. 5.5.89. Council of Europe, Strasbourg.

Council of Europe (1990): Explanatory report on the European Convention on transfrontier television. Council of Europe. Strasbourg.

171

Council of Europe (1991): Achievements and activities. Council of Europe, Strasbourg.

Council of Europe (1991a): Recommendations adopted by the Committee of Ministers of the Council of Europe in the media field. Council of Europe Directorate of Human Rights. Strasbourg.

Council of Europe (1991b): Council of Europe activities in the media field. Council of Europe Directorate of Human Rights, Strasbourg.

Council of Europe (1991c): The three main audio-visual components of the CDCC programme. Council for Cultural Co-operation. Council of Europe, Strasbourg.

Council of Europe (1991d): Recommendations and resolutions adopted by the Parliamentary Assembly of the Council of Europe in the media field. Council of Europe Directorate of Human Rights, Strasbourg.

Council of the European Communities (1986): Council Directive on the adoption of common technical specifications of the MAC-packet family of standards for direct satellite television broadcasting: 86/529/EEC. OJ L 311, 6.11.1986.

Council of the European Communities (1989): Directive on the coordination of certain provisions laid down by law, regulation or administrative action in Member States concerning the pursuit of television broadcasting activities. 89/552/EEC. OJ L 298. 17.10.1989, pp. 23–30.

Council of the European Communities (1990): Decision concerning the implementation of an action programme to promote the development of the European audiovisual industry (media) (1991–1995). 90/685/EEC. OJ L 380. 31.12.90. pp. 37–44.

Council of the European Communities (1992): Directive on the adoption of standards for satellite broadcasting of television signals. 92/38/EEC 11.5.92 OJ L 137. 20.5.1992, pp. 17–20.

Council of the European Communities (1992a): Directive on Rental rights and lending right and on certain rights related to copyright in the field of intellectual property. 92/100/EEC. OJ L 346, 19.11.1192, pp. 61–66.

Crick, B. (ed) (1991): *National identities. The constitution of the United Kingdom.* Basil Blackwell, Oxford.

Crouch, C and D Marquand (1990): *The politics of 1992. Beyond the single European market.* Basil Blackwell, Oxford.

CSO [Central Statistical Office] (1991): Overseas transactions of the film and TV industry (1990). CSO, Newport.

CSO [Central Statistical Office] (1992): Overseas transactions of the film and TV industry (1991). CSO, Newport.

de Bock, H. (undated but probably March 1983): *Eurikon considered: The Eurikonsumers' perspective.*

de Kalbermatten, R. (1985): Letter to Directors General of EBU Member Broadcasters 26.11.85. DAJ/6038.

de Win, P. (1985): *Opportunities and restrictions for international advertising.* Paper given at the IBA Advertising Conference. Television without Frontiers, 30.4.1985. London.

Decaux, A. (1989): *La politique télévisuelle exterieure de la France*. La Documentation Française,. Paris.

Delors, J. (1985): Address to the opening of the European Parliament 12.3.85. Commission programme for 1985 in Debates of the European Parliament. OJ No 2-324.

Dondlinger, J. (1989): Europe's Media Future. *Media Bulletin*, Vol. 6 No. 2, p. 3. European Institute for the Media, Manchester.

Dyson, K. and P. Humphreys ed. (1990): *The political economy of communications*. Routledge, London.

EBU (European Broadcasting Union) (1990): EBU commentary on the Television without Frontiers Directive and the European Convention on Transfrontier Television. *European Broadcasting Union Review. Programmes Administration Law*. V XLI N 4 July, pp. 6–16.

EBU/OTS Operations Group (1983): Eurikon DBS Pan-European Broadcasting. A summarised report on the EBU/OTS Experiment '82. Mimeo.

The Economist Weekly. London.

Eliot, T.S. (1948): *Notes Towards a Definition of Culture*. Faber: London.

Eugster, E.. (1983): *Television programming across national boundaries: the EBU and OIRT Experience*. Artec House, Dedham.

Eurimages (1990): Information sheets EUR/INF 90 1-9. Eurimages, Strasbourg 27.6.90.

Eurimages (1991): Eurimages in brief. EUR/INF (19) 5 REV 2. Eurimages, Strasbourg.

European Council (1989): Conclusions of the Presidency. Commission of the European Communities, 1990b, p. 9.

European Movement (ND [1950]): *The European Movement and the Council of Europe*. Hutchinson, London.

European Parliament (1980): Report on the information policy of the European Community, of the Commission of the European Communities and of the European Parliament (The Schall Report). PE Doc 1-596/80.

European Parliament (1982): Report on radio and television broadcasting in the European Community on behalf of the Committee on Youth, Culture, Education, Information and Sport [The Hahn Report]. PE Document 1-1013/81.

European Parliament (1982a): Resolution on radio and television broadcasting in the European Community [The Hahn Resolution]. OJ C 87 5.4.82, pp. 110–112.

European Parliament (1983): Resolution on the Establishment of a uniform technical standard for television pictures and sound in the Community. OJ C 322 28.11.1983, p. 277.

European Parliament (1984): Report on a policy commensurate with new trends in European television on behalf of the Committee on Youth, Culture, Education, Information and Sport [Arfé Report] 16.3.1984. PE 85.902 final.

European Parliament (1984a): Resolution on a policy commensurate with new trends in European television [The Arfé Resolution] OJ C 117 30.4.84, p. 201-205 30.4.84.

European Parliament (1984b): Hutton Report on behalf of the Committee on Youth, Culture, Education, Information and Sport, 15.3.1984. PE 78.983 final.

European Parliament (1984c): Resolution on broadcast communication in the European Community (the threat to diversity of opinion posed by commercialisation of the new media) [The Hutton Resolution] OJ C 127 14.5.1984, p. 147-150.

European Parliament (1985): Resolution on a framework for a European media policy based on the establishment of a common market for broadcasting especially by satellite and cable. OJ C 288 11.11.1985, p. 113.

European Parliament (1985a): Resolution on the economic aspects of the common market for broadcasting in the European Community. OJ C 288 11.11.1985, p. 119.

European Parliament (1985b): Report on a framework for European media policy especially on the establishment of a common market for broadcasting, especially by satellite and cable on behalf of the Committee on Youth, Culture, Education, Information and Sport [Hahn Report] PE Document A2-75/1985.

European Parliament (1985c): Proposal for a council regulation on a Community aid scheme for non-documentary cinema and television co-productions. (COM (85) 174 final) OJ C 288 8.10.1985 pp. 28–41.

European Parliament (1985d): Amended proposal for a Council Regulation (EEC) on a Community aid scheme for non-documentary cinema and television co-productions. (COM (85) 800 final) OJ C 351 31.12.1985, p. 37.

European Parliament (1986): Baget Bozzo report on the European Community's information policy on behalf of the Committee on Youth, Culture, Education, Information and Sport, 6.10.1986 PE DOC A 2-111/86.

European Parliament (1987): Audio-visual policies of the Community. The role of the European Parliament. Research and Documentation Papers. Economic Series N 10. 8-1987. European Parliament Secretariat, Directorate General for Research.

European Parliament (1987a): Resolution on the European Community's information policy [The Baget Bozzo Resolution]. OJ C 7 12.1.1987, pp. 111–114.

European Parliament (1989): Report on the European film and television industry (de Vries report) 09.01.1989. PE Document A2-0347/88.

European Parliament (1990): Report of the Committee on Youth, Culture, Education, the Media and Sport on the proposal from the Commission to the Council concerning the implementation of an action programme to promote the development of the European audiovisual industry (1991–1995) [Barzanti report] PE 144.275/fin. PE A 3-0293/90 3.11.90.

European Parliament (1991): Opinion for the Committee on Institutional Affairs of the Committee on Youth, Culture, Education, the Media and Sport on the Annual report by the Council of the European Communities on European Union. Part A: Activities in the Community framework. PE Doc 153.030/def. 25.9.1991.

Ficsor, M. (1990): Direct broadcasting by satellite and the Bogsch Theory. *International Business Lawyer*, June, pp. 258–263.

The Financial Times. Six times a week. London.

Fumaroli, M. (1990): La culture et les loisirs: une nouvelle réligion d'etat. *Commentaire* No. 51 Automne, pp. 425–435.

Garnham, N. (1990): *Capitalism and communications*. Sage, London.

Gavin, B. (1991): *European broadcasting standards in the 1990s*. NCC Blackwell, Oxford.

Gellner, E. (1983): *Nations and nationalism*. Basil Blackwell, Oxford.

Gellner, E. (1992): From the ruins of the great contest. *Times Literary Supplement* No. 4641. 13 March 1992, pp. 9–10.

George, S. (1990): *An awkward partner. Britain in the European Community*. Oxford University Press, Oxford.

Great Britain. Parliament. House of Lords (1985): 4th report. Select Committee on the European Communities. Television without Frontiers. (HL 43) HMSO, London.

Great Britain. Parliament. House of Lords (1987): 4th report. Select Committee on the European Communities. European Broadcasting. (HL 67) HMSO, London.

Hallstein, W. (1972): *Europe in the making*. Allen and Unwin, London.

Harriott, J. (1984): European broadcasting policy: some considerations. 7.6.1984. IBA Mimeo.

Heath, S. (1990): Representing television. In *Logics of Television: essays in cultural criticism*, ed. P. Mellencamp. British Film Institute, London.

Hjarvard, S. (1991): *Pan European television news. towards a European political public sphere?* Paper at the Fourth International Television Studies Conference London, 1991.

Hodgson, P. (1992): Foreword. In *Paying for Broadcasting. The Handbook*, eds, Congdon, T. *et al.* Routledge, London.

Karnell, G. (1990): A refutation of the Bogsch Theory on direct satellite broadcasting rights. *International Business Lawyer*, June, pp. 263–266.

Kedourie, E. (1966): *Nationalism*. Hutchinson, London.

Kelly, B. (1991): Mipcom '90. Us and Them; an outsider's view. *Screen* Vol. 32 No. 2 Summer, pp. 224–227.

Knowledge Research (1990): Private communication to R Collins from Knowledge Research Peterborough drawing on research conducted for MERGE (Media Economics Research Group Europe).

Maggiore, M. (1990): *Audiovisual production in the single market*. Commission of the European Communities, Luxembourg.

Maidment, K. (1985): Letter to Leon Brittain (sic) In *Annual Report of the British Film and Television Producers' Association*, 1984/5. London.

Mattelart, A., X. Delcourt and M. Mattelart (1984): *International image markets*. Comedia, London.

Media Policy Review. Monthly. London.

MEDIA (1990): Progress report of the Pilot Projects. September 1990. MEDIA 92. Commission of the European Communities, Brussels.

MEDIA (1990a): *MEDIA 92. Newsletter*, 6 September 1990.

MEDIA 92. Newsletter. Bimonthly.

Melich, A. (1990): *Identité Nationale et Medias Contemporains*. Editions Loisirs et Pedagogie, Lausanne.

Michael, J. (1988): The regulation of broadcasting by European institutions: convention or chaos? PICT Policy Research Paper No. 5. Economic and Social Research Council, Swindon.

Minogue, K. (1967): *Nationalism*. Methuen, London.

Mitrany, D. (1975): *The functional theory of politics*. Martin Robertson, London.

Miyet, B. (1990): The European Audiovisual Conference. *European Broadcasting Union Review. Programmes Administration Law*, Vol. XLI No. 1 January, pp. 10–13.

Moeglin, P. (1991): Télévision et Europe. *Communication* Vol. 12 No. 2, pp. 13–51. Ste Foy.

Monnet, J. (1978): *Memoirs*. Collins, London.

Naef, F. (1990): The EBU's involvement in multilingual audiovisual production as a joint founder of BABEL. *European Broadcasting Union Review, Programmes, Administration, Law*. Vol XLI, No. 4. July, pp. 41–44.

Negrine, R. and S. Papathanassopoulos (1990): *The internationalisation of television*. Pinter, London.

Noel, E. (1988): *Working together. The institutions of the European Community*. Office for Official Publications of the European Communities, Luxembourg.

O'Brien, C. (1992): Pursuing a chimera. Nationalism at odds with the idea of a Federal Europe. *Times Literary Supplement*, No. 4641, 13.3.1992, pp. 3–4.

OECD [Organisation for Economic Co-operation and Development] (1986): *OECD Observer* No. 141, July. Paris.

Office for Official Publications of the European Communities (1988): The audio-visual media in the single European market. Office for Official Publications of the European Communities, Luxembourg.

Owen, R. and M. Dynes (1990): The Times *guide to 1992* (2nd Edition). Times Books, London.

Papathanassopoulos, S. (1990): Towards European Television: The Case of Europa-TV. *Media Information Australia* No. 56, May, pp. 57–63.

Peacock Committee (1986): Report of the Committee on Financing the BBC (Chairman Professor A Peacock). Cmnd 9824. HMSO, London.

Pinder, J. (1991): *European Community*. Oxford University Press, Oxford.

Porter, V. (1991): Film and television in the single European market. Dreams and delusions. Inaugural Professorial Lecture. Polytechnic of Central London, London.

Porter, V. (1991a): *Beyond the Berne Convention. Copyright, broadcasting and the single European market*. John Libbey, London.

Porter, V. and S. Hasselbach (1991): *Pluralism, public service and the marketplace. The regulation of German broadcasting*. Routledge, London.

Prescott, M. (1991): *The need for tax incentives*. British Film Institute, London.

Producer News. Monthly. The Producers Association, London.

Rumphorst, W. (1990): Broadcasting of Films via Satellite. *EBU Review, Programmes, Administration, Law.* Vol. XLI No. 4 July, pp. 34–40.

Schwartz, I. (1985): The Policy of the Commission of the European Communities with respect to Broadcasting. *European Broadcasting Union Review. Programmes, Administration, Law.* Vol. XXXVI No. 6. November, pp. 21–29.

SIICE [Symposium international sur l'identité culturelle européenne] (1988): *Europe sans rivage.* Albin Michel, Paris.

Simon, J.-P. (1992): Aftermath. Deregulation in France in the Eighties. Paper given to PICT National Conference. Newpor,. March 1992.

Sorlin, P. (1991): *European cinemas, European societies.* Routledge, London.

Thatcher, M. (1988): On Europe. Speech given on 20.9.1988 at the College de l'Europe, Bruges.

Truffart, F. (1991): *Guide des télévisions en Europe.* Medias-Pouvoirs (hors série) Paris.

Type, M. (1990): Facing the future with confidence. The EBU celebrates 40 years of achievement. *European Broadcasting Union Review, Programmes Administration Law.* Vol. XLI No. 2 March, pp. 12–15.

UNESCO International Commission on Communication Problems (MacBride Commission) (1980): *Many voices: one world.* Kogan Page, London.

Wangermée, R. (1989): What rules for transfrontier television? *Media Bulletin* Vol. 6, No. 2, pp. 1–2.

Waters, G. (1982): HDTV – The television of the future. *Irish Broadcasting Review* No. 15, Autumn/Winter, pp. 36–40.

Wright, M. (1983): Eurikon reviewed. *European Broadcasting Union Review, Programmes Administration Law,* Vol. XXXIV No. 4 July, pp. 31–38.i65

Media titles available from John Libbey

Acamedia Research Monographs

Satellite Television in Western Europe (revised edition 1992)
Richard Collins
Hardback ISBN 0 86196 203 6

Beyond the Berne Convention
Copyright, Broadcasting and the Single European Market
Vincent Porter
Hardback ISBN 0 86196 267 2

Nuclear Reactions: A Study in Public Issue Television
John Corner, Kay Richardson and Natalie Fenton
Hardback ISBN 0 86196 251 6

Transnationalization of Television in Western Europe
Preben Sepstrup
Hardback ISBN 0 86196 280 X

The People's Voice: Local Radio and Television in Europe
Nick Jankowski, Ole Prehn and James Stappers
Hardback ISBN 0 86196 322 9

Television and the Gulf War
David E. Morrison
Hardback ISBN 0 86196 341 5

Contra-Flow in Global News
Oliver Boyd Barrett and Daya Kishan Thussu
Hardback ISBN 0 86196 344 X

CNN World Report: Ted Turner's International News Coup
Don M. Flournoy
Hardback ISBN 0 86196 359 8

Small Nations: Big Neighbour
Roger de la Garde, William Gilsdorf and Ilja Wechselmann
Hardback ISBN 0 86196 343 1

BBC Annual Research Reviews

Annual Review of BBC Broadcasting Research: No XV - 1989
Paperback ISBN 0 86196 209 5

Annual Review of BBC Broadcasting Research: No XVI - 1990
Paperback ISBN 0 86196 265 6

Annual Review of BBC Broadcasting Research: No XVII - 1991
Paperback ISBN 0 86196 319 9

Annual Review of BBC Broadcasting Research: No XVIII - 1992
Paperback ISBN 0 86196 368 7
Peter Menneer (ed)

European Media Research Series

The New Television in Europe
Edited by Alessandro Silj
Hardback ISBN 0 86196 361 X

Media Industry in Europe
Edited by Antonio Pilati
Paperback ISBN 0 86196 398 9

Media titles available from John Libbey

Broadcasting and Audio-visual Policy in the European Single Market
Richard Collins
Hardback ISBN 0 86196 405 5

Aid for Cinematographic and Audio-visual Production In Europe
(published for the Council of Europe)
Jean-Noël Dibie
Hardback ISBN 0 86196 397 0

BBC World Service

Global Audiences: Research for Worldwide Broadcasting 1993
Edited by Graham Mytton
Paperback ISBN 0 86196 400 4

Broadcasting Standards Council Publications

A Measure of Uncertainty: The Effects of the Mass Media
Guy Cumberbatch and Dennis Howitt
Hardback ISBN 0 86196 231 1

Violence in Television Fiction: Public Opinion and Broadcasting Standards
David Docherty
Paperback ISBN 0 86196 284 2

Survivors and the Media
Ann Shearer
Paperback ISBN 0 86196 332 6

Taste and Decency in Broadcasting
Andrea Millwood Hargrave
Paperback ISBN 0 86196 331 8

A Matter of Manners? – The Limits of Broadcast Language
Edited by Andrea Millwood Hargrave
Paperback ISBN 0 86196 337 7

Sex and Sexuality in Broadcasting
Andrea Millwood Hargrave
Paperback ISBN 0 86196 393 8

Violence in Factual Television
Andrea Millwood Hargrave
Paperback ISBN 0 86196 441 1

Broadcasting Research Unit Monographs

Invisible Citizens:
British Public Opinion and the Future of Broadcasting
David E. Morrison
Paperback ISBN 0 86196 111 0

Keeping Faith? Channel Four and its Audience
David Docherty, David E. Morrison and Michael Tracey
Paperback ISBN 0 86196 158 7

Quality in Television –
Programmes, Programme-makers, Systems
Richard Hoggart (ed)
Paperback ISBN 0 86196 237 0

Media titles available from John Libbey

School Television in Use
Diana Moses and Paul Croll
Paperback ISBN 0 86196 308 3

UNESCO Publications

Video World-Wide: An International Study
Manuel Alvarado (ed)
Paperback ISBN 0 86196 143 9

University of Manchester Broadcasting Symposium

And Now for the BBC ...
Proceedings of the 22nd Symposium 1991
Nod Miller and Rod Allen (eds)
Paperback ISBN 0 86196 318 0

It's Live – But Is It Real?
Proceedings of the 23rd Symposium 1992
Nod Miller and Rod Allen (eds)
Paperback ISBN 0 86196 370 9

Published in association with
The Arts Council

Picture This: Media Representations of Visual Art and Artists
Philip Hayward (ed)
Paperback ISBN 0 86196 126 9

Culture, Technology and Creativity
Philip Hayward (ed)
Paperback ISBN 0 86196 266 4

Parallel Lines: Media Representations of Dance
Stephanie Jordan & Dave Allen (eds)
Paperback ISBN 0 86196 371 7

Arts TV: A History of British Arts Television
John A Walker
Paperback ISBN 0 86196 435 7

ITC Television Research Monographs

Television in Schools
Robin Moss, Christopher Jones and Barrie Gunter
Hardback ISBN 0 86196 314 8

Television: The Public's View
Barrie Gunter and Carmel McLaughlin
Hardback ISBN 0 86196 348 2

The Reactive Viewer
Barrie Gunter and Mallory Wober
Hardback ISBN 0 86196 358 X

Television: The Public's View 1992
Barrie Gunter and Paul Winstone
Hardback ISBN 0 86196 399 7

Media titles available from John Libbey

Seeing is Believing: Religion and Television in the 1990s
Barrie Gunter and Rachel Viney
Hardback ISBN 0 86196 442 X

IBA Television Research Monographs

Teachers and Television:
A History of the IBA's Educational Fellowship Scheme
Josephine Langham
Hardback ISBN 0 86196 264 8

Godwatching: Viewers, Religion and Television
Michael Svennevig, Ian Haldane, Sharon Spiers and Barrie Gunter
Hardback ISBN 0 86196 198 6
Paperback ISBN 0 86196 199 4

Violence on Television: What the Viewers Think
Barrie Gunter and Mallory Wober
Hardback ISBN 0 86196 171 4
Paperback ISBN 0 86196 172 2

Home Video and the Changing Nature of Television Audience
Mark Levy and Barrie Gunter
Hardback ISBN 0 86196 175 7
Paperback ISBN 0 86196 188 9

Patterns of Teletext Use in the UK
Bradley S. Greenberg and Carolyn A. Lin
Hardback ISBN 0 86196 174 9
Paperback ISBN 0 86196 187 0

Attitudes to Broadcasting Over the Years
Barrie Gunter and Michael Svennevig
Hardback ISBN 0 86196 173 0
Paperback ISBN 0 86196 184 6

Television and Sex Role Stereotyping
Barrie Gunter
Hardback ISBN 0 86196 095 5
Paperback ISBN 0 86196 098 X

Television and the Fear of Crime
Barrie Gunter
Hardback ISBN 0 86196 118 8
Paperback ISBN 0 86196 119 6

Behind and in Front of the Screen – Television's Involvement with Family Life
Barrie Gunter and Michael Svennevig
Hardback ISBN 0 86196 123 4
Paperback ISBN 0 86196 124 2

Institute of Local Television

Citizen Television: A Local Dimension to Public Service Broadcasting
Dave Rushton (ed)
Hardback ISBN 0 86196 433 0

Reporters Sans Frontières

1993 Report
Freedom of the Press Throughout the World
Paperback ISBN 0 86196 403 9